SYNGE:
THE MEDIEVAL
AND THE GROTESQUE

Toni O'Brien Johnson

Irish Literary Studies 11

1982
COLIN SMYTHE
Gerrards Cross

BARNES AND NOBLE BOOKS
Totowa, New Jersey

Copyright © 1982 by Toni O'Brien Johnson

First published in 1982 by Colin Smythe Limited, Gerrards Cross,
Buckinghamshire

British Library Cataloguing in Publication Data

Johnson, Toni O'Brien
Synge. – (Irish literary studies,
ISSN 0140-895X; 11)
1. Synge, J.M. – Criticism and interpretaion
    I. Title   II. Series
    822′.912   PR5534

ISBN 0-86140-104-2

First published in USA by Barnes & Noble Books,
81 Adams Drive, Totowa, New Jersey 07512

Library of Congress Cataloging in Publication Data
Johnson, Toni O'Brien.
Synge, the medieval and the grotesque.

(Irish literary studies ; 11)
Bibliography: p.
Includes index.
1.Synge, J. M. (John Millington), 1871–1909 –
Criticism and interpretation.   2. Synge, J. M. (John
Millington), 1871–1909 – Knowledge and learning.
3. Middle Ages in literature.   4. Literature, Medieval –
History and criticism.   5. Grotesque in literature.
    I. Title.   II. Series.
PR5534.J63   1982   822′.912   82-8762
    ISBN 0-389-20307-6   AACR2

Typeset by Inforum Ltd, Portsmouth
Printed in Great Britain by
Billing & Sons Limited, London,
and Worcester

To the Memory
of
Julia Daly

CONTENTS

ACKNOWLEDGEMENTS

I wish to record my deep gratitude to Professor Ernest Giddey for his unfailing support in the preparation of this work. My sincere thanks are due to Professor Patrick Rafroidi for his expertise and valuable advice. I am grateful also to Professor Ian Kirby for lending his Anglo-Saxon clarity to disperse threatening Celtic mist.

The staffs of the following libraries were helpful in a number of ways: the Library of Trinity College, Dublin; the National Library of Ireland; the Bodleian Library, Oxford; the Library of the University of Lausanne; and the British Library. I am grateful to Mrs Lilo Stephens and the Trustees of the Estate of J. M. Synge for permission to quote from the manuscripts, and to Oxford University Press for permission to quote from J. M. Synge, *Collected Works*).

My greatest debt of gratitude is to Professor Ann Saddlemyer, for help and encouragement throughout the long period it has taken to bring this work to fruition.

T. O'B. J.

I INTRODUCTION

As early as 1913 Maurice Bourgeois claimed for John Millington Synge 'a lifelong intimacy with medieval literature'.[1] Since Bourgeois's work has proved a rich and reliable source for subsequent Synge scholarship, it is inviting to examine that claim, together with the suggestion which accompanies it that Synge's bitter-sweet humour may owe something to his intimacy with so many French farces and *fabliaux* of the Middle Ages. Although some studies have been made of individual cases where medieval material has some bearing on Synge's work, no attempt has been made to estimate the global significance of his use of medieval literature.[2] A cursory consideration shows a variety of uses: as a source for *The Well of the Saints*; providing a distant original for *Deirdre of the Sorrows*; analogously for *The Playboy of the Western World*; and, in the case of a few poems, to make his highly individual 'translations'. If one goes beyond circumstantial explanations for Synge's using this medieval material, an intrinsic, literary reason for his choice emerges. The pervading factor common to both Synge's work as a whole and to the medieval literature he used is the grotesque. It underlies the connection which Bourgeois made between the comic medieval material with which Synge was familiar and what he calls Synge's 'bitter-sweet humour'. For although the source for *The Well* is comic, and there is indeed a comic element in much of Synge's work, it is but one aspect of the inclusive, complex vision which can be defined in terms of the grotesque.

Any study of Synge's work concerning questions of source and literary influence is dogged by three major difficulties. First, life, not literature, was his primary source; second, his originality obscures direct links with the traditions within which he was writing; and finally, his intimacy with so many folk tales confounds attempts to identify possible influence from their literary analogues. Some solution to these difficulties is offered by the adoption of a variety of approaches, rather than a single, uniform one. Thus *The Well of the Saints* presents both genetic and generic interests, whereas *The Playboy* lends itself to a comparative approach with the emphasis

1

on analogues. *Deirdre of the Sorrows* is also dealt with comparatively, but within a historical framework; and Synge's translations of medieval poems demand a stylistic treatment. An empirical analytical approach is necessary in the chapters on the grotesque in order to show effectively that the grotesque is indeed an intrinsic literary factor in Synge's work. Such a variety of angles may at times convey a fragmentary effect, but to impose a bold extrinsic framework would put too great a strain on the sometimes slight links which exist between Synge's work and related medieval material.

Since it is in his plays that Synge's use of medieval literature most evidently converges with his use of the grotesque, this study will concentrate on them, with the exception of *Riders to the Sea*, which is uniquely devoid of incompatibles clashing. In addition, his translations of medieval poems will be considered, in conjunction with *Deirdre of the Sorrows*, for the nature of the literary language which Synge evolved.

The concept of the grotesque most readily applicable to Synge's work is that evolved by Victor Hugo in his Preface to *Cromwell*, but such an application is inevitably an oversimplification which merely serves as a point of departure for empirical analysis. According to Hugo's aesthetic, the dualistic, antithetical structure of the world and of man's nature is inevitably reflected in art, which must reflect the whole of life, not just one side of it, if it is to be 'true' and 'complete'. The aesthetic is 'realist', in the sense that it does not seek to exclude the negative aspects of man and his life from art, but rather reinstates them; and Hugo explicitly identifies the aesthetic as Christian and Romantic as opposed to Classical. He expects the Romantic drama to be a mixture of tragedy and comedy, and sees the grotesque there as the vital foil for the sublime.[3] We shall see in the course of this study that Synge's aesthetic of contrast has much in common with that of Victor Hugo, but for a working definition of the grotesque, that of Philip Thomson is adopted: it is *the unresolved clash of incompatibles in work and response*; and there is in addition an anti-rational disposition behind its use, which may be either conscious or unconscious.[4]

This study will be divided into two main parts, the first of which will concern the medieval. This term is used in two ways. First, historically, it is used in the widest sense, denoting material which pertains to the period generally designated as the Middle Ages. This material is sometimes very early, as in the case of some of the Irish literature known to Synge, while it is five or six centuries later in the case of François Villon, some of whose poems Synge translated. Old Irish and Middle Irish (which are known collectively as Early Irish) are here both designated as medieval, since we are not concerned with linguistic properties which would call for recognition of the distinction between them. Second, the term medieval is used in literary reference to denote certain conventions and attitudes which seem characteristic primarily of the Middle Ages. Such conventions and attitudes are not chronologically confined, and may therefore be survivals or revivals. The use of the fool figure, or the professional poet's self-consciousness would serve as examples. The object of this first part of the study will be an analysis of how Synge used medieval material, how he altered it, what he discarded, and what he developed.

The grotesque elements in Synge's work will be analysed in terms of folly, incongruity, ugliness, and the comic, in the second part of this study. In each case it becomes evident that a reductive process is at work: a process which asserts as a structural principle in the work of art a co-presence of the irrational with the rational, of disharmony with harmony, of ugliness with beauty, or of the body with the spirit. This assertion expresses a vision of the actual world which accommodates the grotesque, neither ignoring it nor seeking to eliminate it. It is an earthy vision, with a strong folk affinity. It recognizes the instinct to reinstate the rights of the body beside those of the mind, and to allow them priority over reason. It also recognizes that this instinct is ineradicable because it is hinged with the vital regenerative and degenerative processes of birth and death, processes over which the mind and reason have no ultimate control.[5]

Reason was not quite sovereign either in the society in which Synge lived or in the literature of his day, but both society and literature had, for centuries in Europe as a whole, largely insisted on man's rational and sentimental needs, to the neglect of those which were primarily sensual and instinctual. The distinctions are crudely expressed, but they serve to account for the need which Synge felt to make the clash of incompatibles so loud in his work. Wolfgang Kayser observes that the power of the grotesque is seen in ages which follow on ages which believed in a perfect and protective natural order. 'The various forms of the grotesque', he writes, 'are the most obvious and pronounced contradictions of any kind of rationalism and any systematic use of thought'.[6] But, although the power of the grotesque may be more evident in ages which follow on those when rationalist tendencies dominate, it is by no means confined to them.

In Synge's case one can trace an individual reaction to the prevalent attitudes of his milieu, as well as to the literary fashions of his time. It will therefore be profitable to examine here that biographical material which is relevant to the cultivation of his interest in medieval literature with its grotesque quotient, and also to consider how his grotesque vision, centred on the body, resulted in the Rabelaisian note which he insisted should be recognized in his work.[7]

J.M. Synge came from an educated family and class which followed the 'enlightened' tradition based on the belief that man can improve and advance through learning. It was a tradition which strongly contrasted with that of the majority of Synge's fellow-countrymen who, first of all, had generally had no means of formal education in Ireland since the dissolution of the monasteries at the end of the sixteenth century and the progressive dispossession of the native aristocracy whose professional poets had been the custodians of Irish learning. Secondly, the majority of his fellow-countrymen had retained the 'old faith' and had remained unaffected by the Enlightenment. Synge's grandfather, also called John Synge, provides a typical representative of that educated and enlightened Irishman who came from the Protestant Ascendancy class. Having paid a three-month visit in 1814 to the institute founded by Pestalozzi at Yverdon castle in Switzerland, and having been impressed by the ideas and practice of this Rousseau-inspired educator, he proceeded to establish a school, based on Pestalozzian principles, for twenty poor pupils on his estate in County Wicklow. He also set up a press at Roundwood for the purpose of printing translations of Pestalozzi's works. Such philanthropy provides strong evidence for a firm belief in the power of education.[8]

J.M. Synge was, however, an outsider in the environment into which he was born. It was not that he did not go through its standard process, but that he did not share its beliefs. He renounced his family's religious beliefs early, at sixteen or seventeen, and realized that as a consequence he would be faced with the outraged feelings of almost everyone he knew.[9] He wrote of his ideas then:

> The Common idea of God, among religious people, is a Being supremely good, delighting in virtue and in nothing else. But, if God did, as is generally believed, make man in the state [in

which] he now exists, and if He guides and directs humanity at the present moment, if He gave us our intellects, can we believe that he does not require us to use them?[10]

Synge evidently did not find life as orderly, or man as virtuous as his own family professed they were. Here we see an early development in the direction of the complex vision which could accommodate what was generally considered unacceptable in his inherited environment.

In Trinity College, Dublin, where between 1888 and 1892 he read for a general degree, not concentrating on either English or medieval studies of any kind, Synge found an extension of the environment of his family and class. He usually met the minimum requirements only for remaining 'on the books', preferring to spend his time at music. Having renounced the religious faith of his family, his cultural allegiances also altered, so that he was even further separated from their beliefs:

> Soon after I had relinquished the Kingdom of God I began to take a real interest in the kingdom of Ireland. My politics went round from a vigorous and unreasoning loyalty to a temperate Nationalism. Everything Irish became sacred . . .[11]

His interest in Irish antiquities and the Irish language during his time at Trinity laid the foundation for his later scholarly pursuits in the field of the early literature of Ireland. This interest coincided with the Celtic Revival, so that he was able to procure texts such as *The Children of Lir*, published by The Society for the Preservation of the Irish Language, with both the Irish text and an English translation.[12] Such reading led Synge away from the sympathies of his family and took him further into the 'primitive' and therefore more vital side of Irish culture. This cultural deviation further complicated his vision, bringing to it that medieval dimension so scornfully excluded from his inherited culture.

The range of people with whom Synge had contact was extremely limited up to 1893: it was largely Anglo-Irish Ascendancy, with an occasional admixture of the native Irish servant class. He claimed that, until he was twenty-three, he had never met, or at least never known a man or woman who shared his opinions.[13] But his encounter with his cousin, Mary Synge, a fellow-musician who made her living as a pianist, began for him a whole series of encounters with people and places that contributed to his development. In and around Oberwerth in Germany, which he visited in 1893 through Mary Synge, he found, 'in the strictly historical sense, the scenery of romance',[14] and in the von Eiken sisters he met people who shared his views and interests. Having so far been isolated in his opinions, he here enjoyed a liberation, the importance of which he later recognized.[15] The fact that for the first time he moved in circles where the arts were regarded not as dangerous, but rather as of great value, was particularly disengaging for him, so that although his choice of career was soon to shift from music, it remained confidently within the field of the arts.

Synge's settling in Paris in 1895 further enriched his experience of people and ideas. It is significant that it is then, for the first time, that we find him expressing sure, critical opinion.[16] In the notebooks which he had used up to that time, he had merely made uncritical transcripts from the works he had read.

The Sorbonne played a crucial role in the development of Synge's interest in medieval literature intermittently over the next seven years, up to the effective beginning of his literary careeer in 1902. There, he attended the lectures of Professor Paul Passy on general and comparative phonetics, which were to provide him with the means of acquiring the necessary linguistic equipment for going directly to the medieval texts of the literature of France and of his own country, instead of his having to depend on modern renderings. Also, during that first term of 1895, he attended the lectures on medieval French literature given by Professor Louis Petit de Julleville.[17] Petit de Julleville was one of two medievalists at the Sorbonne who had a deep and lasting influence on the development of Synge's literary taste. The other was Professor Henry d'Arbois de Jubainville, first holder of the chair of Celtic Languages and Literature at the *Collège de France*.

These two men were remarkable for the profusion of their publications, the breadth of their learning, and for adopting the comparative approach to language and literature. Petit de Julleville (b. 1841) had held a chair in the Arts Faculty at Dijon before his appointment as Professor of Medieval French Literature and the History of French Literature in Paris in 1886. By the time Synge first attended his lectures in 1895, de Julleville had already written and published, in addition to his thesis on *L'Ecole d'Athènes au XVe siècle*, the following works: *Histoire de la Grèce sous la domination romaine* (1875); *Histoire du théâtre en France, les Mystères* (1880);

Les Comédiens au moyen âge (1885); *La Comédie et les Moeurs en France au moyen âge* (1886); *Répertoire du théâtre comique en France au moyen âge* (1886); and *Le Théâtre en France, l'histoire de la littérature dramatique depuis ses origines jusqu'à nos jours* (1896). Apart from these, he had also published textbooks for his courses, and the following year (1896) his monumental eight-volume *Histoire de la langue et de la littérature française* started coming out. As well as being general editor of this great work, he wrote most of the medieval sections and many of the others including, notably, the introduction to the Renaissance, where he stresses the continuity between the Middle Ages and the Renaissance, correcting the prevalent tendency to entirely separate them.[18]

Although the range of literature which de Julleville treated in his works was wide, it is perhaps inevitable that among so many publications one should find a great deal of repetition, particularly where he is dealing with medieval literature. *La Moralité de l'aveugle et du boiteux* by André de la Vigne, the source Synge was to use for *The Well of the Saints*, is treated at length in three different works, and referred to more briefly in several other places in the corpus.[19] Besides, de Julleville's works abound in cross-references, some of which are straight quotations of himself. Thus, while he adopts various approaches to his material, the writer continually reinforces his own opinions and literary theories. Given Synge's voracious reading during this period,[20] in addition to his regular attendance at this author's lectures, it is not surprising to find that de Julleville's influence on Synge was considerable.[21] The combination of hearing him lecture regularly during two semesters with reading and taking notes from his reiterative books made it inevitable, particularly when one remembers that Synge's intellectual maturation had not greatly advanced during his undergraduate years at Trinity.

Synge also attended the lectures of Professor de Jubainville during two semesters, the first time in 1898 when the course consisted of a comparison between the ancient Irish and Greek cultures as reflected in their literatures;[22] and the second time in 1902, when the course had a more linguistic basis, being centred on Old Irish. The classes on Old Irish took place twice weekly; Synge faithfully attended them all, and he was sometimes the only student present. Teacher and student thus became so familiar that Synge was invited to de Jubainville's home for lunch on 19th April 1902.[23] Besides, Maud Gonne, who was a friend of de Jubainville, claimed that she had recommended Synge to him for a position as Assistant, although there is no evidence that this recommendation was ever officially acted upon.[24] However, we find a revealing reference to the matter in a letter from Synge to Lady Gregory:

> I am working at Jubainville's lectures now, so I shall not forget my Irish this Winter. He came to see me the other day to ask me to go and give them the pronunciation of modern Irish. I feel rather a blind guide but I do my best.[25]

The zealous patriot Maud Gonne was probably unaware of the highly scholarly nature of de Jubainville's work and of the relatively early stage at which Synge was in his study of Old Irish at that point, although as we shall see, his competence was to become considerable later.

Henry d'Arbois de Jubainville (b. 1827) had a more varied academic background than his colleague Petit de Julleville. He had attended the *Ecole des Chartes* (School of Paleography and Librarianship) from which he took a first class degree in French Feudal Law at the age of twenty-two. Then he went on to a seminary at Nancy where his evident inclination towards broad erudition rather than deep theological studies caused the head of the seminary to declare him lacking in a vocation for the priesthood at the end of a year. For twenty-eight years thereafter he acted as Keeper of Public Records for the district of Aube, continuing meanwhile with his private studies. Celtic Philology became his consuming interest, arrived at through his research and numerous publications on the history of Gaulish France. By 1890, when he retired from his position as Keeper of Public Records to take up the newly created chair of Celtic Languages and Literature in Paris, he had already published important works on subjects of Celtic interest.

The profusion of de Jubainville's publications surpassed that of de Julleville: they ran to well over 420 works, though not all were in the Celtic field. Notable among those of relevance to Synge are *Introduction à l'étude de la littérature celtique* (1883); *Elements de la grammaire celtique* (1903); *Le cycle mythologique irlandais et la mythologie celtique* (1884); and the all-embracing twelve-volume *Cours de littérature celtique*, published between 1883 and 1902. De Jubainville was director of the *Revue celtique* from 1885 to 1899, and was thus responsible for the publication of many Old Irish texts, with scholarly commentaries.[26]

Naturally, such profusion resulted in the same kind of repetitions which we found in the case of de Julleville, so that the Deirdre tale and *Bricriu's Feast*, both of which Synge came to use in different ways in his works, are treated extensively in de Jubainville's. This prolific medievalist was regarded as one of the greatest scholars of his time, yet he was also noted for his remarkable ease in relating to his students. Such ease was borne out in his contact with Synge.

The enthusiasm of de Jubainville, a distinguished Celtic scholar of international reputation, impressed Synge, whereas he had noted a contrasting indifference on the part of his professor of Irish at Trinity College, Dublin, whom he described as:

> an amiable old clergyman who . . . seemed to know nothing, or at least to care nothing, about the old literature of Ireland, or the fine folk-tales and folk-poetry of Munster and Connaught.[27]

In Paris Synge found among the erudite someone who valued Early Irish culture and literature, a rare phenomenon in the Ireland of his day, for although there were a few enthusiasts such as Douglas Hyde, W.B. Yeats and Lady Gregory, they were like himself to some extent outsiders, even in their own class. And although Synge was to discover later on that there were plenty of folk remnants of the ancient culture of Ireland, these were to be found only among simple people in whom, despite his emotional sympathy with them, he felt an intellectual lack:

> In some ways these men and women seem strangely far away from me. They have the same emotions that I have, and the animals have, yet I cannot talk to them when there is much to say, more than to the dog that whines beside me in a mountain fog.[28]

Yet these same men and women of the Aran islands were to provide Synge both with a vitalizing factor in the forging of his literary language, and with a link to that medieval past of which he had grown so conscious through his academic pursuits during the periods he spent in Paris.

Synge's pursuits in that city were not, however, entirely academic. His social contacts were often of a kind that helped to clarify further for him his own individual cultural heritage. Among these contacts was the Irishman Stephen MacKenna, whom Ann Saddlemyer sees as perhaps Synge's closest friend,[29] and who spent a fair amount of time in Synge's company in Paris where they lived near each other.[30] Both from their correspondence and from Synge's references to MacKenna in his letters to Molly Allgood, it is evident that there was close understanding between these two men whose upbringing differed considerably. MacKenna was of Irish Catholic stock and education. He also differed from Synge temperamentally. One might describe him as scholarly and classical: for example, in Thomas à Kempis and Meister Eckhardt he noted the absence of the Greek respect for the intellect which had been brought into religion by the Renaissance;[31] and he worked methodically on translations such as Plotinus's *Enneads*. Synge's literary preferences, on the other hand, were often outside the Classical tradition, and he was essentially an artist, not a scholar, by vocation.

In their letters we can trace the kind of exchanges which show confident, friendly disagreement backed by affection. MacKenna's suggestion to Synge that Ireland needed a 'spring-dayish, Cuchulanoid drama' evoked a strong declaration in favour of a drama that grew out of 'the fundamental realities of life which are never fantastic, are neither modern nor unmodern and as I see them rarely spring-dayish or Cuchulanoid'.[32] Such exchanges forced Synge to articulate for himself what the relationship should be in his own work between 'the fundamental realities of life' and his Irish literary heritage. One aspect of Irish life on which these two men agreed was that it was in some ways medieval. In his journal MacKenna noted: 'I find Ireland is still mediæval, beautifully and dismally mediæval . . .';[33] and Synge, as we shall see, found the beauty of medieval life in the artefacts of Aran, and encountered medieval reasoning in the argument of an Irish peasant.

Another fellow-countryman whom Synge met in Paris was Richard Best, a Celtic scholar who later translated de Jubainville's *Le Cycle mythologique irlandais et la mythologie celtique*, which Synge reviewed. When Best returned to Dublin he continued to share his literary knowledge with Synge and also advised him on practical matters such as preparing manuscripts for publishers.[34] The fact that Best was a friend of Stephen MacKenna's doubtless paved the way for the friendship between himself and Synge, but when they met in January 1898 nothing beyond their shared interest in Early Irish literature was needed, since Synge was newly fired with Celtic enthusiasm contracted from the Breton scholar, Anatole le Braz.

In April of 1897 in Paris, Synge had attended a lecture on Brittany by Anatole le Braz, with whom he spoke afterwards.[35] This occasion provided Synge's first direct personal contact with the Celtic revival. He maintained interest in this writer, which led him to read le Braz's works and to study Breton. In 1899 he spent a fortnight in Brittany.[36] He came to see attempts at establishing a dramatic movement there as 'a survival of the sincere, if sometimes grotesque, religious drama of the Middle Ages',[37] and was thus implicitly recognizing that in his own branch of Celtic literature there was no dramatic tradition as such, although there were countless situations and dialogues with dramatic potential which he was later to draw on.

In reading le Braz's works on Breton culture, Synge was further expanding his knowledge of the Celtic past, a knowledge which embraced all four branches. He had read MacPherson's *Ossian* by 1894, and had doubtless become acquainted with *The Mabinogion* through Professor J. Loth's translation and commentary in Volumes III and IV of *Cours de littérature celtique*, for we later find him sending Molly his 'little book of old Welsh stories – written 900 years ago'.[38] In two reviews he displays his comparative approach to Celtic literature by drawing parallels between its Irish and Welsh aspects, and he notes 'the peculiar delight in clear, natural colour which is so characteristic of Irish and Welsh Romance.'[39]

Although one can trace a pronounced taste for Celtic literature in a listing of Synge's reading according to his articles and notebooks,[40] many other lines of interest are detectable and there is a notable tendency to explore the unfrequented by-ways of literature.[41] Of relevance here is his extensive reading in the medieval field, and that in many languages. In Latin he knew the *Gesta Romanorum*, the work of Geoffrey of Monmouth, and *The Imitation of Christ*, of which he attempted a translation.[42] In Italian he knew the *Pecorone* of Ser Giovanni Fiorentino, in addition to those two great writers who stand at the junction of the medieval and Renaissance literary traditions, Dante and Boccaccio.[43]

The three writers last mentioned were all connected with Florence, in which, according to Edward Stephens, Synge 'saw a city of the Middle Ages, a flower of a particular period'.[44] The literary associations, especially those of the middle ages, of those places Synge visited in Europe before the beginning of his success as a dramatist, seem to have been very much alive to him. Not only did he find 'the scenery of romance' in the area of Oberwerth (see p. 6), but he also saw the tomb of Walther von der Vogelweide in the cloister of Wurzburg cathedral,[45] and went on to translate one of

Walther's poems. This poet's work would also have been brought to his attention through his reading of Gottfried von Strassburg's *Tristan* (fl. 1210), in the literary excursus.[46] Synge read a modern German translation of Gottfried's *Tristan* in a landscape with medieval features, and wrote to Molly about it in 1908:

> Yesterday I went a bit up the Rhine to where another river the Lah[n] joins in, and I sat on a seat in the sunshine opposite a little hill with a big mediaeval castle on it, and read a modern German translation of the Tristram and Isolde that you read the other day. The English version is very much cut down, and things the good lady didn't approve of are left out. Today I went to Rhens – the little old town again – it is extraordinarily quaint. There are houses there that were built in 1400, with ordinary peasant people living in them still. I wish I could get some photos of them, I'll try tomorrow.[47]

His complaint about the 'refinements' in the English translation of *Tristan* –presumably Jessie Weston's –echo the remarks he made in 1902 about Lady Gregory's omissions in her rendering of the Cuchulainn saga (see p. 56), and show his appreciation of an aesthetic which incorporated the grotesque. In his remarks about another medieval German saga, the *Nibelungenlied*, his predisposition to the comparative approach leads him to note a parallel between it and the Cuchulainn sage.[48]

Likewise, Synge related the medieval French romance *Aucassin et Nicolette* to its Irish counterparts in being composed of alternating fragments of prose and verse,[49] and he evidently found its beauty in no way marred by its markedly grotesque features:

> I am very glad you liked Aucassin and Nicolette, it is a very beautiful little thing, I think, filled with the very essence of literature and romance.[50]

Thus he wrote to Molly, giving this work his highest praise and revealing his literary preferences.

He makes the same sort of revelation in an earlier letter to her, where he recommends the Arthurian tales as follows:

> Read your Arthur, that will keep your mind full of wild and beautiful things like the beauty of the world. When I had to live in

London I always kept some book like 'Arthur' on my hands and found it a great plan for keeping myself up when I was in ugly surroundings.[51]

He perceives the combination of 'wild' and 'beautiful' in this medieval romance as a parallel to the beauty of the natural world, and he proposes it as an antidote to the ugliness of the urban one. Like other writers who express a grotesque vision, Synge sought the image which was not composedly beautiful, but which instead contained that disturbing element which gives rise to emotion, and which is thereby related to the beauty of the natural world, which is eternally moving. For Yeats it was a 'terrible beauty'; for Synge it was a wild one, not 'nature methodized', and was therefore more commonly found in medieval literature than in that produced in cultures where reason had curtailed fantasy.

Synge was familiar with all the major versions of the Arthurian tales.[52] He clearly placed the work of Malory together with that of Gottfried von Strassburg in the category 'of a land of the fancy' when he made his division between that category and poetry 'of real life'.

Yet he noted that these medieval writers of romance 'become real here and there'. At the same time he stated that two of the greatest poets, Dante and Chaucer, 'are supremely engrossed with life, and yet with the wildness of their fancy they are always passing out of what is simple and plain'.[53] Synge's taste, therefore, accommodated both those writers who are rooted in reality but whose fancy introduces the necessary vitalizing wildness; and those who, though primarily operating in the realm of fancy, periodically cast anchor in reality.

Wide reading and assiduous study, travel, and stimulating contacts were all contributory forces in the growth of Synge's personality between 1893 and 1902. By his first visit to Aran in 1898 his perception of life on those islands was more European than it could possibly have been before 1893, but it was also more appreciative and understanding of the native Irish culture and of his own altered relationship to it. His individual identity was then sufficiently ripe to be able to respond during his annual visits between 1898 and 1902 to the distinction of the time and place to which he was to give expression in his plays.

Moving from Europe to rural Ireland, from Paris to Aran, provided Synge with a strong contrast of environment. Where the one had been sophisticated, cosmopolitan and intellectually active, the other was simple, isolated and demanded much physical exertion from those who wished to survive. Synge relished the sense of an instinctual life around him on Aran, after the intellectual alertness of Paris. His capacity for blending with the natural world, developed during childhood, always helped him to fit easily into peasant surroundings, as he found even in Brittany: 'Since I came here my daily readings of the saints and Stoics have lost their interest, and I live simply and naturally as the peasants do.'[54]

With his 'prepared personality',[55] Synge now looked at life on remoter Inishmaan in terms of his literary experience:

> It is hard to believe that those hovels I can just see in the south are filled with people whose lives have the strange quality that is found in the oldest poetry and legend.[56]

He is not merely expressing that predilection for the primitive which is common in the Romantic tradition here. Rather, he is revealing the artist's capacity to perceive the wealth of the image: to perceive the present in relation to the past, to perceive life in relation to literature and *vice versa*.

Certain details in the landscape actually reminded him of Europe, but significantly, this occurred at night: '. . . the groups of scattered cottages on each side of the way reminded me of places I have sometimes passed when travelling at night in France or Bavaria . . .'.[57] While the night-time blanketed differences, they remained quite apparent in the day-time. When Synge came across a tinkers' camp on a country road in Wicklow, he was alert to the distinction of their way of life:

> People like these, like the old woman and these two beautiful children, are a precious possession for any country. They console us, one moment at least, for the manifold and beautiful life we have all missed who have been born in modern Europe . . .[58]

His identity, while consciously European and modern, could relate to what was distinctly local with warmth. Survivals from the distant past had a special appeal for him.

This appeal is also evident in his account of a group of men in a 'half-sensual ecstasy of laughter' evoked by 'a man of extraordinary ugliness and wit':

14

These strange men with receding foreheads, high cheek-bones, and ungovernable eyes seem to represent some old type found on these few acres at the extreme border of Europe, where it is only in wild jests and laughter that they can express their loneliness and desolation.[59]

That this 'old type' has survived 'at the extreme border of Europe' shows that in Synge's mind he is descended from a continental prototype. The 'medley of rude puns' and 'wild jests and laughter' which Synge perceives as combined with 'loneliness and desolation' suggest that the prototype is the fool figure to whom Synge had been introduced by Petit de Julleville (see Chapter VI). While the fool provokes laughter he is in fact a sad outcast.[60]

Synge also saw a remnant of medieval life in the artefacts of Aran: 'Every article on these islands has an almost personal character, which gives this simple life, where all art is unknown, something of the artistic beauty of mediaeval life.'[61] The simplicity there was the more apparent to him after the contrasting sophistication of life in Paris. His statement that 'all art is unknown' in Aran refers to the plastic arts, because, as he repeatedly recalled, the art of storytelling was still alive and strong there.

The storytellers reminded him most directly of Europe and its medieval literary tradition:

It gave me a strange feeling of wonder to hear this illiterate native of a wet rock in the Atlantic telling a story that is so full of European associations.

The incident of the faithful wife takes us beyond Cymbeline to the sunshine on the Arno, and the gay company who went out from Florence to tell narratives of love. It takes us again to the low vineyards of Würzburg on the Main, where the same tale was told in the middle ages, of the 'Two Merchants and the Faithful Wife of Ruprecht von Würzburg'.[62]

Synge's response to Pat Dirane's story of *The Lady O'Connor* here shows his pre-disposition to react to the folk tales he heard in Ireland in terms of an extended literary tradition, going back to the Middle Ages, and in this case with European analogues. He went on to write several drafts for a play based on this story, and although he never brought that near completion, he incorporated certain analogous features in *The Shadow of the Glen*, thus further extending a tradition of which he was sensitively aware (see pp. 163–165).

15

The folk version of the Diarmuid tale which Synge heard from the old man of the house when he was staying in West Kerry evidently belonged to the native tradition:

> When we had gone some distance, the old man pointed out a slope in front of us, where, he said, Diarmuid had done his tricks of rolling the barrel and jumping over his spear, and had killed many of his enemies. He told me the whole story, slightly familiarized in detail, but not very different from the version everyone knows. Then he told me about Oisin.[63]

The aliveness and immediacy of that tradition to Synge is apparent in how readily its associations came to his mind in relation to a particular place: 'As I was resting again over the Behy where Diarmuid caught salmon with Grania, a man stopped to light his pipe and talk to me.'[64]

His sensitivity to the native cultural heritage is also striking in his account of old Mourteen reciting Old Irish poetry to him in Aran:

> Then he sat down in the middle of the floor and began to recite old Irish poetry, with an exquisite purity of intonation that brought tears to my eyes though I understood but little of the meaning.[65]

That Synge admits to not understanding the meaning may appear on the surface to be an admission of a poor knowledge of Irish. However, while it is true that Synge's knowledge of Old Irish was not deepened in a scholarly way until 1902, when he attended de Jubainville's Old Irish course, it was not entirely lacking. He is more likely expressing his awareness of the actual obscurity of much Old Irish verse.

Mourteen went on to give Synge another account of Diarmuid and Grainne, which Synge revealingly connects with Greek mythology:

> [He] went on to talk of Diarmid, who was the strongest man after Samson, and of one of the beds of Diarmid and Grainne, which is on the east of the island. He says that Diarmid was killed by the druids, who put a burning shirt on him, – a fragment of mythology that may connect Diarmid with the legend of Hercules, if it is not due to the 'learning' in some hedge-school master's ballad.[66]

It is, of course, the influence of de Jubainville's lectures comparing the early Irish and Greek civilizations which is responsible for this association with Greek mythology. And perhaps that is also what made Synge think of early Greek festivals when he heard a feeble ballad on Puck Fair being sung:

> At the foot of this platform, where the crowd was thickest, a young ballad-singer was howling a ballad in honour of Puck, making one think of the early Greek festivals, since the time of which, it is possible, the goat has been exalted yearly in Killorglin.[67]

Continuity of tradition impressed Synge, and he had by now developed a synthesizing habit of mind, which led him to the view expressed in his preface to *The Playboy* that 'All art is a collaboration'.[68]

In the wealth of collaboration behind Synge's own literary art, the role of rural Ireland is self-evident. The factors so far stressed as contributing to the growth of Synge's personality and confidence – reading and study, travel, and personal contacts – informed his selection of material from life in rural Ireland. But, what was most fundamental to this selection was that element in his own nature which exulted in joy, hardness, wildness, passion, and ecstasy. The Rabelaisian note in his own work, consciously introduced as a counteraction to what was sweet or pitiful, was a single reply to three denials: the denial in Synge's upbringing of what was joyous, wild, passionate, and ecstatic; a similar denial in the Irish mores of his time; and its denial in much Victorian literature. In order to express his own personality,[69] Synge had to assert himself in the face of these denials, and in his writings came to insist on the Rabelaisian note which he heard among the folk of rural Ireland:

> The crimeless virtuous side of Irish life is well known and cannot be disputed. The wilder – the Rabelaisian side of the Irish temperament is so wild it cannot be dealt with in book or periodical that is intended for Irish readers. I have come across a great deal of this side of the life in the months and months that I have spent in living among the people or wandering about the roads of Ireland.[70]

He came across it often at collective events, such as Puck Fair where

17

the ballad mentioned above was being sung, and where for three days every August a male goat is raised on a platform to reign over a notoriously riotous throng. Apart from the traditional drinking, other pleasures and entertainments were available there. Synge observed 'a number of women – not very rigid one could see – selling, or appearing to sell, all kinds of trifles'; and he also noted that 'a crowd is as exciting as champagne to these lonely people, who live in long glens among the mountains'.[71]

The instinctual and sensual urges felt and expressed at such collective events are representative of those informing the whole of Rabelais' *Gargantua and Pantagruel*. Thus Synge's Rabelais, in his projected 'Rabelaisian Rhapsody', says in reply to the asceticism of St Thomas à Kempis:

> At a fair also with ale and the sound of fiddles and dancers and the laughter of fat women the soul is moved to an ecstasy which is perfection and not partial.[72]

So, the Rabelaisian note asserts the rights of the instincts and of the body to gratification: at its crudest, to drink, food, and sex. Synge's work opposes the denial of these rights. As Ronald Gaskell's article 'The Realism of J.M. Synge' points out, he has no wish to see nature altered, although he fully grasps the hardness of the struggle with it. His reality is the life of the passions, the senses and the natural world, and it is expressed in bodily terms.[73]

Mikhail Bakhtin, in his work on Rabelais, develops the concept of grotesque realism focused on the body. He suggests that it is a mistake to see a rehabilitation of the flesh after the ascetic Middle Ages in such writers as Rabelais, Boccaccio, Cervantes, and Shakespeare. That, he writes, is a narrow, modern interpretation of materiality and of the body:

> Actually, the images of the material bodily principle in the work of Rabelais (and of the other writers of the Renaissance) are the heritage, only somewhat modified by the Renaissance, of the culture of folk humour. They are the heritage of that peculiar type of imagery and, more broadly speaking, of that peculiar aesthetic concept which is characteristic of this folk culture and which differs sharply from the aesthetic concept of the following ages. We shall call it conditionally the concept of grotesque realism.[74]

18

Synge's grotesque images of the body certainly come from the Irish folk culture, but he selects them as an assertion against the three denials mentioned above, denials which, in the context of his 'Rabelaisian Rhapsody', are essentially ascetic. However, this assertion can also be seen in terms of Synge's aesthetic of contrast,[75] and of his recurrent use of counterpoint in his work.

The bodily principle in grotesque realism includes cosmic, social, and individual human bodily elements, all forming an indivisible whole: it resides not only in the biological individual but in the people as a mass, continually decaying but continually being renewed. Although grotesque realism is degenerative, it is also gay, positive, and festive. It is a resistance against attempts at severance from the material and bodily roots of the world, and is therefore degrading in the sense that it brings down to earth all that is high, spiritual, ideal, and abstract.[76]

The fair, a popular, festive occasion with carnivalesque aspects which are a visible, social expression of the merging of the individual with the throng, became a recurrent background event in Synge's plays. Although Irish fairs as Synge knew them differed in opulence from possible historical Rabelaisian counterparts, he nevertheless recorded the gaiety and animation, the many extravagant remarks made, the stories told and the bawdy songs sung there. He also recorded 'the extraordinary tumult of swearing, wrestling and laughter' among the spectators, and the 'many mediaeval jokes' of the clown at another collective event, the circus.[77] In his 'Rabelaisian Rhapsody', Rabelais thinks of the dancers (that traditional image for conveying man's shared destiny) at a fair, as well as of ale and fat women, for the gratification of the flesh and the lowering of social and sexual boundaries between men. The fair as a social phenomenon provides the writer of comedy with a ready-made form for the drawing together of characters at the end. Ben Jonson made use of it for this purpose in *Bartholomew Fair*, a play which in Yeats's view, expressed in a letter to Allan Wade, 'was one of the things that influenced Synge'. Here Yeats was probably thinking of Jonson's use of a living idiom, for Synge nowhere uses the fair as a framework. It remains a background event, and none of his plays have a traditional comic ending.[78]

Alternating with the wildness Synge detected among the rural Irish was a certain reticence and reserve. He experienced this travelling on the train from the west of Ireland to Dublin, sitting next to a shy young woman while shrieks and obscene songs hailed from the next compartment:

> This presence at my side contrasted curiously with the brutality
> that shook the barrier behind us. The whole spirit of the west of
> Ireland, and its strange wildness and reserve, seemed moving in
> this single train . . .[79]

On the Aran islands, a man called Patrick sold his honour by going
to work as a bailiff, informing the police during evictions. This
denial of his bond with the islanders caused his mother to stand up
and denounce him with vindictive fury, so that Synge thought the
man would be stoned:

> In the fury of her speech I seem to look again into the strangely
> reticent temperament of the islanders, and to feel the passionate
> spirit that expresses itself, at odd moments only, with magnifi-
> cent words and gestures.[80]

The passionate spirit resists the severance of the part from the
whole, of the individual man from his kin: it is the 'all or nothing'
disposition which does not respect rational dissent.

Whereas the inter-relationships within the social body of the rural
Irish varied between wildness and reticence, their relationship to
the cosmic body or natural world was one of close intimacy. The
artefacts of Aran, which Synge saw in medieval terms, were an
expression of this intimacy for him:

> The curaghs and spinning-wheels, the tiny wooden barrels that
> are still much used in the place of earthenware, the home-made
> cradles, churns, and baskets, are all full of individuality, and
> being made from materials that are common here, yet to some
> extent peculiar to the island, they seem to exist as a natural link
> between the people and the world that is about them.[81]

As he here perceives the external world in terms which are inter-
related and fluent, so Synge saw man's inner life:

> The emotions which pass through us have neither end nor begin-
> ning, are a part of eternal sensations, and it is this almost cosmic
> element in the person which gives all personal art a share in the
> dignity of the world.[82]

The education provided by nature was the right education in Synge's view, because it brought the inner man into direct communication with his world, rather than providing him with some mechanical system or framework to apply to it. He noted the full integration of the Aran islanders with the elements during an attempt to beach a curagh in a rough sea 'when the curagh seemed suddenly to turn into a living thing. . . . This sudden and united action in men without discipline shows well the education that the waves have given them'.[83] Elsewhere, he recorded the candour which the islanders felt was necessary in the face of the sea, quoting one of them on the subject: ' "A man who is not afraid of the sea will soon be drownded," he said, "for he will be going out on a day he shouldn't. But we do be afraid of the sea, and we do only be drownded now and again." '[84] In a notebook Synge also emphasized the concord which he found existed between the people of Aran and their world: 'I cannot say it too often, the supreme interest of the island lies in the strong concord that exists between the people and the limited but powerful impulses of the nature that is around them'.[85]

This harmony between the inner and the outer world, this merging of the unit with the whole, was for Synge a concrete expression of his early view that ecstasy should be sought in the blending of the individual life with the whole:

> We do wrong to seek a foundation for ecstasy in philosophy or the hidden things of the spirit – if there is spirit – for when life is at its simplest, with nothing beyond or before it, the mystery is greater than we can endure. Every leaf and flower and insect is full of deeper wonder than any sign the cabbalists have invented.
> . . . We must live like the birds that have been singing or will soon be singing over the way. They are shot and maimed and tortured, yet they go on singing – I mean those that are left – and what does the earth care or what do we care for the units? The world is an orchestra where every living thing plays one entry and then gives his place to another. We must be careful to play all the notes; it is for that we are created. If we play well we are not exorbitantly wretched.[86]

Only through the acceptance of nature, both without and within, can the unit blend successfully with the whole.

The men of Aran beaching a curagh were accepting their part in
the natural orchestra, and they played their part well by harmoniz-
ing their instincts with the waves. Although there is no ecstasy in
question, there are the right conditions for it according to Synge's
view, and he did find an ecstatic quality in the keening of the Aran
women:

> Each old woman, as she took her turn in the leading recitative,
> seemed possessed for the moment with a profound ecstasy of
> grief, swaying to and fro, and bending her forehead to the stone
> before her, while she called out to the dead with a perpetually
> recurring chant of sobs.[87]

Each old woman taking her turn in leading the recitative is reminiscent of those birds, or of each living thing playing its entry only to be
replaced by another. The expression of grief is collective, and death
is experienced not as an isolated, personal event, but as something
which reminds survivors of their common fate. The normal reticence of the islanders retreats in the presence of death, and the
people 'shriek with pitiable despair before the horror of the fate to
which we are all doomed'. The ritualized mourning of the keen is
'no personal complaint for the death of one woman . . ., but seems
to contain the whole passionate rage that lurks somewhere in every
native of the island'.[88]

Yet despite this passionate, ecstatic grief which Synge witnessed
on Aran, he also saw a gay side to the rituals surrounding death.
After one burial he recalled: 'We walked back to the village, talking
of anything, and joking of anything, as if merely coming from the
boat-slip, or the pier'. Earlier, he had been served poteen in his
room, and he records an account which one man gave him of the
great drinking that takes place at some funerals. Although Synge
was acquainted with the tradition of 'waking the dead', we have no
record of him attending a full-blown wake, possibly because
economic conditions in the parts of Ireland he knew best were such
as to make the cost of much festive food and drink prohibitive for
the people there. However, fertility rites and obscene games were
still performed at wakes during the nineteenth century, and written
as well as oral accounts of these would have been available to Synge,
in addition to his certain experience of those consisting largely of
poteen-drinking.[89]

The point to be stressed is that in rural Ireland, although Synge found a sadness and deprivation which coincided with one side of his vision of life, there was, nevertheless, a vital and gay side to that life, which he also included in his creative work. The collective folk response to death and degeneration was healthy because it was instinctive and balanced by passion, vitality, and humour. Health of this kind was consciously sought by Synge, who was well aware of a morbid tendency in his own nature: one should remember his detestation of his 'Etude morbide', which he described to Yeats in 1908 as 'a morbid thing about a mad fiddler in Paris, which I hate', and which he clearly grouped among those works he considered bad and did not want rashly printed.[90] His insistence on gaiety expresses his striving to correct that morbidity: 'I believe in gaiety which is surely a divine impulse peculiar to humanity and I think Rabelais is equal to any of the saints.'[91] Thus he wrote in connection with his 'Rabelaisian Rhapsody', the very title of which betrays the musical nature of its conception, and the relevance of counterpoint in any analysis of the Rabelaisian note in Synge's work as a whole. Gaiety as a corrective for morbidity is not a static absolute to be attained, but rather a counter-movement to pity.

The limitations of the musical analogy in discussing drama must be recognized, and were implied by Synge himself:

> Every life is a symphony and the translation of this sequence into music and from music again, for those who are not musicians into literature or painting or sculpture, is the real effort of the artist.[92]

Yet his recurrent use of musical concepts in those theories where he is following Pater, together with his use of musical terminology in marginal notes to scenarios and drafts, confirms those cases where counterpoint appears to be a structural principle in his work.

The Rabelaisian note is an ecstatic one which, he says, '*must* have its climax no matter who may be shocked' (his emphasis). That it is gross and coarse, he concedes.[93] That it often implies sexuality was the main reason for so much objection to his work in his own time. Among the fragments which remain of his projected satirical 'National Drama: A Farce', we find the Cyclopian, chauvinistic prig Fogarty declaring: 'The National Drama of Catholic Ireland must have no sex.'[94] But, in a letter to Stephen MacKenna, Synge makes it clear that he deliberately restored the sex element with his own drama:

Heaven forbid that we should have a morbid sex-obsessed drama in Ireland, not because we have any peculiar sanctity which I utterly deny – blessed unripeness is sometimes akin to damned rottenness, see percentage of lunatics in Ireland & causes thereof, – but because it is bad as drama and is played out. On the French stage you get sex without its balancing elements: on the Irish stage you get the other elements without the sex. I restored the sex and people were so surprised they saw sex only.[95]

In all his plays after *Riders to the Sea*, that ecstatic, often sexual, Rabelaisian note is played. In his translation of the symphony it serves a contrapuntal purpose for the romantic theme,[96] for 'Gaiety and pity are essentially in coexistent conflict' and Synge's Rabelais is the personification of gaiety: 'The gaiety of life is the friction of the animal and the divine.'[97] No constant or mechanical definition of that Rabelaisian note should be posed because of the continual movement of the music in the context of which it was conceived, and because of the multifarious possibilities for dissonance and assonance. But it is unquestionable that it is rooted in the instincts and the body.

Without dwelling on questions of Synge's personal psychological make-up here, it should be mentioned in passing that despite the sureness of his thought on the rights and integrity of the instincts and the body, his feelings on the matter were uneasy. On a train journey from Dieppe to Paris, for example, the presence of a party of eight dancers in his compartment was highly disturbing for him. While they were awake he was conscious of their boisterous gaiety, and when they fell asleep their physical vulnerability struck him, so that he questioned their having nightly 'to exhibit the strained nudity of their limbs to amuse the dregs of masculine cupidity'. This sensitive response did not prevent him from seeing something grotesque in them, nor blind him to their crumpled clothes and drawn faces. Eventually, he was so anguished that he had to wake them up:

After a while I grew so bitter in my strange and solitary watch that I sprang up and cried out to them that we were nearing Paris. They roused themselves with stiff and dreary expectation. I could have kissed and comforted them each in turn despite the rouge and sea salt that lay upon their lips. In a few moments their traditional gaiety reasserted itself. They threw aside their shawls and hats and began to do their hair with combs and looking-glasses, plying me with questions about Paris life and theatres, throwing in at times a remark of naïve yet frank obscenity.[98]

In similar mood, he thought of 'the lewd-tongued girls and low contaminated men' who frequented the back-streets of Dublin or Paris as 'rousing admiration and abhorrence with pity it is not possible to gauge'. Such conflicting feelings are typical of those aroused by the grotesque, and Synge was markedly susceptible to such material:

> More than any other thing I yearn to acquaint myself with the true personalities of these women – these bastard daughters of the Enduring Life – and perpetually I wander among them reading in their faces and their transient gesticulation the mysterious record of their divinity. I have seen the young hands of girls straying lewdly on their comrades, I have seen the crude animal propensities known still always to exist in men and women laid forth with plain indifference, yet these things stir not within me the instinctive blame pure men profess to cherish, for no action is more lawless than a thought, no thought than the black mood from whence it may arise . . .[99]

This clearly shows Synge's ability to endorse intellectually the coexistence of the divine and the animal in mankind, while at the same time fearing 'the mood' from which this ambiguity comes. His fear explains why the treatment of sexuality in his work is implicit rather than explicit.[100]

However, bodily images there are in plenty in Synge's work, and they contribute to that Rabelaisian note. The body, like music, is continually moving. In the course of its natural functions, some movements are regenerative while others are degenerative. Those movements connected with procreation are very subtly handled in Synge's work, while the degenerative processes of decay and death are emphasized. One might say that, whereas in the work of Rabelais grotesque realism focuses largely on the consumption and discharge of food and on the immediate physical and social merging of bodies, in Synge's work the focus is on the decay of the individual body which then merges with the earth and the cosmic body. While sex moves Synge's characters through the unconscious, there is a direct confrontation with death or decay in every play.

The emphasis on the degenerative aspect of bodily life is so strong in Synge's vision that his epitaph on Rabelais, which avowedly follows Ronsard's, radically shifts the focus on the *bon viveur*. Where Ronsard makes extensive use of elaborate images which convey the sensuality released by imbibing, Synge deserts him and takes up only his striking proposition that generation takes place out of putrefaction:

> Si d'un mort qui pourrit repose
> Nature engendre quelque chose,
> Et si la génération
> Est faite de corruption,
> Une vigne prendra naissance
> De l'estomac et de la panse
> Du bon Rabelais, . . .

> If fruits are fed on any beast
> Let vine-roots suck this parish priest,
> For while he lived, no summer sun
> Went up but he'd a bottle done,
> And in the starlight beer and stout
> Kept his waistcoat bulging out.

> Then Death that changes happy things
> Damned his soul to water springs.[101]

The opening lines of Ronsard's poem 'Epitaphe de François Rabelais' compared with Synge's poem show the French poet starting from the general supposition that nature can cause 'something' to grow from a rotting corpse, then shifting to the abstractions 'generation' and 'corruption', before arriving at the vine sprouting from Rabelais' stomach. The Irish poet, on the other hand, lashes out with the concrete image of fruit-feeding-on-beast, which directly recalls the original meaning of 'grotesque'. The verbs he chooses, like 'feed' and 'suck', are coarse and animalistic. He translates the meridional drink of the neo-Classical poem into 'beer and stout' for his implied northern audience, thus avoiding any elevation of tone through distancing or rarifying. And his final couplet sees what for Ronsard was the rowdy, carousing Rabelais through the refraction of death, whereas Ronsard's poem ends with a celebratory finale. This example of Synge's literary practice illustrates the tendency of his vision to hold those images which disturb, even when his subject allows, and even invites a quite different emphasis and treatment.

The sounding of the Rabelaisian note in Synge's work balanced its denial in his family and class, and in the correct formality of his social behaviour. In *The Playboy*, where he particularly insisted on that note, the scenes where the Widow Quin appears are marked as Rabelaisian in the drafts.[102] She is the most lustful of Synge's women, though not overtly so. In one draft Synge planned 'a scene of grotesque futile lovemaking' in which she would propose to Old Mahon.[103] But as she evolved she became more associated with the spilling of blood, being responsible for the death of her own husband and relishing the rent in Old Mahon's crown when she takes it in both hands 'examining it with extreme delight'.[104] Such delight, inconceivable both from the point of view of social propriety and of Classical literary principles, is a vigorous alternative to squeamishness, and a heightening of ambiguity instead of a purging. In effect it is comparable to the passage where Rabelais writes of the response of Gargantua to the simultaneous birth of Pantagruel and death of Badebec.[105]

The review of relevant biographical information above shows that the experience of medieval literature which Synge acquired, notably under the tutelage of Louis Petit de Julleville and Henry d'Arbois de Jubainville, contributed to the preparation of his personality, apparently cultivating certain conflicts inherent in it; and it also coloured his subsequent view of life in rural Ireland. The heightening of conflicts in his vision is reflected in his writing, particularly in the recurrent clash of the passionate, instinctive, Rabelaisian note with a profound sense of pity and compassion.

Style for Synge was a 'portrait of one's own personality, of the colour of one's own thought', and he found a suitable subject for his style in the clashes and ambiguities peculiar to the life of the Irish peasants who, according to Jack B. Yeats, 'had all his heart'.[106] Such a subject added distinction of time and place to that of his own personality, so that in his work he was able to achieve the triple distinction he sought when he wrote 'the great artist . . . adds his personal distinction to a great distinction of time and place'.[107] The conclusion is that Synge, in his use of medieval literature greatly altered it by locating it in his chosen time and place, and by expressing it in his own style. The grotesque elements of that literature were rendered with the increased pathos of a post-Romantic sensibility, but without sentimentality. Besides, a whole new range of grotesque effects were achieved with the tendency in the artist's vision to perceive antithetically, and to accommodate disharmony.

II THE WELL OF THE SAINTS AND THE QUESTION OF GENRE

There are two of Synge's plays where he undeniably uses medieval material, though in two different ways: *The Well of the Saints* and *Deirdre of the Sorrows*. Both W.B. Yeats and Padraic Colum reported him as having told them that the idea for *The Well* had come to him from a 'pre-Molière French farce', but Gertrude Schoepperle in her search for this farce discovered that what Synge had used was not actually categorized as a farce, but as a *moralité* of the late fifteenth century.[1]

La Moralité de l'aveugle et du boiteux, composed by André de la Vigne in 1496, consists of the exchanges between a blind man and a cripple, in some two hundred and twenty lines, concerning their unsought, miraculous cure in the presence of the corpse of Saint Martin. It appears in the same MS as two other compositions for the same occasion by the same author: a long rambling version of the *Mystère de Saint Martin*, about forty times the length of the *moralité* and with one hundred and fifty-two characters; and *La Farce du Meunier*.[2]

André de la Vigne was, like several writers whose work Synge used, such as Villon, Colin Muset and Walther von der Vogelweide, dependent on patronage and therefore resorted to writing 'occasional verse' and other commissioned entertainments to supplement his income.[3] This is how he came to write *La Moralité de l'aveugle et du boiteux* for the burghers of Seurre, where it was performed by a troupe of players, either that of *Les Enfants-sans-Souci*, or of *La Mère-Sotte*. The laxity which has been noted in its versification is doubtless the result of the pressure under which the author was working in order to finish it, together with the lengthy *mystère* and the farce which accompanied it, in a period of five weeks.[4] This impediment is, however, compensated for by the situational comedy and the liveliness of the dialogue.

In creating this *moralité*, André de la Vigne had amputated the amusing incident of the beggars being cured in spite of themselves from the end of his source, which was an older, anonymous *mystère* of some four thousand lines and fifty-three characters, based on the life of Saint Martin. This anonymous *mystère* was published in Paris

29

.

in 1841, and it is therefore possible that Synge read it.[5] Miss Schoepperle did not believe that he did, however, for two reasons: that 'Synge did not read Old French, or indeed any foreign language with great ease'; and that there is no indication that he was interested in mystery plays.[6] In the light of later research, however, neither of these points holds true.

To begin with the question of Synge's lack of knowledge of Old French, the biographical information now available suggests the contrary view. The level of proficiency in Modern French which he must have attained in order to follow the various courses he took at the Sorbonne has to be recognized. One does not have to rely on the possibly biased evidence of his mother who claimed that he spoke French so well that 'he might easily pass for a Frenchman if he got mixed up in a row'.[7] Besides, there are the certificates of Petit de Julleville stating Synge's assiduity in following his courses. Such assiduity certainly brought a fair amount of experience of Old and Medieval French, which are not, after all, so inaccessible to someone with a sound knowledge of Modern French, especially since so many of the early French texts were published with glossaries. For example, one can cite two editions of *La Moralité de l'aveugle et du boiteux* where the text is glossed at the bottom of the page, Edouard Fournier's and P.L. Jacob's, both of which were available to Synge at the time he was following de Julleville's courses.[8]

Synge's grounding in comparative phonetics from Professor Paul Passy also contributed to his linguistic versatility, and he would doubtless have used de Julleville's concise history of the French language, which gives an ideal introduction for such a student. Some facility in languages can be assumed in a man who in his life-time learned nine: English, Irish, Hebrew, Latin, Greek, French, German, Italian, and Breton. Although his knowledge of Hebrew, Latin and Greek was confined to requirements for examinations, these 'dead' languages added to the breadth of his linguistic basis for the learning of the six modern languages, all of which he used *in situ* at one time or another. Besides, one must recognize that a less profound knowledge of a language is required for mere cognitive, as opposed to operative use.

The impression that Synge knew little French arose from a statement made by Stephen MacKenna at a National Literary Society meeting in 1912, defending him against those charges of 'foreign influence' so often brought against him by hostile nationalists. Since MacKenna was something of a genius at languages himself, he would have disparaged Synge's ability in any case.[9] But it is clear from the evidence above that Synge could well have read either the incident of the two beggars being cured in spite of themselves at the end of the anonymous *mystère*, or André de la Vigne's version in the original, in the context of de Julleville's courses at the Sorbonne.

Whether Synge had actually read the play or not, he made detailed transcriptions from Petit de Julleville's account of *La Moralité de l'aveugle et du boiteux* in *La Comédie et les moeurs en France au moyen âge* the year he began writing *The Well* (1903), which was six years after his studies with the author had come to an end. It was this re-reading of de Julleville that recalled for Synge the 'pre-Molière French farce', as well as some questions related to genre which affected his own literary practice. Certain factors bearing on literary composition, such as the taste of an epoch, the function of particular genres and their relation to 'real life' are discussed in *La Comédie et les moeurs*, and throughout the works of de Julleville there is a marked preoccupation with the question of genre.[10]

That Synge described the *moralité* which was his source for *The Well of the Saints* as a farce is significant. De Julleville had pointed out that the title *moralité* was little justified; that it ended a little too gaily for a *moralité*; and he categorized it as a *moralité joyeuse*.[11] Edouard Fournier, whose edition of this *moralité* is noted by de Julleville and is therefore likely to have been read by Synge, says in his introduction to it: 'Cette moralité, qui, on le verra, est bien plutôt une farce, a pour nous bien des points intéressants . . .' (This *moralité* which is, as we shall see, more like a farce, has some interesting features . . .).[12] And P.L. Jacob writes in his introduction to it:

> Cette moralité, qui a tous les caractères d'une farce, et qui diffère de la plupart des moralités, proprement dites, en ce qu'elle ne met pas en scène des personnages allégoriques, se trouve à la suite du Mystère de Saint Martin . . . (This *moralité*, which has all the characteristics of a farce and differs from the majority of true *moralités* in not presenting allegorical characters, comes after the *Mystère de Saint Martin* . . .)[13]

With these comments on *La Moralité de l'aveugle et du boiteux* in mind, one concludes that Synge used the term 'farce' not in ignorance, but because he was aware that the play was exceptional, and

31

that it did, indeed, have all the characteristics of a farce. Criticism to date has not credited him with the knowledge he had acquired of the finer distinctions to be made in genres. The fact that he had forgotten the established title of this play, but had at the same time put it in a category which displays information rather than ignorance, reflects the interest of the practicing artist concerned with form, and not that of the codifier: an interest in the nature of the creation rather than in the label by which it might be identified.

The *moralité* as a genre is distinguished by its didactic purpose, and it mostly uses allegorical characters (as, for example, *Bien Avisé, Mal Avisé*) to show how the good are rewarded and the wicked punished.[14] *La Moralité de l'aveugle et du boiteux*, however, bears no didactic burden, and its characters are certainly not allegorical in the usual sense of that word, hence its repeated identification as an exception and its ready classification as a farce. The question of didacticism is discussed at length in *La Comédie et les Moeurs*, and de Julleville argues strongly against the idea that the drama, or indeed any art form, actually has the power to teach – a view echoed in Synge's theory recorded in his preface to *The Tinkers*: 'The drama, like the symphony, does not teach or prove anything'. The function of the farce, defined according to French medieval practice, was to provoke laughter by portraying the absurdities and failings of social and private life, by using, in the words of de Julleville 'anything of a grotesque nature'.[15] Synge decided that the grotesque subject of his medieval farce could be treated in such a way as to produce a more complex effect than simply provoking laughter.

La Moralité de l'aveugle et du boiteux portrays the singularly grotesque bodily interdependence of a blind man carrying a cripple, the clash being between the accepted notion of the autonomy of the individual human body and that of two-men-in-one. The cripple, to be whole, requires the legs of the blind man, while the wholeness of the blind man depends on the eyes of the cripple. However, whereas the original subject of this *moralité* is grotesque, the treatment of it is not, for the cure effected by the body of Saint Martin brings about a resolution. Thus we have an ending which is indisputably happy: the blind man is delighted by his new-found sight, while the cripple is undaunted by the possibility of his wholeness depriving him of his living, because he has decided to feign disease in order to continue receiving alms.[16] The effect of this play is precisely that of the farce as defined by de Julleville:

La gaieté y déborde, sans arrière-pensée ni sous-entendu; sans retour amer ou serieux sur nous-mêmes, sur nos défauts, sur nos vices, dont elle s'amuse, sans perdre le temps à s'en plaindre, sans prétendre à nous corriger.[17]

(Gaiety is brimming over, without either intellectual reservations or implications; it evokes no bitter or serious self-reflection, nor consideration of those failings or vices of which it makes fun without wasting time complaining of them or aiming to improve us.)

Such gaiety is clearly not designed to call forth any sense of emotional conflict in the audience. The simplicity of the blind man and the patent insincerity of the cripple leave the audience emotionally detached from them, so that their ultimate fate is of no concern. There is a distinct difference, however, in the case of Synge's play, where the fate of the blind couple, Martin and Mary Doul, is left uncertain at the end, and where the complexity of their natures and sublimity of their dreams move the audience to the point where conflicting feelings of gaiety and pity coexist.

In his choice of the subject of the blind man carrying the cripple, Synge was following a fundamental tendency in grotesque images of the body to show two bodies in one.[18] His treatment of that subject, while extending the grotesque effect to the end of the play, was, however, more subtle. To refine the effect he changed the interdependence from a bodily to an emotional one, and was thus able to alternately evoke pathos and laughter. The concrete presence of physical interdependence on the stage has an immediate impact, while the less striking emotional interdependence moves the audience gradually. Beckett, after Synge's example and with his knowledge of French drama, went on to elaborate both effects in his pairing of the emotionally interdependent Estragon and Vladimir, and the more physically interdependent Pozzo and Lucky in *Waiting for Godot*.[19]

Synge's dual evocation of laughter and pathos in *The Well* is effected through contrapuntal movements which come to rest in the final uncertainty about what Martin and Mary will find in 'the towns of the south'. Against Martin's hope that 'the people will have kind voices maybe', which pathetically conveys the exaggerated importance of sound for those lacking in sight, we have Mary's anticipation of the hardship of 'walking with a slough of wet on the one side and a slough of wet on the other, and you going a stony path with a north wind blowing behind'.[20] The audience, having witnessed the painful disillusion of the couple in the course of the play, is susceptible to the expectations uttered by Timmy the Smith for them after they have left the stage:

> There's a power of deep rivers with floods in them where you do have to be lepping the stones and you going to the south, so I'm thinking the two of them will be drowned together in a short while, surely.[21]

While so mundane a character as Timmy is no candidate for a prophetic role in Synge's canon, and his expectation might be regarded as an expression of mere malice, it still contributes to the fear of the audience concerning the blind couple. This fear coexists with delight at their escape from a conformity imposed from without, with the result that the delight is free neither from intellectual reservations nor bitter reflection, unlike in Synge's medieval source. In his own play he creates an unresolved clash of incompatibles which is reflected in the response to it. The ending is but a rest in an ongoing sequence of which the play is one cycle. The emotions of the audience have been kept in continual movement, apart from the brief rests following the peaks of intensity at the end of each of the first two acts.

The pattern of emotional response to the medieval play follows a single line from a clear opening predicament to a final resolution. By the time of André de la Vigne, the blind beggar was already an established comic character in the French tradition, starting with the anonymous farce *Le Garçon et l'Aveugle* two centuries before.[22] At the opening of *La Moralité de l'aveugle et du boiteux*, the complaint of the blind man that he has been robbed makes a direct link with that anonymous farce, and would have immediately alerted the audience to the key in which the work was pitched, had that not been already clear from the point at which the work was introduced in relation to the *mystère*. The blind man's punning on the death of his good 'servant' Giblet further establishes the comic note.[23] The plight of the individual beggars is quickly resolved by their joining forces, which gives rise to low comic exchanges and doings of an excretary nature, after which the alternative solution of a miraculous cure is introduced. The negative response of the cripple to this, based on the loss of his livelihood as beggar which would ensue, is extended to the blind man, so that both try to escape, thus providing some further comic stage business. When, despite this attempt at escape, they are cured, the blind man is delighted by his sight and the cripple decides to feign his disability so as to maintain his livelihood. Thus, with a minimum of complexity, the process of resolution is complete, and the original position is entirely altered.

The movement of Synge's play differs in a number of ways. From amusement at the good-natured bickering between Martin and Mary at the opening, the audience is taken through the excitement of the cure with a great deal of unease at the high expectations of the couple, in particular of Martin, because it can see the ugly reality before it. The vigour in Martin's expression of his horror partially relieves the tension, but the bitterness of the couple's quarrel at the end of the first act carries a violence which is far from comic in effect. Indeed Synge clearly indicated the tragic quality of this scene in his analysis of the play.[24] However, to end this first act he moves the audience away from these two characters, in whose fate it has become involved, by giving a long, final speech to the remote saint who states the pious, ascetic view-point of the existing solution.

In the opening scene of the second act, there is no emotional 'current' (Synge's word),[25] since the function of that scene is to realize the nature of the new life being led by Martin and Mary. But the arrival of Molly introduces the latent lechery between herself and Martin, which results in a somewhat confused shift of sympathy towards the repulsive victim, Martin. His fine words, which express sentiments far from ignoble, are in strong contrast with the physical reality before the audience, and once again we find a revealing description in Synge's analysis: he identifies the scene as 'traPoetical' (sic).[26] This Syngean coarctation of tragic and poetic strains comes to rest in Martin's final speech, which moves from dejection to a vigorous escape from his immediate situation into the land of fancy.

In the long opening scene between Martin and Mary in the third act, increasing confidence is felt in the new-found harmony between the couple. However, in counterpoint to this there is the beginning of apprehension about the possibility of an unwanted cure. The sense of intrusion is heavy when the Saint, Molly, Timmy and the crowd arrive, from which point emotions among the characters are intense and varied: Martin moves from piteous dejection through increasing anger to his final violent assertion; Mary is comparatively passive, but moves through doubt to despondency; the saint is by turns severe, persuasive, and dismissive, but finally returns to his conventional piety; and Timmy and Molly are angry, threatening and vindictive. Last, the background crowd, of which the men are most active, shows itself mindless and cruel, going so far as to throw things (presumably stones) at the blind couple in its rejection of them for refusing to be cured. This crowd, let us not forget, is the same one which is bent on celebrating Molly's marriage with Timmy, and thus provides us with loudly clashing attitudes to the young and old couples.

It is significant that Synge altered the ending of the original drafts for his play, where Timmy invited all the people 'to the green below for the piper has come and we'll have dancing till the fall of night'.[27] He evidently wanted to avoid the conventional comic ending with nuptials attended by a harmonous throng, and therefore omitted this feature. Although his crowd forms a procession to leave the stage for the wedding of Molly and Timmy, its final expressive gesture and words of rejection are what remain uppermost in the mind of the audience. Society, which had not been represented at all in the medieval play, and was therefore not actively concerned with the fate of the beggars, is depicted by Synge forcefully rejecting them for their insistence on their peculiar concept of joy. There is no rational explanation for this rejection, for the blind couple's choice in no way impinges on the well-being of the other characters, but the social body violently sets apart those members who refuse to conform.

Synge, besides creating a much more complex plot with a correspondingly manifold emotional response in his audience, also elaborated a number of individual features of his medieval source. The physical decay and decrepitude which is present in the corpse of Saint Martin and in the infirmities of the medieval beggars is variously transformed. The dead saint is replaced by a living one whose ascetic way of life has markedly impaired his physical vitality, and the subject of physical ageing and decay becomes a recurrent concern for the blind couple. Whereas the infirmities of the medieval beggars are differentiated, and each is corporally dependent on the other, Synge's beggars both suffer from the same affliction, and their emotional interdependence is recognized only in the course of the play. The functional interdependence of eyes and legs is transmuted into the process of a growing combination for resisting the impositions of society, as well as a mutual recognition of what is shared. While the coming together of the two individuals temporarily

36

strengthens their physical state for the medieval beggars, the union for which Synge's beggars fight serves to identify them as scapegoats for the crowd. Synge's focus is on the cruelty evoked in the 'normal' body of society when it is confronted with the 'abnormal'.

The idea of being cured in spite of oneself is present in the medieval play, but is developed only insofar as it becomes a fact. Synge took this idea and wove his play around it, placing the issue of the conflict between the individual and collective wills at the centre. His interest in this idea can be detected in his noting the phrase 'si ce saint allait nous guérir, malgré nous' (if, in spite of us, the saint were to cure us), which is de Julleville's synthesis of the cripple's argument for escape and the attempt which follows, but which does not appear in the text of the *moralité*.[28] In the medieval play the supernatural power, both ultimate and immediate, is vested in the body of the saint, and human will and intervention play no effective part in the evolution of the plot. In Synge's play the ultimate supernatural power is attributed to the water, and its implementation to the hands of the saint. The will of Martin and Mary Doul are in accord with that of the saint at the first cure, so that there is no question of being cured in spite of oneself; but by the time the second cure is proposed, there is a direct conflict of wills. In the medieval setting the will of man is conceived as powerless and therefore insignificant, whereas there is a humanistic concern with the inherent capacity for choice in the modern play where, consequently, the power of frustrating the tyrannical imposition of a cure is vested in the hands of the blind man.

The idea of the necessity of working for a living is voiced in André de la Vigne's play only as a possibility to be feared, but Synge puts it directly on the stage, using it for structural purposes. The biblical maxim 'By the sweat of thy brow thou shalt eat bread' is well understood by the medieval cripple, who has been able to identify the single advantage of being crippled:

> Quant seray gary, je mourray
> De faim, car ung chascun dira:
> 'Allez, ouvrez!' Jamais n'yray
> En lieu où celuy Sainct sera.[29]

(When I'm cured I'll die of hunger, for everyone will say 'Go and work'. I shall never go anywhere that saint is.)

37

Martin Doul, however, learns about this fact of life only by the experience through which the audience sees him living. At the opening of the second act Martin, reproached by Timmy for his slowness in cutting sticks for the forge fire, replies:

> It's destroyed I'll be whacking your old thorns till the turn of day, and I with no food in my stomach would keep the life in a pig. (*He turns towards the door.*) Let you come out here and cut them yourself if you want them cut, for there's an hour every day when a man has a right to his rest.[30]

And he goes on to recognize retrospectively: '. . . it's more I got a while since, and I sitting blind in Grianan, than I get this place, working hard and destroying myself, the length of the day.'[31] Martin's strenuous work of cutting sticks at the opening of this act provides a structural link with the blind couple's occupation of stripping rushes for lights at the beginning of the first and last acts, where it draws attention to their blindness; and the irony inherent in having the blind, themselves unable to benefit from light, working towards making it for others, adds to the grimmness of the intrinsic irony of the play.

Petit de Julleville recorded the joyous reaction of the blind man at seeing the world for the first time, and Synge in his notes selected from that passage the words *'le monde'*, and the blind man's speech identifying that world as Burgundy, France, and Savoy.[32] This visible concrete world reflects the limits of the concept of sight for the medieval dramatist and his audience, limits which are not observed by Synge, although he tangibly explores the concrete world in its immediate, repulsive physical features. The world of Martin and Mary Doul is primarily the people in it (perhaps Synge was inspired by the secondary meaning of *monde* = people): people who drive him to seek again that ugly, weatherbeaten wife whom he had earlier rejected for her physical appearance, because of the illusions they share.

In the medieval play the prerequisite that the candidates for cure should be merry is mentioned by the cripple when he reports the miracles of the recently dead Saint Martin:

> Malladies les plus perilleuses
> Que l'on sçauroit penser ne dire,
> Il guerist, s'elles sont joyeuses:[33]

(He cures the most dangerous diseases imaginable if the sick are merry.)

It is noteworthy that de Julleville does not include this reference in his description of the play, and since Synge uses it in his, it is an argument for his knowing the original text. In Synge's play it is introduced not exactly as a prerequisite, but a merry disposition is attributed to the blind couple, of which the saint explicitly approves:

SAINT. Are these the two poor people?

TIMMY (*officiously*). They are, holy father, they do be always sitting here at the crossing of the roads, asking a bit of copper from them that do pass, or stripping rushes for lights, and they not mournful at all, but talking out straight with a full voice, and making game with them that likes it.

SAINT (*to Martin Doul and Mary Doul*). It's a hard life you've had not seeing sun or moon, or the holy priests itself praying to the Lord, but it's the like of you who are brave in a bad time will make fine use of the gift of sight the Almighty God will bring you to-day.[34]

It is an added irony that Martin and Mary's mirth evaporates in the face of the world they eventually perceive.

The wiliness of the medieval cripple's plan to retain his beggar's livelihood through pretence is echoed in Martin's wily avoidance of the second cure. What was a verbal decision in the medieval play becomes a highly dramatic reaction in Synge's hands. It is Mary who first proposes that Martin outwit the determination of the world: '. . . you'd have a right to speak a big terrible word would make the water not cure us all'.[35] When reasonable argument fails him, Martin uses his blind man's sharp hearing to gauge the right moment for knocking the can of water across the stage. Thus wiliness, from being an amusing attribute in an idle rogue, becomes a necessary defence for an individual whose personal choice is in danger of being denied.

The above comparison of features from the medieval play with Synge's elaboration of them reveals that, whereas de la Vigne shows a series of static views, Synge presents life in flux. In Synge's play, decay and decrepitude become a process instead of simply being given facts; the will of man is given an active role, producing actual conflict where it had been powerless in the presence of a super-natural force. Work, instead of being a given necessity to be either endured or avoided, is one kind of hardship among others. The world, rather than a tangible external constant, consists of human relationships, with the myriad of uncertainties they imply and bring-ing with them both conscious and unconscious changes of disposi-tion. These differences convey not only the general shift of *Weltans-chauung* in the centuries intervening between the two plays, and the particular stamp of the individual artists, but also they reflect the essential generic distinction between them.

The genre which Synge was developing in *The Well*, already initiated in *The Shadow of the Glen*, was to some extent a response to external needs. Anglo-Irish drama, at the point where Synge entered, was an emergent, not an established tradition (unlike the tradition out of which his medieval source came), so that almost of necessity he became an innovator. He was fully aware of the move-ment which was afoot, of the foundations which were being laid, and of future possibilities:

> For the future of Anglo-Irish writers everything is hopeful. The Irish reading public is still too limited to keep up an independent school of Irish men of letters, yet Irish writers are recognized, to some extent, as the best judges of Irish literary work, and it may be hoped that we have seen the last of careless writing addressed to an English public that was eager to be amused, and did not always take the trouble to distinguish in Irish books what was futile and what had real originality and merit.[36]

The hope for a discriminating Irish reading public expressed here is also implied in his declaration of the need for Irish critics for the emerging Irish drama:

> . . . our real critics must come from Dublin. It is only where an art is native, I think, that all its distinctions all its slight gradations, are fully understood.[37]

It was dissatisfaction with the understanding of the London critics in their reception of Yeats's *The King's Threshold* and his own *Shadow of the Glen* that drove him to this apparently chauvinistic view. The view is not, however, narrowly nationalist, but rather reflects Synge's belief that great art must express a national mood:

> Goethe's weakness [is] due to his having no national and intel-
> lectual mood to interpret. The individual mood is often trivial,
> perverse, fleeting, [but the] national mood [is] broad, serious,
> provisionally permanent. Three distinctions [are] to be sought:
> each work must have been possible to only one man at one period
> and in one place.[38]

The Irish dramatist, then, from Synge's point of view, had to interpret a national mood for a national audience. For his purposes, he
had found the traditions of the London stage inadequate as early as
1900, before any of his own plays had been completed or staged.[39]
At the same period he saw the Irish Literary Theatre as 'an attempt
to replace the worthless plays now familiar to the public by artistic
work'; and by 1906, with three of his own plays already staged, he
was confident that the Irish movement had lost 'all resemblance to
the movements fostered by purely artistic cliques in London and
Paris'. The difference on which he remarks here arose from the
intimate relationship which existed at the Abbey between 'actors,
writers and a part at least of the audience'.[40]
   The intimacy noted here assured the kind of homogeneity necessary for the production of drama which was national, so that Synge
strongly objected to Yeats's idea of enlarging the Abbey repertoire
to include a variety of foreign classics in the manner of the continental municipal theatres:

> So far our movement has been entirely creative – the only
> movement of the kind I think now existing – and it is for this
> reason it has attracted so much attention. To turn this movement
> now – for what are to some extent extrinsic reasons – into an
> executive movement for the production of a great number of
> foreign plays of many types would be, I cannot but think, a
> disastrous policy . . . I think Yeats's view that it would be a good
> thing for Irish audiences – *our* audiences – or young writers is
> mistaken.[41]

Although by this time the process of interpreting the national mood
was under way, in Synge's view it was far from sufficiently evolved
yet to permit any enlargement of the aims of the movement.
Goethe's admission that he and Schiller had confused the German

public at Weimar with the variety of their repertoire, as well as the failure of the municipal theatres in Europe to produce a 'new stage literature', convinced Synge of the need to consolidate the national element in the Irish drama. Thus, in his own search for a new dramatic form, two informing aims can be assumed on his part: the production of a 'new stage literature' which would be different from that current in Europe, and the expression of a 'national mood'.

At the time Synge was writing his plays, their most ready classification was as peasant plays or folk drama. While it is true that this classification distinguishes them from other non-Irish stage literature of the period, his additional brief of interpreting a national mood led to that more intrinsic, lasting distinction which was particularly evident in the language of his characters. Retrospectively, it is possible to define a significant grouping of four of Synge's plays based on the manner in which their characters use language. They are *The Shadow*, *The Well*, *The Tinker's Wedding*, and *The Playboy*. In addition to the use of Hiberno-English idiom, which is common to all of Synge's plays and will be analysed in the context of his translations, the characters of these four express themselves with a degree of daring, extravagance, and energy beyond those of *Riders to the Sea* and *Deirdre*. Of the four of them, *The Well* serves best to identify the genre, partly because it has an identifiable dramatic source, comparison with which clarifies the differences between them.

La Moralité de l'aveugle et du boiteux not only came from an established comic tradition, but was a response to the specific need to reward the crowd with amusement after the performance of the edifying *mystère*.[42] Synge, in *The Well of the Saints*, transformed the traditional comic beggars into their Irish equivalent of 'one or more centuries' before 1903, thus indicating a certain timelessness in the beggar's existence.[43] This timelessness results from what is common, first of all between all men who have been reduced to the lowest possible social status, and second, between all those who live in close relationship with the natural world. The primitivist preference implicit in the choice of such an existence was not simply the result of the common Romantic rebellion against the polish of the town. It also helped to express Synge's grotesque vision, which insisted on allowing full exposure to elemental opposites without reduction or modification. The order of values implicit in his play is neither primarily supernatural like his medieval source, nor social like many contemporary European playwrights. Instead, the values emerge as a statement of the validity of a dual reality, one external, which has a social dimension and is rationally perceptible, and the other internal, of individual importance but not rationally express-ible.

An urbane language which polished and conceptually sifted would not have effectively conveyed the coexistence of those ele-mental drives and feelings on which Synge wished to insist in *The Well*. Such a language, because of its tendency to antithesise and distinguish, could not have yoked pity and cruelty as Martin does when he says 'there's cruel hardship in the pity of your like'.[44] In availing himself of the reputed richness of Irish peasant idiom, Synge was better able to convey those values which required equal recognition for conscious and unconscious life. Thus Martin was able not only to have necessary designatory exchanges with his fellow-men, but also to convey the unconscious cruelty behind the conscious pity, and to portray adequately the invisible world of his fancy behind the contrasting external world the audience can actu-ally see.

Viewed historically, what Synge was doing was creating a genre which would bring forward the unconscious and integrate it on the stage in a manner relative to what was being done in the novel. He is in this the precursor of dramatists like Pirandello, Ionesco, and Beckett, but he is distinguished from them by a certain faith in the power of language: he believed that the Anglo-Irish drama tried to be 'literature first . . . and drama afterwards', also indicating that sincerity was one of its attributes.[45] For this reason his characteriza-tion does not flounder in inarticulacy, for the unconscious remains only one aspect of the whole.

The nature of Synge's characterization beyond the question of language also distinguishes the genre in question. Despite the usual custom of using 'low' characters for comic purposes, and although his source did just that, he presents us with protagonists of some depth and considerable variety. While there is humour in the characters of Martin and Mary, they do not become stereotypes, partly because Synge was consciously opposed to the cult of the stage Irishman and the cheap laughs he could win.[46] The social roles of the characters is significant only to the point of distinguishing between those who are outsiders and those who are not. Sympathy and alienation evoked in the audience in relation to the characters form two currents which flow in a musical pattern through the play, sympathy going with the fleeing outsiders at the end so that there is no endorsing of the values of society.

The ending of *The Well* has been discussed in relation to that of *La Moralité de l'aveugle et du boiteux*, but here certain characteristics which this ending shares with the three other plays in question call for comment. The heroes or heroines in all cases take flight from the 'established' characters at the end, and what sense of enlightenment there is belongs with the outsiders. Yet it would be a mistake to attribute any gain in power to these outsiders because of this enlightenment: it is rather that each of them gives full recognition to some ineluctable force within himself, and thereby comes to terms with it. That inner force reveals itself in various but related forms: to Nora in *The Shadow* as the psychic energy, notably in its sexual aspect, which was being stifled by her way of life; to the tinkers as their inalienable right to satisfy their basic needs without the sanction of society – 'it's little need we ever had of the likes of you to get us our bit to eat, and our bit to drink, and our time of love'; to Martin and Mary as their need for fantasy, which was in danger of being denied by society; and to Christy Mahon as that myth-making power within himself which would allow him to go 'romancing through a romping life-time' once he had the courage to detach himself and express his creativity, like the artist who weaves romance.[47]

The inconclusive ending of these four plays is related to the kind of use Synge makes of death, the traditional tragic solution, and marriage, the traditional comic one. Death is present in the course of the plays, but only as a possibility: feigned by Dan Burke in *The Shadow*; the drowning envisaged by Timmy for the blind couple in *The Well*; the threat for the priest of being put 'headfirst in the boghole' in *The Tinkers*; and the apparent murder of Old Mahon in *The Playboy*. Insofar as there is a connection in the attitude to death behind these various possibilities, it is that death is no solution, because the same contrary forces continue regardless. Similarly, marriage is no solution, so that we see at the end of *The Shadow* one marriage failed and another *manqué*; a dreary one forthcoming and a fruitless one repaired in *The Well*; one thankfully avoided in *The Tinkers*; and in *The Playboy*, one miscarried and one shunned.

The particular genre which Synge evolved is not readily classifiable, nor perhaps would it be especially useful to do so since no other dramatist has employed exactly the same combination of features. One could say, broadly speaking, that these four plays belong to that category commonly but unsatisfactorily called tragi-comedy which will be further discussed in the context of the comic (see pp. 166–167). But the plea that Synge was an innovator in this falls down because, depending on definition, certain plays which preceded Synge's might also be put in this class. The most significant distinction is Synge's order of values, concerned with the recognition of ineluctable forces in both inner and outer reality, and the ongoing quest of individual characters to find a path where they can accommodate both. The staging of such values was new, and it anticipated such later dramatic explorations of reality as Sartre's *Huis Clos* and Beckett's *Waiting for Godot*.

Synge, in identifying his source for *The Well* as a 'pre-Molière French farce', was revealing his sense of its place in tradition. The oldest extant French farce, the anonymous *Le Garçon et l'Aveugle*, had exploited blindness on the stage for comic purposes over two hundred years before André de la Vigne. Petit de Julleville gives a synopsis of this play in his *Répertoire du théâtre comique au moyen âge*, and points out that it prefigures several fifteenth-century farces in its subject-matter.[48] Synge's reference to his source as 'pre-Molière' shows that he was conscious of the fact that Molière, in his turn, had exploited the comic potential of the blind man on the stage in his *Fourberies de Scapin*.[49] Once again, the teaching of de Julleville emerges, because almost every time he mentioned Molière he commented on his literary debts. Because of the importance of Synge's view of art as a 'collaboration', it is of interest here to look at two statements by de Julleville on the subject of borrowing, the first in his Introduction to *La Comédie et les moeurs*, and the second in the chapter on contemporary drama (1889) in *Le Théâtre en France*:

1. ... chaque époque a instruit, formé, enrichi l'époque suivante; et la tradition comique ininterrompue est arrivée jusqu'à Molière, qui se vantait, on le sait, 'de prendre son bien partout ou il le trouvait'. – 'Ses vols étaient des conquêtes', a-t-on dit. Mot plus éclatant que juste. Ne disons ni vol ni conquête; mais legitime héritage; toute l'immense matière comique accumulée depuis près de quatre siècles, est tombée en ses mains puissantes; il l'a comme pétrie et refaite, et marquée à la marque de son génie ...

    (... each age informed, shaped, and enriched that which followed, and the unbroken comic tradition came down to

45

Molière, who prided himself, as we know, on helping himself
to whatever material he could lay his hands on. 'His thefts
were victories', the saying goes, but the expression is more
striking than true. It would be more accurate to speak of a
legitimate heritage than of thefts or conquests. The entire
vast accumulation of almost four centuries of comic material
fell into his capable hands. He moulded it and re-made it and
gave it the stamp of his genius.)

2.   On fait grand bruit des emprunts ou, comme on a dit, des
plagiats de M. Sardou. Il n'emprunte pas plus que Molière;
souhaitons seulement qu'il use aussi bien de ce qu'il
emprunte. La matière comique est éternelle et toujours la
même; elle passe de main en main comme une argile com-
mune, dont chacun, tour à tour, tire des effigies différentes.
L'important c'est d'ajouter sa marque à sa signature . . .[50]

(Much fuss is made of Mr Sardou's borrowings, or plagiar-
isms as they are called. He does not borrow any more than
Molière did, only let us hope that he makes as good use of
what he borrows. Comic material is perennial, and always
the same; it passes from hand to hand like common clay from
which each one in turn creates a different image. The important thing is that each should add his own mark to his
signature.)

Petit de Julleville's teaching that comic material is a common heritage, and that Molière's and others' use of such material is legitimate,
encouraged Synge's theory of art as a collaboration. Besides, that
teaching gave Synge both confidence in his own practice of borrowing, and determination to apply his own individual stamp to borrowed material. His consciousness of tradition, particularly of
dramatic tradition, and his appreciation of the value of the contribution of individual talent to it were both increased by de Julleville.
   Sensitivity to tradition means not only consciousness of the literary past but also awareness of current literary practice, and here too
the work of de Julleville guided Synge. There the great variety of
genres, including various mixtures, which were then being produced
in the French theatre, are noted. Alexandre Dumas is singled out as
the playwright who most successfully mixes the comic with the
pathetic, and even with the tragic, often in the same scene.[51]

Naturalism of style and determinist values are identified as the main pitfalls of the contemporary drama: naturalism for the incoherence it can produce, which, de Julleville insists, must be precluded by creating an overall sense of unity in a play;[52] and determinism for its being essentially antidramatic in demoting the will, so that passionate internal conflict is not possible.[53]

It is indicative that despite the painstaking attention Synge gave to naturalistic detail in costume, set, and props, he was careful to produce a unified effect, meticulously orchestrated, in his plays, achieved through exhaustive drafting and re-writing;[54] and that where individual will was powerless in his source, as in the case of *The Well* and *Deirdre*, he created volitional protagonists. Both practices suggest that he was avoiding those very dangers which de Julleville had identified in contemporary dramatic practice in France.

The most fundamental influence from de Julleville was perhaps his cultivation of Synge's sense of audience, and cognate with that, his awareness of changes in sensibility. In his reiterative works, it is striking how strong de Julleville's historical sense was and how clearly he perceived the difference in sensibility reflected in medieval and contemporary drama. He noted particularly that the medieval audience expected, and was always presented with, situations which were clearly sad or gay, but never ambiguous, whereas contemporary audiences saw situations and characters as essentially complex – half pitiable, half laughable.[55] Besides, his awareness of the relatively exaggerated sense of pity in the contemporary drama and its audience caused him to publish the following remarks verbatim in two different books:

> Le moyen âge ne craignait pas de tourner au comique des situations pénibles ou même atroces, dont nous ne pourrions supporter aujourd'hui l'horreur. Mais l'époque, sans être plus méchante qu'une autre, était dure à la souffrance, et peu accessible à l'attendrissement. Dans les farces on rit très souvent à gorge déployée de bien des choses qui de nos jours seraient mises en scène pour nous tirer des pleurs. Cette facilité à rire des misères de l'homme, le moyen âge l'a transmise, adoucie, mais non diminuée, d'abord à la Renaissance (qu'on se rappelle dans Rabelais l'histoire des Chicanoux, et celle du sacristain écartelé par Villon), ensuite, au XVIIe siècle. Il y a chez Molière, il y a chez Regnard des situations comiques sur la scène, dans notre

siècle, deviendraient purement pathétiques. Est-ce à dire que
nos coeurs soient plus sensibles, ou notre sensibilité plus
emphatique?[56]

(In the Middle Ages, there was no fear of turning to comic
purposes painful or even agonizing situations, the horror of
which we would not be able to bear to-day. But the times,
without being worse than any other, were hard towards suffering
and not very susceptible to pity. Often, in the farces, things which
would be staged today to wring tears from us were laughed at
heartily. The Middle Ages transmitted this capacity to laugh at
man's miseries, softened but not reduced, first to the Renaissance (remember the story of Chicanoux in Rabelais, and Villon's deposed sacristan), and then to the 17th century. In Molière
and Regnard there are comic situations on the stage which would
become purely pathetic in our day. Does that mean that our
hearts are more sensitive or our sensitivity more inflated?)

This raising of the question of changing sensibility and increased
susceptibility to pathos encouraged the formation of Synge's view
on the place of pity and gaiety in art: 'Gaiety and pity are essentially
in coexistent conflict' (see p. 23 above). Holding such a view, he
clearly had no design to evoke the easy tear of the Victorian melo-
drama, any more than the easy laugh at the stage Irishman, the first at
the cost of gaiety and the second at the cost of pity. Accordingly,
when he transfigured a medieval French farce into his own terms,
while he alternated the flow of the Rabelaisian and the pathetic
streams, he neither denied their distinction nor did he attempt to
segregate the sources of pity and laughter.

Synge's debt to Petit de Julleville is immediate in the matter of
developing his aesthetic theory, but there is another influence at
work which may not be entirely direct. The numerous striking
parallels between the few statements on literary theory which Synge
has left us and the ideas of Victor Hugo in his Preface to *Cromwell*
suggest that Synge had thoroughly absorbed those ideas.[57] However, it would be difficult to distinguish definitively between ideas
taken directly from Victor Hugo and those ideas of Hugo transmitted via de Julleville, and even those which had by Synge's time
saturated current French literary theory.

Hugo's rejection of the claim that ugliness and the grotesque
should be excluded from art is perhaps the most pertinent of his

views to Synge's practice in *The Well*:

> Ainsi, que des pedants étourdis (l'un n'exclut pas l'autre) pré-
> tendent que le difforme, le laid, le grotesque, ne doit jamais être
> un objet d'imitation pour l'art, on leur répond que le grotesque,
> c'est la comédie, et q'apparemment la comédie fait partie de
> l'art.[58]

> (When scatter-brained pedants (the one does not preclude the
> other) claim that the deformed, the ugly and the grotesque
> should never be imitated by art, one replies that the grotesque is
> comedy, and that comedy obviously is a part of art.)

This idea of the grotesque as something essentially comic will be
further discussed in the course of examining the comic element in
Synge's work. What concerns us here is Hugo's refusal to exclude
the grotesque, and the related refusal to separate comedy and
tragedy on the basis that the Christian view of man recognizes both
the animal and the divine in him:

> ... si ... ils renouvellent leur prohibition du grotesque allié au
> sublime, de la comédie fondue dans la tragedie, on leur fait voir
> que, dans la poésie des peuples chrétiens, le premier de ces deux
> types représente la bête humaine, le second l'âme.[59]

> (If they renew their objections to the grotesque mixed with the
> sublime and to comedy blended with tragedy, show them that in
> the poetry of Christian peoples the first of these two examples
> represents the animal aspect of man, the second the human soul.)

The separation of these two aspects of man results in abstraction,
which is unfaithful to reality and thus fails to truly depict man:
'après ces abstractions, il restera quelque chose à représenter,
l'homme; après ces tragédies et ces comédies, quelque chose à faire,
le drame' (after these abstractions, something else remains to be
depicted: man; and after these tragedies and comedies something
else remains to be created: drama). True drama, in Hugo's view,
must be based in reality:

> Dans le drame, tel qu'on peut, sinon exécuter, du moins le
> concevoir, tout s'enchaîne et se deduit ainsi que dans la réalité.

49

Le corps y joue son rôle comme l'âme; et les hommes et les événements, mis en jeu par ce double agent, passent tour à tour bouffons et terribles, quelquefois terribles et bouffons tout ensemble.[60]

(In the drama, so far as possible, everything is linked just as it is in reality, if not in its execution then at least in its conception. The body plays its part there as well as the soul; and instigated by this dual agency, men and incidents proceed, funny and terrible by turns, and sometimes terrible and funny together.)

Since the grotesque in art should reflect that in life, and since the course of events in drama should imitate that confused course of man's body and soul in life, then tragi-comedy is implicitly desirable and the grotesque is not simply a convention, but something essential:

C'est donc une des suprèmes beautés du drame que le grotesque. Il n'est pas seulement une convenance, il en est souvent une necessité . . . Il s'infiltre partout, car de même que les plus vulgaires ont mainte fois leurs accès de sublime, les plus élevés payent fréquemment tribut au trivial et au ridicule. . . . Parfois enfin il peut sans discordance, comme dans la scène du roi Lear et de son fou, mêler sa voix criarde aux plus sublimes, aux plus lugubres, aux plus rêveuses musiques de l'âme.[61]

(The grotesque, then, is one of the supreme beauties of the drama. It is not simply a convention, but is often a necessity there . . . It infiltrates everywhere because, just as the most vulgar persons often have bouts of sublimity, so the most elevated frequently pay tribute to the trivial and the ridiculous . . . Sometimes, even, it can add its shrill voice to the most sublime, the most gloomy, or the most dreamy music of the soul, without discordance, as for instance in the scene between King Lear and his fool.)

Thus Hugo justifies the admission of the grotesque to drama, and Synge put this theory into practice in *The Well*, and in the three other plays which assert the coexistence of inner and outer reality, by giving the body due place beside the soul.

The distinction of place which Synge sought in each work (see

50

p. 27) echoes another Hugo principle:

> On commence à comprendre de nos jours que la localité exacte est une des premiers éléments de la réalité. Les personnages parlants ou agissants ne sont pas les seuls qui gravent dans l'esprit du spectateur la fidèle empreinte des faits. Le lieu où telle catastrophe s'est passée en devient un témoin terrible et inséparable; et l'absence de cette sorte de personage muet décompléterait dans le drame les plus grandes scènes de l'histoire.[62]

> (In our days we have begun to understand that precision of place is one of the primary elements of reality. The characters who speak and act are not alone in etching a faithful impression of the facts in the mind of the spectator. The place where a particular catastrophe occurred becomes an awful and inseparable witness of it; and the absence of this sort of dumb character would leave the greatest scenes of the story incomplete in the play.)

Further on the question of creating a sense of place, Hugo urges that it is insufficient to add 'local colour' afterwards to a total situation which is quite artificial and conventional. He continues: 'Ce n'est point à la surface du drame que doit être la couleur locale, mais au fond, dans le coeur même de l'oeuvre . . .' (Local colour should not be at all superficial in the drama, but should be fundamental to the work, at its very heart . . .). And besides this fundamental sense of place, he also seeks the sense of a specific time:

> Le drame doit être radicalement impregné de cette couleur des temps; elle doit en quelque sorte y être dans l'air, de façon qu'on ne s'aperçoive qu'en y entrant et q'en sortant qu'on a changé de siècle et d'atmosphère. Il faut quelque étude, quelque labeur pour en venir là; tant mieux.[63]

> (The drama should be impregnated with the colour of the times at its very roots; this colour should in a certain way be in the atmosphere, so that one only notices that one has changed centuries or atmosphere as one enters and leaves. To achieve this requires some study and labour. So much the better!)

In order to avoid producing what is common, which he sees as killing the drama, Hugo asks the dramatist to create the sense of a particular place and time, and warns that he must also avoid becoming a parasite on other artists, no matter how great they might be, and that he must not hope for success by following rules. Here we find the hub of Romantic theory as it was articulated by Hugo – that act of faith in the power of the genius of the individual artist to give organic form to his creation. This is the basis for the third distinction sought by Synge: '. . . the great artist, as Rembrandt or Shakespeare, adds his personal distinction to a great distinction of time and place'.[64]

Synge, in addition to echoing certain theories of Hugo, could also have been faithfully following all of Hugo's recommendations for the drama when he evolved the genre typified in *The Well*. The medieval source with its grotesque conception was a promising point of departure. To it Synge added the sublimity of Martin and Mary's dream, thus creating the kind of contrast which Hugo saw as vitalizing. The chosen distinction of time and place gave expression to a 'national mood', as well as according with Synge's conception of his characters as elemental; and it provided a credible setting against which he could illuminate both their inner and outer lives, once again in accordance with the multiple objective of art as defined by Hugo:

> . . . le but multiple de l'art, qui est d'ouvrir au spectateur un double horizon, d'illuminer à la fois l'intérieur et l'extérieur des hommes; l'extérieur, par leurs discours et leurs actions; l'intérieur, par les *a parte* et les monologues; . . .[65]

> (. . . the multiple objective of art, which is to open up to the spectator a double horizon, to illuminate man's interior and exterior at the same time; the exterior through speech and actions; the interior through asides and soliloquys . . .)

Even Hugo's recommendation as to the means of illuminating man's inner life was among those adopted by Synge in *The Well*. The soliloquy, which fits ill with notions of naturalism on the stage, is used for revealing the true state of Mary's feelings at the opening of act three. Her blindness helps credibility here, as does Martin's when he comes in and delivers his soliloquy after hers. In *The Tinker's Wedding* Synge was again able to justify soliloquy through Mary Byrne's drunkenness. But in *The Playboy*, which was the culmination of the genre, the justification for it was in the characters to whom it was attributed, Christy and the Widow Quin: Christy because of his growing self-satisfaction, and the Widow because of her woman-of-experience self-confidence. Besides, the burden of self-revelation was by then being adequately borne by dialogue and action, so that Synge felt ready for another change: 'I wanted a change from Peasant Comedy – or thought I did'.[66] By the time he had finished *The Playboy* he had exploited the possibilities of the genre he here refers to as 'Peasant Comedy' to the full. To pursue it further would have been to follow his own rules, and that could have been to fossilize.

III THE PLAYBOY OF THE WESTERN WORLD: MEDIEVAL ANALOGUES

The Playboy of the Western World has a number of features which are analogous to one of the heroic tales from the Ulster cycle, *Fled Bricrend (Bricriu's Feast)*. In this tale Bricriu, on of the Ulster lords renowned for his evil tongue and *penchant* for trouble-making, threatened to set father against son among his peers unless they accepted his invitation to a vast feast which he had prepared. Although Cuchulainn, Conall Cearnach, and Loigaire then came to his feast, he still instigated strife by promising the 'hero's portion' to each of the three heroes in turn. Likewise he incited each of the wives of these warriors to assume precedence over all the women of Ulster. Since no solution to the question of superiority was found, judgement was referred to Curoi, who lived in the south of Ireland. The three warriors set out, and each in turn, with his gillie, encountered an ugly giant who overcame Conall and Loigaire but was mastered by Cuchulainn. Cuchulainn then returned to Emain victorious, but the other two would not acknowledge his victory on the grounds of magical interference. Judgement was then referred to Aillil of Connacht, who, with Maeve's intervention, again attributed the 'hero's portion' to Cuchulainn, but once again the other two disagreed. Finally the question was settled by the arrival of a huge, ugly churl at Emain announcing that he sought 'fair play'. His proposal, a reversal of his original suggestion, was that he should have his head cut off by a warrior and return the following night to cut off that warrior's head. Only Cuchulainn kept his 'champion's covenant' and duly turned up to receive the reciprocal blow from the churl, so that from that time his right to the 'hero's portion' went unchallenged.

None of the extant manuscripts preserves a complete text of this tale, but collation of them all has restored a version reflecting that told in the eighth or early ninth century.[1] The oldest MS version of *Bricriu's Feast* is in the pre-1106 *Book of the Dun Cow*, which is in the Royal Irish Academy; and the ending of the tale is to be found in a MS in the Edinburgh Advocates' Library. A facsimile of a copy of *The Book of the Dun Cow* made by the scribe Joseph O'Longan was published by the Royal Irish Academy in 1871. This, or indeed the original MS, may well have been brought to Synge's attention by his friend Richard Best. He much admired the work of Best, who had a particular interest in this MS and was eventually responsible for showing that it had been compiled by three different scribes.[2]

Although Synge has left no direct reference to this tale, he was well acquainted with the cycle as a whole, and several discussions of it are to be found in works with which he was familiar. Extensive treatment of it is to be found in Eleanor Hull's collection of Cuchulainn tales, *The Cuchullin Saga in Irish Literature*, which Synge had studied in sufficient detail to publish a critical reference to it.[3] Miss Hull tells us of Professor de Jubainville's translation of the tale into French in *L'Epopée celtique en Irlande*, which Synge would certainly have known.[4] Besides, the tale would have been included in the material dealt with in his lectures by de Jubainville, who gives a detailed account of it in his *Introduction à l'étude de la littérature celtique*.[5] In that account he refers to Windisch's edition of the tale, which is accompanied by a German translation,[6] and since Synge has commented on the admirable erudition of Windisch, it is also likely that he examined the latter.[7]

Reviewing Keating's *History of Ireland* in 1902, Synge wrote: 'This volume is the fourth published by the Irish Texts Society, and in some ways the most important that they have brought out'.[8] Such a judgement coming from Synge can be taken as based on at least a fair knowledge of the material against which he rates the importance of this fourth volume. Therefore it is safe to assume that he knew the second volume in the series: *Fled Bricrend* (Bricriu's Feast), edited by George Henderson in 1899.

Henderson, in his Introduction, selects certain Irish words which he examines philologically in relation to Welsh, Greek, Latin, German and Sanskrit, displaying the kind of interest reflected in the philological entries to be found in Synge's notebooks. This expansive, comparative approach is similar to that of Professor de Jubainville in his philological works. Also in his Introduction, Henderson has a striking literary comment to make on *Bricriu's Feast*:

> With a realism true to fact, the wild and the grotesque are intermingled, here and there crossed with a vein of broad primitive humour, in keeping with the rougher, if withal naïve and simple childhood of the world.[9]

There is much here that is reminiscent of comments on Synge's work as a whole, and on *The Playboy* in particular. His use of the wild, the grotesque, the humorous, and the primitive, as well as the nature of his realism, are of ongoing interest, and that such factors should also be recognized in *Bricriu's Feast* is conducive to comparison of the two.

Synge knew Lady Gregory's rendering of this tale under the headings 'Bricriu's Feast' and 'The Championship of Ulster' in her *Cuchulain of Muirthemne*. She had used Windisch, de Jubainville and Henderson to produce a comparatively free rendering,[10] and one can see in this tale in particular that she omitted certain barbarous features. This aspect of her method, which had been commented on by Synge, leads one to concentrate on the work of those 'who translate without hesitation all that has come down to us in the MSS' for our comparisons,[11] therefore Henderson's edition and translation, which is based on all the MS texts, will be mainly used for comparison in this work, with some reference to de Jubainville's translation.

The first analogous feature to be considered is the setting of father against son. In the Early Irish tale this remains a threat, but one which is powerful enough to alter the decision of the Ulster warriors. Bricriu's threat, as Synge would have known from de Jubainville, was a danger to one of the eight unions recognized by Old Irish law, and father set against son is a recurrent feature in Early Irish tales. Synge makes the archetypal struggle between youth and age concrete, both in Christy's reports and in the physical combat between Mahon and Christy. Finally the struggle is resolved by the adoption of a new attitude to each other by father and son, thus avoiding the social disruption which was the key to the power behind Bricriu's threat.

Synge did not present in *The Playboy* the actual reaction to parricide which he had encountered on Aran, and which was accepting of a certain uncontrollable passion: 'Would any one kill his father if he was able to help it?', they would ask in relation to the parricide whom they had sheltered.[12] In the fact that the people of Aran had hidden a parricide fleeing from the law, Synge saw not only a refusal to allow public justice to discount an individual state of mind but also a striking contrast with the honoured law of the heroic world of the Early Irish tale. There the threatened social disruption implied dire, far-reaching effects, but the conflict in Synge's play is largely limited to Christy and Old Mahon. Where mass slaughter is repeatedly averted in *Bricriu's Feast*, an individual case of parricide is apparently nearly missed three times in the play. Those consequences which are far-reaching that can be divined at the end of *The Playboy* are in the realm of personal consciousness, where great disruption has occurred: it might be said that the old Christy is dead, and his father's relationship to him is on a quite different footing.

The next feature common to the Early Irish tale and the play is the 'hero's portion'. It was customary at the kind of feast set up by Bricriu that one man should be offered the 'hero's portion' in recognition of his superiority over the other warriors. In *Bricriu's Feast* the host promises the 'hero's portion' in turn to three of the greatest heroes of Ulster: Cuchulainn, Conall Cearnach and Loigaire. Since it can only go to one, various contests result between the contenders. Traditionally the 'hero's portion' consisted of the thigh, which was claimed by the bravest man when the joints were set before the guests. But at Bricriu's feast there was an exceptionally elaborate hero's portion, described by Bricriu himself as consisting of a seven-year-old boar and a seven-year-old cow, both having been fed on a special diet for sweetness' sake; five score wheaten cakes baked in honey; and a cauldron full of pure wine.

There are four distinct elements in this 'hero's portion' and each one is marked for its luxurious quality. It is feasible that when Susan, Nelly, Honor and Sarah arrive to see Christy, the food which they bring him should be viewed as the 'hero's portion'. No other character is offered food in the play, and this food, brought by the admiring young girls to the man that killed his father, is a tribute to his bravery. Furthermore, their tribute consists of four elements: a brace of duck's eggs, superior to Pegeen's; a pat of butter, a distinct luxury in a Mayo cottage; a cut of cake, another luxury; and finally a laying pullet with a fat breast, killed only the previous evening, therefore fresh.[13] What Christy has been given is in itself a feast in local terms, and he has the whole portion. That he is a champion is explicitly recognized by the Widow Quin who calls him 'the champion of the world', while she calls Old Mahon 'a civil warrior'.[4] The hand of Pegeen might also be regarded as forming part of the hero's portion, since it is the bravery and distinction of Christy's 'deed' which wins him her love. Besides, Christy contends for the 'hero's portion' in three ways, a pattern which follows the arrangement of contests in threes in *Bricriu's Feast*: first, he commands interest and admiration by his telling of his story, which sets him far above the local men; then he competes in the local sports and wins all before him; and finally he shows willing to fulfil his undertaking and meets his father quite prepared to kill him and hang for it.

Christy's preparedness to fulfil his undertaking is comparable to Cuchulainn's fulfilling the 'champion's covenant' with the churl in *Bricriu's Feast*, but Christy is not a simple hero since he also embodies the cowardice of the other warriors who failed to keep the covenant. In the tale, when the churl challenges the Ulster warriors to 'fair play', his initial proposal is that he should cut off a warrior's head and return the following night to have his own cut off. Since this is unacceptable, he reverses the proposal to having his own head cut off by a warrior the first night and coming back the following night to cut that hero's head off. This proposal is agreed to by the warriors. Each cuts off the churl's head but fails to keep the bargain the following night. Eventually on the last night the churl returns furious, and challenges Cuchulainn, who has since returned to Emain. Cuchulainn beheads the churl, who, as on the previous occasions, nevertheless gets up and leaves, carrying his head. The following evening Cuchulainn, in spite of his fear, keeps his covenant with the churl, who brings the blunt side of the axe down on Cuchulainn's neck and recognizes his bravery.

In *The Playboy*, it is Christy who keeps the 'champion's covenant'. Initially he thinks he has killed his father, but when it transpires that he has not, and the admiration he had won wanes, he undertakes the killing a second time. Everyone, including himself, now believes that he has killed his father and prepares to take Christy to be hanged. This at first brings back Christy's fear of the rope,[15] but when he sees the villany of those around him, he grows brave and boasts '. . . if I've to face the gallows I'll have a gay march down, I tell you, and shed the blood of some of you before I die'. And further on he says:

> If I can wring a neck among you, I'll have a royal judgement looking on the trembling jury in the courts of law. And won't there be crying out in Mayo the day I'm stretched upon the rope with ladies in their silks and satins snivelling in their lacy kerchiefs, and they rhyming songs and ballads on the terror of my fate.[16]

Christy's interest in the effect of his fate on his spectators is an inversion of the power of reputation in *Bricriu's Feast*. Where in the Early Irish tale Cuchulainn has his reputation as a champion to maintain, in *The Playboy* Christy's reputation is only in the making, so that contemplation of its possible effects spurs him towards a heroic concept of himself. As a consequence, when Christy's 'dead' father appears for a third 'killing', Christy is quite ready to carry it out. In both cases, however, the hero is ultimately reprieved. Christy's right to the hero's portion goes unchallenged as he leaves with his father 'like a gallant captain with his heathen slave', to go 'romancing through a romping lifetime,' leaving behind Pegeen who has lost 'the only playboy of the western world'.[17] The reward for Christy's bravery in keeping his covenant is this title undisputed, while Cuchulainn's reward is his undisputed title to the 'hero's portion'.

The beheading motif is also common to *The Playboy* and *Bricriu's Feast*, though in the play beheading is transmuted into various forms of assault on the head. Christy's announcement on arrival that he is faced with hanging for his crime is met with disbelief on the part of Pegeen, who threatens Christy (because he calls her disbelief a lie) in terms which horrify him: 'Would you have me knock the head of you with the butt of the broom?'. Such a threat touches a raw spot in Christy's memory: 'Don't strike me . . . I killed my poor father, Tuesday was a week, for doing the like of that'.[18] In all the four accounts which Christy subsequently offers of how he killed his father, the assault is concentrated on the head. First he says 'I just riz the loy and let fall the edge of it on the ridge of his skull'; then he says: 'I did up a Tuesday and halve his skull'; next we get the most elaborate version, when he is playing to the gallery and dramatically reports the argument between his father and himself, complete with light effects:

> CHRISTY (*impressively*). With that the sun came out between the cloud and the hill, and it shining green in my face. 'God have mercy on your soul,' says he, lifting a scythe; 'or on your own', says I, raising the loy.
> SUSAN. That's a grand story.
> HONOR. He tells it lovely.
> CHRISTY (*flattered and confident, waving bone*). He gave a drive with the scythe, and I gave a lep to the east. Then I turned around with my back to the north, and I hit a blow on the ridge of his skull, laid him stretched out, and he split to the knob of his gullet.

Finally Christy makes the extravagant claim that he had 'cleft his father with one blow to the breeches belt'.[19]

Such use of concrete physical detail in accounts of assault is in the same tradition as that commonly found in Early Irish tales. Where the play accounts convey first, an immediate sense of the human skull, progressing through a splitting 'to the knob of his gullet' to a cleaving 'to the breeches belt', those accounts in *Bricriu's Feast* of the giant's attacks on the three gillies similarly mention specific parts of the body: thus Loigaire's gillie receives a blow from the ear to the heel. Another instance of this kind of specified physical assault occurs in one of the Táin tales, where Cuchulainn strikes Etarcomol through the crown of his head and splits him to the navel.[20]

In *The Playboy*, when eventually Old Mahon appears, much is made of the rent in his crown, and of his son having broken his head. Again, his desire for vengeance is expressed in specific physical terms: 'Let me out the lot of you! till I have my vengeance on his head to-day'. Later he challenges Christy to 'retribution', so that the idea of 'a head for a head' which coincides with the reciprocal beheading of *Bricriu's Feast* is reinforced.[21] While there is not a beheading as such in *The Playboy*, it should be remembered that no true beheading takes place in *Bricriu's Feast* either. Although in the 'champion's portion' episode Cuchulainn knocks off the head of his challenger, hurls it to the rafters and shatters it to pieces, it transpires that the challenger returns intact for the reciprocal beheading: thereby the audience is assured that he is no ordinary mortal but a supernatural figure impervious to human harm.[22] The parallel to be drawn between the tale and the play is the heightening of the sense of the body in assault, and particularly of the head.

Similarly, old Mahon's coming back to life parallels the repeated incident of the churl picking up his head and walking off after being beheaded. When Christy first sees his supposedly dead father he says: 'It's the walking spirit of my murdered da!'. Later, alone with the Widow Quin he says 'To be letting on he was dead, and coming back to his life'. And when Pegeen sees old Mahon she asks 'Is it rose from the dead?'. Finally, old Mahon's reappearance after Christy has 'finished' him for the second time evokes this query from Christy: 'Are you coming to be killed a third time or what ails you now?'.[23] Here one sees an acceptance of the marvel similar to that found in *Bricriu's Feast*, where it is the result of the supernatural powers of Curoi.

The reference to the peelers not coming to Michael Flaherty's 'if the dogs itself were lapping poteen from the dung-pit of the yard' calls for some explanation. While the image of poteen in the dung-pit is understandable as an expression of abundance to the point of waste, dogs, or indeed any other animals, are not noted for being partial to spirits. I would suggest that the association came to Synge from the scene in *Bricriu's Feast* where the host suffers a shocking indignity as a result of Cuchulainn's display of strength in raising the whole side of the dwelling to make a passage for his wife Emer and her fifty attendants. Over that side of the dwelling was the balcony or lodge which Bricriu had had constructed so as to be able to watch the Feast after Conchubor had refused to have him present in the midst of the Ulster warriors for fear of his evil tongue. When Cuchulainn released the wall after the passage of Emer and her train, it collapsed, together with the lodge housing Bricriu and his wife, who were consequently flung onto the dung-pit among the dogs in the yard outside. The excess of liquor and other fare at such feasts as Bricriu's, as they are described in Early Irish tales, would have predisposed Synge to think of dogs and dung-pits in that context.[24]

Another feature common to the tale and the play is the figure of the 'wild man'. This figure is recurrent in tales of the middle ages both in Ireland and elsewhere. For example one might cite *Aucassin et Nicolette* and *Sir Gawain and the Green Knight*, in both of which he embodies something of the supernatural, as he does in *Bricriu's Feast*. The 'wild man' traditionally appears from outside the established community, and his function is to challenge the claims of its warriors or heroes, particularly in the matter of prowess and courage in combat. In *Bricriu's Feast* he can be identified in the ugly giant who attacks the three gillies of Loigaire, Conall Cearnach and Cuchulainn in turn, and with whom each of these warriors is therefore obliged to fight. He can also be seen in the ugly churl who comes to issue the reciprocal beheading challenge in Emain.

The arrivals of both Christy and Old Mahon in *The Playboy* can be viewed as serving a similar function to the 'wild men' of *Bricriu's Feast*, although the question of heroic reputation is inverted. Christy, who hails from 'a distant place, . . . a windy corner of high distant hills', eventually calls into question the eligibility of mousy Shawn as suitor for Pegeen, and also challenges the local sportsmen victoriously. The scene directions describe him as 'dirty'; he is mistaken for a tinker (another outside figure with qualities of the 'wild man'); and he is perceived as 'a wicked-looking fellow' by other characters.[25] Old Mahon, who 'never gave peace to any saving when he'd get two months or three, or be locked in the asylum for battering peelers' (meaning that he desisted from assaulting others only when in prison or hospital), calls into question Christy's boasts and eventually forces him to realize them. Both in their function as challengers and in their physical appearance these two characters are analogous to the challengers of *Bricriu's Feast.*

Each of these is described in hideous terms: among the giant's attributes, for instance, are a huge head, fat lips, bulging eyes, and eyebrows like bushes. Besides, he is ill-clad. Also, the axe carried by the ugly churl and used in the carrying out of his challenge, can be related to the loy which Christy uses, both in the accounts he gives of killing his father and in certain scenes of the play. In each case these are the implement of aggression used in the combat for the 'hero's portion' and the 'champion's covenant'.[26]

One final feature to be found both in the tale and the play is the contest of the women for precedence. In *Bricriu's Feast* this occurs at the instigation of Bricriu, who tells the wife of each of Loigaire, Conall Cearnach, and Cuchulainn that she should be the first to enter the hall where the feast is to be held. As a result, there is an unseemly, comic charge made at the entrance by these ladies, in which Cuchulainn's wife, Emer, is the winner. This charge can be related to the hasty arrival of the Widow Quin to spy out Christy, which is described in these terms by Pegeen: 'and you gasping with the rage you had racing the hill beyond to look on his face'.[27] It can also be related to the hurried arrival of the quartet of admiring girls, described by one of themselves as follows: '. . . and we after rising early and destroying ourselves running fast on the hill'.[28] Again the parallel between the medieval tale and the modern play is not exact, but taken together with the other common features it is plausible, and here Synge echoes the comic spirit. Although there is no comic resolution at the end of his play, in these incidents of contesting women he follows the spirit of a tale which is outstandingly comic in the Ulster cycle.

However, in most cases where Synge adopts features from *Bricriu's Feast* the same sort of inversion can be seen as prevailed in his treatment of the French medieval source for *The Well of the Saints.* After a tale where the prevalence of heroic qualities is assumed, and those qualities are manifestly embodied in Cuchulainn, his drama portrays a society in which no vestige of heroism remains and a 'hero' who initially appears as a coward in spite of the heroic qualities attributed to him by the other characters. Where Cuchulainn had been performing feats to maintain his existing heroic reputation, Christy undergoes experiences, unconsciously at first, which bring him to a totally new evaluation of himself and draw to his attention latent qualities hitherto unrecognized. Cuchulainn had a routine to go through in order to prove once again to his society that he was worthy of their esteem, whereas Christy comes to a favourable estimate of himself for the first time. The values at stake in the early Irish tale are primarily social; those established in the course of *The Playboy* are relevant particularly to the hero, although they are not without a social dimension.

Recognition of Synge's tendency to invert material he adopted makes the question of whether he knew *Sir Gawain and the Green Knight* more pertinent. On the surface, there is no apparent connection between this Middle English romance and *The Playboy* beyond those features which are analogous to *Bricriu's Feast*: the champion's covenant, the wild man, and the beheading ordeal. Besides, there is no 'hero's portion' in *Sir Gawain and the Green Knight*. Synge pursued no course of formal studies where he would have received any detailed scholarly information on *Gawain* as he had done on *La moralité de l'aveugle et du boiteux*, *Deirdre* and *Bricriu's Feast*, and no reference to it by him has come to light. Yet the inversion referred to above, which results in Christy's altered perception of his own value, could be compared with Gawain's altered perception of his.

In the Introduction we saw that Synge identified several European literary analogues to Pat Dirane's story of the Lady O'Connor (see p. 15 above). Given this kind of awareness of analogues it is reasonable to expect him to be aware of those to *Bricriu's Feast*. He would have found a resumé of the analogous passages from *Sir Gawain and the Green Knight* in George Henderson's edition of *Bricriu's Feast* apart from any first-hand knowledge he might have had of the Middle English romance.[29] Henderson notes two editions of *Gawain*, one by Sir F. Madden and one by Dr Richard Morris for the Early English Text Society; and he comments on the special interest and importance of the beheading incident in *Bricriu's Feast* because of its being paralleled in *Gawain*.[30]

Eleanor Hull's book, *The Cuchullin Saga in Irish Literature*, also draws attention to the connections between *Bricriu's Feast* and *Sir Gawain* in all their salient features.[31] It contains a resumé of the

63

latter and mentions Jessie Weston's book, *The Legend of Sir Gawain: The Possible Interpretation of the Facts in Connection with Irish Literature*, which was published in 1898. Such a title would surely have attracted Synge's attention, and even if he did not examine the critical work itself, his curiosity would have been sufficiently aroused to pursue the connection.

In the course of *Sir Gawain and the Green Knight*, the hero, so far as we can tell, mistakenly assumes that the ordeal he is to endure is to test his reputation for courtly honour. Within the bounds of the conventional code he acquits himself socially, and is warmly received by Arthur and his court at the end. Here, however, the blood rushes to his face when he contemplates the token of his failure, for he realizes that the testing was also on the higher plane of absolutes, where he was guilty of a breach of faith. Thus he perceives the indelible effects of his experience, indicating the green girdle which he had accepted from Bertilak's lady:

> Þis is þe token of vntrawþe þat I am tan inne,
> And I mot nedez hit were wyle I may last;
> For mon may hyden his harme, bot vnhap ne may hit,
> For þer hit onez is tachched twynne wil hit neuer.[32]

(This is the token of the perfidy of which I am guilty, and I must wear it while I live. For although injury may be hidden it cannot be cast off, because once it is fixed it cannot be loosed.)

Similarly, Christy believes that he must endure the consequences of having murdered his father. Not only is he mistaken in this but, when his true testing comes it is confounded by a 'lady' with designs on his virility, as happened in the case of Gawain. The challenge to Christy comes from his father, who unwittingly causes his son to leave his own territory and go north to discover the appeal he had for the Mayo girls, and for Pegeen in particular. The new-found confidence which results from this makes him 'master of all fights from now' so that he leaves the stage with the following conception of himself:

> Ten thousand blessings upon all that's here, for you've turned me a likely gaffer in the end of all, the way I'll go romancing through a romping lifetime from this hour to the dawning of the judgement day.[33]

Whereas Gawain's ordeal is chastening in its ultimate effects, Christy's is exonerating. From being the gallant knight *par excellence*, Gawain becomes a more complex being who has to reckon with the supernatural and recognize his frailty. Christy, on the other hand, moves from a cowering and fearful disposition to one of vigour and confidence. For the first time he assumes a gallant social role (as gallant captain to his father's heathen slave), ending up where Sir Gawain began.

There are two incidental features in relation to *The Playboy* for which one should be able to account. Each is apparently unwarranted, yet it would be unseemly to attribute carelessness to a writer so painstaking in his revisions. The first is Christy's describing the sun as 'shining green' in his face in his penultimate account of his fight with his father, quoted above. While it might be argued that the sun is described as shining green for scientific reasons (on the basis of a 'complementary colour' theory), we have no evidence that Synge's mind worked in that manner. We do know, however, that he was particularly interested in folk-tales and customs, and that he made use of the image of the 'green man' in a one-act draft of *The Tinker's Wedding*.[34]

There, the tinker's children have a part in the play, and the following dialogue occurs:

1ST CHILD. We'll make a drum from this bit of a can the way we'll be like the green man we seen in the fair.
2ND CHILD. How would we be like the green man, and not a green rag on us at all?
1ST CHILD. We'll put a bit of rushes round our heads, and then we'll be like the green man surely, and it's a power of money we'll get for sweets beating that thing through the fair.[35]

Robin Skelton has already reminded us of the association between the figure of the 'green man' and *Sir Gawain and the Green Knight*, in his discussion of this passage.[36] I would like to suggest that an additional reason for making that association here is that the above exchange takes place before 'the chapel'. I am making no claim for any similarity of significance between the green chapel of *Sir Gawain* and Synge's chapel: they are, if anything, contrastive. The suggestion is that in the writer's mind there was an association between the ideas 'green man' and 'chapel'. Such an association would readily come to one who knew *Sir Gawain*.

To return to *The Playboy* and the significance of the sun 'shining green' in Christy's face, it is evident that Christy, with his loy, is something of a fertility figure, in the way that the 'green man' and the Green Knight are. The appeal of his virility is borne out in his capturing not only the bevy of girls and the spider-widow, but the betrothed Pegeen. Also, he embodies the regeneration process, which is central to the role of the 'green man' in the folk context and, in its seasonal aspects, plays a considerable part in *Sir Gawain and the Green Knight*.

Furthermore, there are some details in draft C of *The Playboy* which strengthen the argument for the folk connections of the use of the colour green applied to Christy, and bring us to the second feature which needs explanation: Why did Synge contemplate having Christy describe his father 'with a great thorn branch' in his hand?[37] The explanation for this is to be found in a marginal note which reads 'give folk-political basis to murder quarrel?'.[38] Evidently Synge was thinking of the 'green man' with his traditional branch (which appears as the Green Knight's holly cluster in *Sir Gawain*, 1.206), because a thorn branch is not an apt implement for splitting a skull, which is the threat delivered by Christy's father. Later, of course, Synge transferred the whole skull-splitting business to Christy, but it is noteworthy that at the stage of this draft the sun was also 'shining green' in Christy's face. The significance of the great thorn branch was later incorporated in the loy, while the sun 'shining green' remained unchanged.

Synge's intention of using a folk basis for the quarrel is explicit, therefore 'the green man' theory is well founded. Only by implication, however, can the Green Knight analogue be claimed for *The Playboy*. Nevertheless, it can safely be assumed that Synge, conscious as we have seen him elsewhere of literary analogues to folk tale, was not unaware of one here. While he may not have intended his audience to make any direct connection between *Sir Gawain and the Green Knight* and *The Playboy*, he was carrying on a tradition.

Nowhere in Synge's account of the real-life story on which he based *The Playboy* is there any indication that the people who protected the parricide were ripe for a marvel, nor that there was any distinction impressed on them between 'a gallous story and a dirty deed'.[39] Yet, in *The Playboy* these two factors play an important part in the socio-critical emphasis of the work. At first Christy satisfies the need for diversion and entertainment among the people living in the confined society in which he alights. His recounting of the story of the beheading is valued because it's 'a grand story' and 'He tells it lovely'. So long as it is removed from them it is not only acceptable but delectable. However, the moment it is brought to their own 'back yard', it becomes a source of fear, and is intolerable.

Likewise in *Sir Gawain*, the Green Knight enters a confined society which is ripe for a marvel. There we see King Arthur, boyish and restless, refusing, as was his custom, to eat before some marvel was recounted to him or some knight engaged another in jousting (11.85–106). The beheading challenge issued by the Green Knight, under pretext of a Christmas game, stuns the whole court (1.30lf). Turning in his saddle and, *nota bene*, his eyebrows 'shining green' (blycande grene, 1.305), he taunts them for cowering. When the year has passed and the time has come for Gawain to leave, his fellow-courtiers fear for him, although they keep their fear secret (11.558ff). And ultimately, Gawain flinches from the blow (1.2267), thus reinforcing the idea that what was desirable as a 'gallous story' is unacceptable as a reality. In both *Sir Gawain* and *The Playboy*, the question is raised as to how close to real violence those with a need for diversion and excitement can comfortably be. The answer in each case is 'not at all close'. Luckily for both groups, the violence which was brought close was only apparent and finally returns to the realm of the marvellous.

It can be argued that the interests and features which have been identified here as common to *Sir Gawain* and *The Playboy* are also common to many other works of literature. So, even if one could be certain that Synge knew *Sir Gawain and the Green Knight* at first hand, the fact that these features appear in his work is no proof that he was using Gawain or any other literary source consciously. Nevertheless, to evaluate and interpret his work effectively it is essential to relate him to a tradition. Too often Synge is relegated to lonelihood, treated as a writer of peasant plays, and deprived of the company envisaged for all writers by T.S. Eliot when he wrote:

> No poet, no artist of any art, has his complete meaning alone. His significance, his appreciation is the appreciation of his relation to the dead poets and artists. You cannot value him alone; you must set him, for contrast and comparison, among the dead. I mean this as a principle of aesthetic, not merely historical criticism.[40]

In the case of *The Playboy* we can set Synge for contrast and comparison among the nameless makers of the heroic tales of the Ulster cycle and of English medieval romance. As with his earlier plays, he here set about expressing a 'national mood' by using as his primary material incidents and characters from his experience of life and story in rural Ireland. This material was perceived not so much ambivalently as inclusively: courage and cowardice, the sublime and the ridiculous coexisted. Once this material was transferred to a literary plane, it became a fertile medium for growing shoots from the deep and distant roots of Early Irish literature – roots which in the case of *Bricriu's Feast* were of a heroic nature, where Cuchulainn embodies the concept of the hero as a being of absolute courage, daring, and strength.

The fact that Christy Mahon's heroic qualities are offset by apparently contradictory ones has led those who have recognized his connection with Cuchulainn to view Synge's treatment of the heroic concept as parodic or ironic.[41] Such a view fails to give due weight to the aesthetic function of the co-presence of clashing qualities, and it assumes a mocking disposition on the part of the writer, that is a desire to knock at the literary convention of heroism, or at some actual cowardice, or at both. But Synge's disposition was not of the mocking kind.

The society which he portrays is demotic, not the aristocratic world of the saga, but that does not preclude an individual nobility of nature. On the contrary, Synge perceived the simple rural life in Romantic terms: 'The courtesy of the old woman of the house is singularly attractive ... I could see with how much grace she motioned each visitor to a chair, or stool, according to his age, and said a few words to him till he drifted into our English conversation'. And again:

> Their way of life has never been acted on by anything more artificial than the nests and burrows of the creatures that live round them, and they seem in a certain sense to approach more nearly to the finer types of our aristocracies – who are bred artificially to a natural ideal – than to the labourer or citizen, as the wild horse resembles the thoroughbred rather than the hack or cart-horse. Tribes of the same natural development are, perhaps, frequent in half-civilized countries, but here a touch of the refinement of old societies is blended, with singular effect, among the qualities of the wild animal.[42]

But in addition to this natural nobility, Synge also saw the natural cruelty of the peasants, and in *The Playboy* he included both. He attempted, and by concensus achieved, that synthesis for which he sought when he wrote 'Art is so essentially synthetic that if it can be classed as idealistic or realistic it is nearly always inferior'.[43] True, he does not idealize heroism, but neither can his hero be reduced to a parody of Cuchulainn since he is not a parasitic literary growth but one with roots nourished both by 'the clay and worms' of life in the west of Ireland and something of the heroic ideals of *Bricriu's Feast*, all illuminated by the artist's vision.

IV DEIRDRE OF THE SORROWS

The revelation that Synge had used a medieval source for *The Well of the Saints* came from himself, whereas it was common knowledge that for his *Deirdre of the Sorrows* he was drawing on that Early Irish tale which had a wider appeal than any other during the period of the Celtic Revival. Although the tale was widely known in Synge's time, accurate and scholarly knowledge of the original was reserved for the few who could read Old and Middle Irish. He was among those few.

It is not that he approached the tale primarily as a scholar, however. He displayed his sympathies in the matter of approach when he wrote to Lady Gregory the day after he first received her *Cuchulain of Muirthemne*:

> Many of the stories, of course, I have known for a long time, but they seem to gain a new life in the beautiful language you have told them in . . . I told old Jubainville about what you were doing a few weeks ago, and he was very much interested, but I am afraid he looks at Irish things from a too strict point of view to appreciate their literary value as fully as we do.[1]

As he did in the case of his medieval farce, Synge took this 'common' material and moulded it to his own particular shape. But he brought to his handling of it an intimate knowledge of the nature of the basic material, as well as of many of the forms which had emerged from the hands of others over the centuries.

Since such a great number of recensions of the Deirdre tale were available to Synge, it is difficult to single out precisely which individual features he took from which version. Both an Old and Middle Irish version of the tale survived in MS, each of which was edited and variously translated in the nineteenth-century. Besides, the Old Irish version was given a seventeenth-century rendering by Geoffrey Keating, and Andrew MacCurtin made an eighteenth-century rendering of the medieval one. These and the works of Synge's contemporaries Lady Gregory, Yeats and George Russell were the most important versions for him as far as the adoption of incidents

70

and motifs were concerned, though he was acquainted with some, if not all, of the numerous literary adaptations of the nineteenth century. From a stylistic point of view, the two most significant versions were Lady Gregory's in Kiltartanese and Andrew MacCurtin's, of which Synge made a translation.

The oldest written form of the story of Deirdre and the fate to which she and the sons of Uisneach were doomed has survived in two MSS to which Synge had access in his own college library: *The Book of Leinster* and *The Yellow Book of Lecan*. These MSS have been dated as mid-twelfth century and late fourteenth century respectively, but the language which the compilers were recording goes back to the ninth century. The same version of the tale appears in a third MS, in the British Museum (Egerton 1782, dated c. 1517), and a transcript of this made in 1746 by Aodh O'Dalaigh is also to be found in the library of Trinity College, Dublin.[2] Synge's interest and pride in the early literature of his country, increased by the teaching of Henry d'Arbois de Jubainville, is likely to have sent him to peruse the literary treasures housed in his old college during one of his visits home from Paris. Such perusal is clearly implied when in an article for *L'Européen* he writes of *The Book of Leinster*, *The Yellow Book of Lecan*, and two other MSS in the Royal Irish Academy, *The Book of the Dun Cow* and *The Speckled Book of MacEgan*: 'Quand on se met à déchiffrer leurs pages vermoulues, on est étonné par la variété des matières.' (When one begins to decipher their worm-eaten pages, the variety of subject matter is astonishing). Writing of the contents of these MSS, he mentions that among the epic tales are love-stories, the majority of which are tragic: a grouping which would include Deirdre. Since Synge was no poseur, the reference to deciphering the worm-eaten pages of these old MSS can be taken as authentic.[3]

However, even if the claim that Synge had gone so far as to read the oldest version of this tale in manuscript form were refuted, he certainly had learned of that version in the course of his studies with de Jubainville. In Volume V of this scholar's *Cours de littérature celtique* (1892), details are given of the then existing published editions of these MSS, as well as his own French translation of the tale based on a collation of these texts.[4] The texts referred to were edited by Ernst Windisch and Eugene O'Curry, both of whom were praised by Synge for the high quality of their scholarship.[5]

The events of the oldest version of the tale cover the period from before Deirdre's birth to her death. They include the feast at the house of Deirdre's father, Fedlimid, at which Deirdre is heard to cry out in her mother's womb before her birth; Cathbad the druid's prophecy concerning her fate and that of the sons of Uisneach; and the decision of Conchubor, the king, to have Deirdre reared to be his own wife. Deirdre is reared in seclusion, but before Conchubor can claim her she flees to Alba with her young lover, Naisi, son of Uisneach, and his two brothers. Eventually, Conchubor sends to Alba inviting the sons of Uisneach to return, which they do, with Fergus for surety. After the killing of the sons of Uisneach by Eoghan at Conchubor's behest, Deirdre spends a year with Conchubor during which she never raises her head, and when, at the end of that time she is being sent by Conchubor to live with Eoghan for a year, she dashes her head against a rock and dies. The language of the account is direct and terse, the style unornamented; and the world portrayed, where Deirdre is essentially a victim of fate, is heroic and harsh.

Later, another version of the Deirdre tale, sometimes referred to as medieval, was evolved.[6] It reflected not only the social changes against which it was being told, but also the development of a more convoluted and ornamented style. This version was preserved in a fifteenth-century MS known as the Glen Masain MS in the Advocates' Library in Edinburgh. Although it is considerably longer, the range of events it covers is less. It begins only with Conchubor's decision to send to Alba for the exiled sons of Uisneach, omitting Deirdre's birth, upbringing, courtship of Naisi, and their sojourn in Alba. The end of the tale is missing from this MS, and in the editions of it available to Synge was supplied from an eighteenth-century paper MS in the same library. In it, Naisi and his brothers are killed by Maine, after which Deirdre becomes distracted, drinks Naisi's blood, and after uttering her final lay, lies down on his grave and dies.[7]

The more elaborate style in which this version of the tale is recorded accounts for its greater length. There are many devices common to the oral tradition, such as repetition, the piling up of adjectives, and recurrent motifs like that of the black raven/red blood/white snow combination. Besides, the combats are greatly elaborated and characterization is expanded. Finally, although the versified predictions of Cathbad are lost through the omission of events before the end of the sojourn in Alba, the number and length of the poems in the later version is greater because Deirdre is attributed many lyrical lays. As a character, she has become a creature of some insight and complexity. Because of her pre-vision of the betrayal, she warns Naisi of it repeatedly, and endeavours to hide the identity of Fergus. The themes of racial identity and divided loyalties are developed, notably in connection with Fergus.

In the same volume of *Cours de littérature celtique* which deals with the oldest version of the tale, Professor de Jubainville also introduces this later one. He gives details of the edition published by Whitley Stokes in the second part of the second volume of *Irische Texte*, mentioning both the erudite introduction and the English translation by Whitley Stokes which accompany it: highly inviting information for a student with Synge's interests. De Jubainville also notes the similarity between this version and that published in Dublin in 1808 by Theophilus O'Flanagan, and he follows with Georges Dottin's French translation of Whitley Stokes's text.[8]

Synge's scholarship and interest in the field of Old and Middle Irish literature were extensive. His reviews of translations and renderings of this material, including the Deirdre tale, assure one of his confident and knowledgeable judgement of how others handled it. In particular there is his praise of Lady Gregory's approach for popular, literary purposes:

> This version ... should go far to make a new period in the intellectual life of Ireland. Henceforward the beauty and wonder of the old literature is likely to have an influence on the culture of all classes ... The beauty of this old literature has been known to Celtic scholars all over Europe for a considerable time, but the works in which they have dealt with it are addressed to scholars only, and are too learned, and too expensive for general use.[9]

Yet Synge warns of the omission of 'certain barbarous features' and recommends the scholarly translations of the Germans and others who 'translate without hesitation all that has come down to us in the MSS' to those with more than a literary interest.

In contrast with his essentially laudatory disposition towards Lady Gregory's work is Synge's dissatisfaction with a lack of uniformity of style and inadequate arrangement of the stories in Eleanor Hull's *Cuchullin Saga in Irish Literature*, which is a conglomeration of the work of Theophilus O'Flanagan and Whitley Stokes.[10] But it was A.H. Leahy's translation of the *Book of Leinster* which evoked Synge's severest criticism in 1905. He singled out Leahy's translation of Cathbad's prophesy (displaying his own special interest in the Deirdre tale) to illustrate the 'deplorable misrepresentation' and 'facile parody' to which 'the Book of Leinster, a twelfth-century text' had been subjected. Conscious that most of his readers would know no Irish, and would therefore be unable to appreciate his judgement, he refers them to some modern Irish poems translated by Douglas Hyde:

> Those who know no Irish can get some idea of what Gaelic poetry has suffered in this kind of treatment by comparing the beautiful prose translations which Dr. Douglas Hyde wrote of the 'Love Songs of Connacht' with the verse translations – in themselves often pleasing enough – which he put in the same volume. When one is dealing with old texts, like those translated in the present volume, the matter is much worse.[11]

English verse, then, appears to Synge an unlikely medium for translating early Irish tales, yet he can praise Leahy's prose sections for showing 'many of the qualities of an excellent translator – fearlessness, enthusiasm, and the scholar's conscience'.[12] On the basis of the criticism Synge has left us of such translations, it is clear that he had evolved an implicit theory of translation with its focus on style. It should therefore be of some interest for a student of Old and Middle Irish to make a linguistic comparison between the style Synge used in his own *Deirdre* and that of the earliest texts. With a knowledge of only Modern Irish, although comparisons of subject and content can be made with the two early versions, the earliest texts with which a stylistic comparison can be made are Geoffrey Keating's early seventeenth century one, and Andrew MacCurtin's of 1740.

Andrew MacCurtin (d. 1749), 'a learned Irish scholar', entitled his version *Oidhe Chloinne Uisnigh* (The Fate of the Children of Uisneach), writing it in his capacity as bard to the O'Briens of Thomond: an interesting late survival of the professional Gaelic poet.[13] This text is of particular importance in relation to Synge's knowledge of the Deirdre tale, since he made his own translation of it during one of his visits to Aran in 1900 or 1901.[14] It had been published together with an English translation, notes and glossary, by the Society for the Preservation of the Irish Language in 1898, the year Synge made his first visit to Aran and began using Irish for daily communication.

Andrew MacCurtin follows the later medieval version of the tale as it had been recorded in the Glen Masain MS. However, in his pre-tale MacCurtin fills in the early events (i.e. from the birth of Deirdre up to the feast at which the decision is made to recall the sons of Uisneach) from the oldest version, quoting as his source Geoffrey Keating.[15] Thus the MacCurtin text provides an example of the kind of inconsistency on which Synge had occasion to remark in connection with the oldest MSS: 'The tales in these MSS continually overlap and are often contradictory'.[16] In the oldest version, transmitted through Keating, it is the nobles of Ulster who prompt Conchubor to receive the sons of Uisneach back from Alba where they are being hounded in a manner unfitting for their kin, whereas in the later version, in accordance with the Glen Masain MS, the idea of bringing them back comes from Conchubor, who is bent on vengeance.[17]

Because of the intimate knowledge Synge acquired of the MacCurtin text in the process of translating it, it is of considerable interest to compare *Deirdre of the Sorrows* with it. However, it must be constantly borne in mind that where there is common material it is impossible to ascertain whether Synge was taking the events he dramatized from MacCurtin or from the Glen Masain text. Moreover, since this later medieval version of the tale was by far the more popular, Synge may well have heard a form of it from the storytellers of Aran. Therefore, although the comparison will ostensibly be made with MacCurtin, in effect it is with what has become known as 'the later version'.

Synge's DEIRDRE *Compared With MacCurtin's Narrative*

The great feast at which Conchubor publicly announces his intention of inviting the sons of Uisneach back to Emain opens MacCurtin's narrative, providing the typical scene-setting plot-seed for this type of tale. Three of the outstanding Ulster heroes are present: Cuchulainn, Conall Cearnach and Fergus. The process of Conchubor's enquiring about loyalties and retaliation reveals his own concealed intention and the compromised position of Fergus, as well as the danger in which the sons of Uisneach stand.

The point in time at which Synge opens his drama is when the period of the rearing and preparation of Deirdre to be the wife of the king, Conchubor, is coming to an end. Thus, when her meeting with Naisi takes place she is 'ripe'. Such an opening provides the point of departure for all the conflicts of the romantic love which follows. The audience is made aware of the sexual awakening of Deirdre, and of the desperation of the ageing king to possess her. The interests reflected in Synge's opening are in the inner drives of the protagonists, whereas those of the MacCurtin opening are in the social effects of Conchubor's decision.

In addition to altering the emphasis in his opening, Synge also omits certain incidents which are structurally important in the MacCurtin version, such as Deirdre's dreams of foreboding, and her advice to Naisi and his brothers not to return to Emain. Both of these omissions are related to Synge's change of conception both of Deirdre's role and of motivation. With his increased emphasis on inner motivation, he finds the use of *geas*, which is vital to the plot of the narrative, superfluous. The *geas*, which is a solemn injunction, the infringement of which will lead to misfortune or even death, is used in the narrative as a device for crystallizing the division of Fergus's loyalties. He has given his word to Conchubor that the sons of Uisneach will arrive at Emain on the same day that they arrive in Ireland; he has also undertaken the safeguard of Naisi, Ainnle, and Ardan; and Conchubor, knowing that Fergus was under *geas* never to refuse a feast, enlists an invitation for him from Borach on his arrival in Ireland with the sons of Uisneach. Thus, in the more socially orientated narrative, by placing Fergus in such an impossible position much attention is focused on the question of loyalty. Synge's characters, on the other hand, are presented in more intimate conflict. Accordingly, his explanation for Fergus's absence is reduced to a simple reference to his having been 'stopped in the north' because of Conchubor. As the play stands, unfinished, this feature is inadequately integrated.

The more intimate conflict in which Synge's characters are depicted owes something to the reduction of their number. Synge avoids feast scenes and extended combats, as well as the conventional attendant figures in large numbers. Thus he gives prominence to the principal trio, Deirdre, Naisi, and Conchubor, whose characters are more developed and who acquire some new traits.

Synge's Deirdre becomes wilful, and she has no initial fear of death. Her wilfulness is not only evident in her behaviour, but is indicated in a reference to her by Lavarcham at the beginning of the play:

Who'd check her like was made to have her pleasure only, the way if there were no warnings told about her you'd see troubles

76

coming when an old king is taking her, and she without a thought but for her beauty and to be straying the hills.[18]

Also, when Conchubor arrives and indicates his intention of taking Deirdre, Lavarcham warns him 'It's wilfuller she's growing these two months or three'.[19]

Her fearlessness of death can likewise be seen in her actions and in this early speech to Naisi:

> I will not live to be shut up in Emain, and wouldn't we do well paying, Naisi, with silence and a near death? . . . I'm a long while in the woods with my own self, and I'm in little dread of death . . .[20]

Besides, Lavarcham warns Conchubor: 'It's not the dread of death or troubles that would tame her like'.[21]

The crowning of Deirdre's fearlessness in Synge's play is the manner in which she takes her own life, which she does with Naisi's knife. The dignity in her treatment of those around her makes her every inch a queen. Her detachment, her mood and movement towards a 'higher sphere' is more reminiscent of the grand departure of Shakespeare's Cleopatra to join her lover than that of MacCurtin's Deirdre, whose death is a passive affair in that she simply lies down on the grave and dies after uttering her final lay.

In the same way that her awakened sexual instincts prompt her to don her fine garments to lure Naisi at the outset, Synge's Deirdre's impossible dream of eternal beauty, youth and love drives her to opt for the grave. The fear of being united with an unfit mate in the ageing Conchubor precipitates that first action, just as the fear that the passion between herself and Naisi will fade with her beauty prompts her to send Naisi to his death with a pitiless word. This idea of the pitilessness of beauty, which is the central 'clash of incompatibles' in *Deirdre*, will be further developed in the context of ugliness in Chapter VIII.

MacCurtin's Deirdre had not been 'modernized', so that she remains a victim of prophecy or fate: something of a beautiful object without power in a man's world. She moves in a milieu where her dreams are ignored and her advice unheeded. When she lies down on the grave of her lord and lover, she is doing little more than her duty in dying with him.

As a pivotal character, Synge's Deirdre is flanked by Conchubor and Naisi, of whom Conchubor has the greater power. Yet, although his schemes and decisions affect the progress of the play, the figure he makes at the close of the play as a broken old king in the care of Lavarcham is pathetic. Being somewhat villainous, he overshadows the noble-spirited Naisi in a similar way to that in which Milton's Satan, Shakespeare's Iago, and other literary villains tend to overshadow characters more virtuous than themselves. Beside him, Naisi plays the role of the conventional lover to Deirdre. Whereas Owen's attempt to perturb Deirdre's view of Naisi with warnings of old age are unsuccessful, Fergus's warning of the ephemeral nature of love, as well as Deirdre's harsh words at the end, both sway Naisi.

MacCurtin's Naisi is brought to the attention of Deirdre by Lavarcham, and is a more evidently decisive character than Synge makes him. In the narrative, when Fergus arrives as Conchubor's emissary appealing to Naisi's feeling for his homeland, Deirdre proclaims how much better off Naisi would be to remain in Alba. This has no influence whatsoever on Naisi who says 'is annsa liom féin Éire 'ná Alba, gídh mó do gheabhainn a n-Albain 'ná a n-Éirinn' (Ireland is dearer to me than Alba, though I would get more in Alba than in Eire), and he subsequently returns against Deirdre's wishes.[22] Not only is he more decisive than his counterpart in Synge, but his demeanour and reputation are altogether more warrior-like. Thus, in accordance with this reputation, Conchubor has blood-feuds to exploit. By reminding Treundorn that Naisi had killed his father and three brothers, he can persuade him to spy on Naisi and Deirdre; and likewise Maine of the Rough Hand is prepared to kill Naisi because *his* father and three brothers had been killed by him too.

The blood-feud from the narrative is reduced in Synge's play to two passing references by Owen to Naisi's having 'put in his sword among my father's ribs'.[23] And although Synge's Owen in the role of spy seems to be related to Treundorn, he had taken this role up only in a half-hearted way. He is not a medieval warrior thirsting for revenge, but a passionate fool caught up in the conflicts and confusions around him, and besotted with the beautiful Deirdre. Owen owes more to the oldest version of the tale, as we shall see. His character will be further discussed in the context of folly, as will that of Lavarcham.

Whereas the principal male characters in MacCurtin's version are warlike heroes who are primarily concerned with possession and reputation, in the play they act in accordance with their feelings, notably those for Deirdre. It is the fear that the pitch of their reciprocal feeling cannot be sustained which leads to Naisi's decision to return to Emain, and it is Conchubor's blindness to the intensity of Deirdre's feeling for Naisi that prevents him from seeing she cannot be queen in Emain after Naisi's death. Deirdre is conscious of the power arising from the feelings these two men have for her, and she uses it: she almost succeeds in making peace between Naisi and Conchubor, but the events which Conchubor had earlier set in motion overtake them; and she despatches Naisi to fulfil his heroic role in relation to his brothers with a taunt.[24] In the MacCurtin version, no personal exchange takes place between Conchubor and Deirdre after the death of Naisi. There, once Conchubor has re-established his reputation and possession, he is of no further interest, and attention is transferred to the public revenge which follows his perfidy.

Synge portrays a strong bond of affection between Deirdre and Lavarcham, whose stature is considerably greater than MacCurtin's. Not alone is this affection evident at the opening of the play, but it brings Lavarcham, old though she is, across the sea to Alba with warnings for Deirdre at the beginning of the second act. Also, at the opening of the third act, the Old Woman says to Conchubor: 'It's Lavarcham coming again . . . She's a great wonder for jogging back and forward through the world . . .'[25] This notion of Lavarcham always on the move comes from the MacCurtin version, but there it arises in connection with the affection Lavarcham has for Naisi, not for Deirdre. There she is described as follows:

> ba h-annsa léi Naoise 'ná neach eile 'san domhan; óir ba mhinic léi dul ar feadh an domhain d'iarraidh Naoise, agus ag breith sgeul chuige agus uaidh.[26]

> (She loved Naisi above anyone else on earth, for it was often she went the length of the world looking for him, bringing messages to and from him.)

Another idea Synge took from MacCurtin is the provision of a separate hut for eating when Ainnle, Ardan, and the other characters have to leave the stage in order that Deirdre and Naisi can have their first lover's encounter alone. Since there is a storm raging outside, and the scene is Lavarcham's lonely house on Slieve Fuadh, the characters could not credibly be sent out without shelter. Synge could, of course, have simply sent them into the next room, but instead Deirdre instructs Lavarcham and the Old Woman: 'Take Ainnle and Ardan, these two princes, into the little hut where we eat'; and she says to Ainnle and Ardan: 'Do not take it badly that I am asking you to walk into our hut for a little. You will have a supper that is cooked by the cook of Conchubor . . .'. This lodging arrangement clearly comes from MacCurtin who describes the way Fergus found Deirdre and the Sons of Uisneach housed in Alba as follows:

> Is amhlaidh do bhádar Clann Uisnigh agus trí fiannbhotha aca; agus an bhoth ann a m-bruithidís a b-proinn, ní h-innte d'ithidís; agus an bhoth ann a n'ithidís, ní h-innte do chodlaidís.[27]

> (This is how the Sons of Uisneach were: they had three hunting-booths in the forest, and the booth in which their food was baked was not where they ate, nor did they eat in the one where they slept.)

Separate huts, Lavarcham's travelling about, and various other features from MacCurtin are all found in the Glen Masain text, therefore when we say that Synge took such features from MacCurtin, or that he altered others, what is really meant is that MacCurtin provided Synge with an immediate source for the matter of the later medieval version of the tale. The most striking overall alteration Synge made in that material is the internalizing of motivation. His autocratic Conchubor grows increasingly determined to foil old age with a young queen. His Naisi enters as a lusty youth eager for wine and a woman, saying to Lavarcham:

> At your age you should know there are nights when a king like Conchubor would spit upon his arm ring and queens will stick their tongues out at the rising moon. We're that way this night, and it's not wine we're asking only . . . Where is the young girl told us we might shelter here?[28]

And his Deirdre spiritedly rejects an improper pairing and is willing to pay the ultimate price for love, youth, and beauty.

What need thus for dreams and predictions to account for the clash and destruction which takes place? If these inner forces weren't enough to move things towards the outcome predefined in the old tale, the sharp realization of mutability that Synge gives Deirdre and Naisi assures it. The heroic and chivalric basis of the narrative with its accompanying predictions is replaced by a realistic conception of character and motives, accompanied by a preoccupation with time's havoc. And the use of stylistic techniques appropriate to a narrative rendering is replaced by devices more fitting to a poetic drama, such as an enriched imagery, using notably colour and animals.[29]

MacCurtin's version can therefore be seen as a firm stepping-stone for Synge between the later medieval version of the Deirdre tale and his own play. Its most important contribution was perhaps the part it played in the development of the language he came to use in his plays. When he translated it at the turn of the century, before he wrote any of his published plays, it provided him with a pattern for the style of dialogue he was to evolve. Making that translation gave him his first extended practice at using in English those Irish constructions with substantival weighting which characterize his drama and later translations. He was fully conscious of the literary idiomatic evolution to which he was but one contributor, as is clear from his remarks in his 1902 review of Lady Gregory's *Cuchulain of Muirthemne*. While he grants her considerable praise, he does not allow that she discovered the language she uses:

> Some time ago Dr. Douglas Hyde used a very similar language in his translations of the 'Love Songs of Connacht', and more recently Mr. Yeats himself has written some of his articles on folklore with this cadence in his mind, while a few other writers have been moving gradually towards it . . . the translation of the old MSS into this idiom is the result of an evolution rather than of a merely personal idea.[30]

He also notes 'her plaintive Gaelic constructions that make her language, in a true sense, a language of Ireland.'

When he wrote these remarks about Lady Gregory's language, he was not in a position to name himself among those who were using such a language, but was surely remembering that he had done so a year or so before in translating MacCurtin's *Oidhe Chloinne Uisnigh*. In that translation, he has on the whole, followed MacCurtin's text faithfully. He omits much of the pre-tale, translating only the first paragraph and part of the second. He then proceeds to the middle of the second paragraph in the body of the tale, and continues to translate up to Cathbad's prediction about Emain at the end. It is interesting that he omits the final lay which explains the close blood relationship between the nobles of Ulster. One wonders whether this was because he knew that this lay does not appear in the Glen Masain MS.[31]

Synge also omits the nine adjectives describing the fight between Fiachra and Iolann the Fair, as well as the names of the three waves of Erin, doubtless for reasons of style. He strongly criticized what he calls 'the abuse of adjectives that has been the curse of Irish literature.'[32] But these two omissions can also be justified on the grounds that they are features whose function is more relevant to the oral tradition than to a written tale. There they provided the bard with a relaxation of concentration while the audience had the pleasure of hearing what was familiar and high-sounding.

The account of the separate booths used by the Sons of Uisneach in the MacCurtin text which was noted above, reveals a purely literal approach in the language of the published translation:

> Thus were the sons of Uisneach, with three hunting-booths, and the booth in which they cooked their meal, not in it they ate, and the booth in which they ate, not in it they slept.[33]

This approach is representative of the translation as a whole, and does not suggest that the translator aimed to exploit the English language for stylistic purposes. There is no feeling shown for the nuance or the syntax of 'standard English', nor for its possible use in conveying the rhythm of the Irish original.

Where Synge begins his translation of the main text, the published translation reads: 'Conor raised his great royal voice on high, and this is what he said – "I desire to know from you ..." ' (thógaibh Conchobhar a ollghuth rioghdha ós árd, agus is é so ráidh, "Is áil liom a fhios d'fhághail uaibhse ..."). First, one must criticize the use of the verb 'to raise' in conjunction with 'voice' here, because in English it commonly evokes notions of anger, whereas in the context Conchubor is not expressing anger. The phrase 'on high' smacks more of a prayer-book than of an early Irish tale; and 'I desire to know from you' is pompous, without being particularly regal. Synge's translation of the same passage reads: 'Then Conor lifted up his great voice that was the voice of a king and said "Let me learn this thing of you ..." '.[34] The periphrastic 'that was the voice of a king' is preferable to the curt term 'royal' because it characteristically weights the noun 'voice', both through syntax and through repetition. Besides, it echoes the dominant rhythm of the Irish. The stateliness of 'Let me learn this thing of you' is fitting for the command of a king at a feast. And in not separating 'great' from 'voice', Synge is remaining close to his original 'ollguth', 'guth' meaning 'voice' and 'oll' being a superlative prefix.

It would be pointless and out of place here to extend the comparison between Synge's translation of MacCurtin and that published by the Society for the Preservation of the Irish Language. To do so would be merely to show that the two translators had different aims. Where the one wished to make intelligible to a largely non-Irish-speaking public what had been recorded in the eighteenth century, the other was experimenting, playing one language against the other to create a new linguistic vitality. Synge made no attempt to publish his translation. He was using MacCurtin's text to increase his working knowledge of Irish while on Aran, and at the same time to add to his versatility in the use of those 'Gaelic constructions' which were to make the English of his plays 'in a true sense, a language of Ireland', as he was to say of Lady Gregory's.

Although his own knowledge of Irish was extensive, he did not have great hopes for its future, and was reported by Stephen Mac-Kenna as loathing the Gaelic League for using the argument that Modern Irish would give those who learned it access to the grand old saga literature: 'That's a bloody lie; long after they know modern Irish, which they'll never know, they'll still be miles and years from any power over the Saga.'[35] Such a remark conveys implicitly Synge's own privilege in belonging to the coterie which possessed the necessary diachronic knowledge of the language to have 'power over the Saga'. Nevertheless, he put his creative energies into adapting the English language to Irish thought-structures.

Geoffrey Keating

Synge's curiosity about the rendering by Geoffrey Keating (1570?–1644?) of the Deirdre tale was doubtless aroused by Mac-Curtin's use of it to fill in the early events leading up to the decision to recall the Sons of Uisneach from Alba. MacCurtin gives this part of Keating's text *verbatim*, apart from occasional orthographical variations, transcribing the first page and a half out of a total of four pages. Synge, after beginning to translate the first sentence of this quotation from Keating, left it aside, as was noted above. He was sensitive to the more spare style in which Keating's account is given, and probably decided to confine his efforts then to rendering Mac-Curtin's own style, which is baroque.

This is not to say that Synge disliked Keating's work. On the contrary, the two reviews Synge wrote of new editions of it show both an intimate knowledge and a high esteem: acquaintance with existing editions, as well as an appreciation of a 'remarkable literary talent' and a 'plaintive dignity' of style. Moreover, in his review of the first volume of Keating's *Foras Feasa Ar Éirinn: The History of Ireland* in 1902, Synge was eagerly awaiting the second:

> The members of the Irish Texts Society intend to publish the remainder of the history in several succeeding volumes, which will then form the first complete edition of this important work, and be of the greatest service to students of Irish literature and history. . . . In the succeeding volumes of the history, Mr. Comyn will have a less well known portion of the work to deal with, and their interest will be proportionately greater. It is to be hoped that the Irish Texts Society will be able to bring them out without much delay.[36]

The second volume was in fact published three years later, in 1905, and it is there that the Deirdre tale appears.[37]

We have two reasons to believe that Synge's attention to Keating's version of the Deirdre tale would have been close. First, he attached sufficient importance to the fact that Keating had access to MSS which had since perished to mention it three times in the small body of his published criticism.[38] And second, he valued Keating's 'knowledge of old or, at least, of Middle Irish'.[39] These advantages enhanced Keating's worth as a reliable transmitter of the old tales for him, so that he saw his transcriptions from the MSS as being of 'high antiquarian value'.[40]

Whereas the MacCurtin proto-text was that of the Glen Masain MS, Keating's was one or more of the oldest version of the tale. It is from here that Synge takes the name Eoghan/Owen, although the role which his Owen plays differs considerably from that played by Eoghan Mac Durrthacht, the slayer of Naisi in Keating's version. Eoghan Mac Durrthacht breaks his warrior's trust when, acting under Conchubor's instructions, he thrusts his spear through Naisi in the act of welcoming him. Synge's Owen is the paid spy of Conchubor, and his detraction of Naisi echoes faintly the physical treachery of Eoghan. The explanation for the enmity between Owen and Naisi, beyond Owen's desire for Deirdre, lies in Naisi having, in Owen's words, 'put in his sword among my father's ribs and when a man's done that he'll not credit your oath'.[41] There is no mention of this blood-feud in Keating's narrative, but there is such a basis for enmity between Treundorn, Conchubor's spy in the Glen Masain version, and Naisi. Thus, although the name for Synge's Owen originates in the oldest version of the tale, perhaps via Keating, his character is an amalgamation of various characters from the early texts, plus, as we shall see, something of the sage fool.

Synge's Owen's lust for Deirdre could also have originated in Eoghan Mac Durrthacht, because in Keating (and in the Old Irish version), Conchubor decides to send her to live with Eoghan for a year after her joyless year with himself. Conchubor, when he sees Deirdre standing in the chariot between Eoghan and himself, makes the raw jest which causes her to leap to her death: 'is súil chaorach idir dá reithe an tsúil sin do-bheir tú oram-sa is ar Eoghan' ('The eye you are giving Eoghan and myself is the eye of an ewe between two rams').[42] Synge's Owen echoes this simile, but in connection with Naisi: 'Then I tell you you'll have great sport one day seeing Naisi getting a harshness in his two sheep's eyes and he looking on yourself'.[43] The simile was anticipated in Synge's Deirdre's first admission of her desire for Naisi: 'Since that, Naisi, I have been one time the like of a ewe looking for a lamb that had been taken away from her . . .'.[44] It is of interest that the animal associations of sexual desire are less prominent in Keating than in the Old Irish version, where Naisi in his first greeting of Deirdre addresses her as a heifer, she calls him a bullock, and he alludes to Conchubor as the bull of the province.[45] Keating omits all this, as well as Cathbad's prophecy that Deirdre would be the cause of Eoghan's death. Yet it is she who is the cause of Owen's death in Synge's play too, although for different reasons. Overall, from the viewpoint of borrowed features, the Old Irish original appears to have been more influential on Synge than Keating's rendering of it.

While both Keating's and MacCurtin's texts were acceptable to Synge as bridges to the two original versions, there were also many nineteenth-century editions and translations of the tale available to him. Of these, some were accurate and scholarly, such as those of Ernst Windisch and Eugene O'Curry, while others, like James MacPherson's, altered fundamental details of the tale. Although it can be assumed that scholarly works, recommended by de Jubainville, contributed to Synge's understanding of the tale, it would be pointless to seek parallels where there is so much repetition. Literary renderings such as Samuel Ferguson's and Standish Hayes O'Grady's were doubtless known to him too, but there is no evidence of influence. In all, Adelaide Duncan Estill in *The Sources of Synge* mentions fourteen literary variations available to him, but of those, only the works of Synge's contemporaries bear fruitful comparison.

Synge's Contemporaries

Four of Synge's contemporaries produced literary renderings of the Deirdre tale: Douglas Hyde, Lady Gregory, W.B. Yeats, and George Russell (Æ). Of these, Hyde and Lady Gregory were very important for him because of their use of Irish constructions in English; while the example of Yeats and Russell in dramatizing the narrative helped him to identify the approach which he should adopt for his own dramatic purposes.

Douglas Hyde is the only one of these writers whose knowledge of the Irish versions of the tale was comparable to that of Synge, although Lady Gregory went to great lengths to consult a wide range of texts and had learned some Irish. Hyde's was published in 1895 as one of the *Three Sorrows of Storytelling*, but it had been written in 1887, when it won the Vice-Chancellor's prize at Trinity College. Hyde's experience and opinion of the attitude to things Irish at Trinity was similar to that of Synge, who entered there in 1888, the year following Hyde's award. If one recalls Synge's remark about his professor of Irish not knowing or caring about the old literature of Ireland, it expresses a like feeling to Hyde's remark on the response to Deirdre as the subject of the Vice-Chancellor's prize: '. . . the students did not know what the word meant, or what Deirdre was, whether animal, vegetable, or mineral.'[46]

Although these two writers shared a deep attachment to the Irish language, they held opposed views on the position of the English language in Ireland. Hyde, especially during Synge's lifetime, was a fierce campaigner for the reinstatement of Irish as the daily language of the country, whereas Synge's view was as follows:

No small island placed between two countries which speak the same language, like England and America, can hope to keep up a different tongue. English is likely to remain the language of

Ireland and no one, I think, need regret the likelihood. If Gaelic came back strongly from the West the feeling for English which the present generation has attained would be lost again, and in the best circumstances it is probable that Leinster and Ulster would take several centuries to assimilate Irish perfectly enough to make it a fit mode of expression for the finer emotions which now occupy literature. In the meantime, the opening culture of Ireland would be thrown back indefinitely, and there would, perhaps, be little gain to make up for this certain loss.[47]

Hyde's active political interests, reflected in the question of a national language, distinguish him from Synge, who was essentially a-political although something of a cultural nationalist. However, their differing views of the feasibility of reinstating the Irish language did not prevent Synge from following Hyde in, for instance, his view of Keating as a naïve and uncritical historian.[48] Besides, when Synge complained of 'the abuse of adjectives that has been the curse of Irish literature', that too was an echo of Hyde's comment about 'a great deal of verbiage and piling up of rather barren names'.[49]

Any influence Hyde had on Synge was in the nature of a general encouragement of interest in Early Irish material, and a linguistic example, set notably in his prose translations of *Love Songs of Connacht*. There is no question of direct influence from Hyde's *Deirdre* on Synge's. The rhythm of Hyde's iambic pentameter is strong and regular to an almost mechanical degree. There is none of the ebb and flow of English based on Irish thought-structures, and the vocabulary is that of standard late-Victorian versifiers. The poem opens with a wordy preamble before coming to the first event of the oldest version of the tale: the feast during which Deirdre is born and the prophetic warnings are given. Hyde includes all the standard features of the story, without significant alteration. Although he pointed out in his notes that Deirdre did not die over the grave of the sons of Uisneach in all MSS, but that she leapt out of a chariot after a year with Conchubor in the oldest version, he gave her a most proper death in his own poem. There 'her heart-strings snapt' as she uttered her praise of Naisi, and she simply fell into his grave. All strife is precluded, both between Naisi and Deirdre and within Deirdre herself, which is quite different to what Synge does. The circumstances in which Hyde wrote his poem (for a University prize), as well as those in which it was published (by mistake according to his own avowal in his preface) account for its undistinguished though readable quality. Also, it was produced before the young Hyde had assumed any public linguistic responsibilities.[50]

Lady Gregory's *Cuchulain of Muirthemne*, which was greatly appreciated as literature by Synge, was another advance in that linguistic evolution in which he was himself to become an outstanding figure. In singling out of its twenty chapters Deirdre's lament for the sons of Uisneach to quote on the grounds of its excellence, he displayed his particular interest in the Deirdre tale.[51] That lament had been the last of the lays he translated when he made his own translation of MacCurtin's *Oidhe Chloinne Uisnigh*.

It is surprising how close Lady Gregory's version of this lament is to the published English translation of MacCurtin, which, although it is set out in four-line stanzas, reads as prose. Yet the few variations in Lady Gregory's text immediately create a more pliant effect with markedly more appeal to the ear. Comparison of the passage quoted by Synge is revealing, therefore we shall look first at Lady Gregory's and then at the published English translation of MacCurtin:

1. 'That I would live after Naoisi let no one think on the earth; I will not go on living after Ainnle and after Ardan.
   'After them I myself will not live; three that would leap through the midst of battle; since my beloved is gone from me I will cry my fill over his grave.
   'O young man, digging the new grave, do not make the grave narrow; I will be along with them in the grave, making lamentations and ochones!
   'Many the hardship I met with along with the three heroes; I suffered want of house, want of fire, it is myself that used not to be troubled.
   'Their three sheilds and their spears made a bed for me often. O young man, put their three swords close over their grave.

2. 'That I would live after Naoise,
   Let none on earth imagine;
   After Ainnle and Ardan,
   In me there will not be life.

'After them I will not be alive;
Three who would rush through the midst of battle;
Since my mate has gone from me,
I will shed showers over his grave.

'O man, who diggest the new grave!
Make not the grave narrowly;
Beside the grave I will be, –
Making sorrow and lamentations.

'Much hardship did I encounter,
Along with the three heroes;
I used to endure without house or fire;
It is not I that used to be melancholy.

'Their three sheilds and their spears,
Were for me a bed oftentimes;
Place their three swords hard
Over the grave, O henchman![52]

Since it has already been established that MacCurtin's translator's objective was a literal rendering without ambitions in the domain of English style, literary evaluation of these two passages is not in question. It is evident straight away that Lady Gregory's lament is more colloquial: she avoids strained inversion and archaism. She uses colloquial phrases such as 'I will cry my fill' in place of 'shed showers', although the latter is more faithful to the Irish. At the same time, she uses the Irish word 'ochone', which had passed into Hiberno-English usage. The increased substantival weighting characteristic of such usage can be seen in her use of pronouns: the nominal group 'no one' is used in preference to the pronoun 'none'; following Irish, the emphatic form 'myself' is used in addition or in preference to the weaker 'I' in the phrases 'After them I myself will not live' and 'it is myself that used not to be troubled'; and 'that' is substituted for the standard relative pronoun 'who' in the phrase 'three that would leap'. The concrete form 'many the hardship' is preferred to the abstract 'Much hardship', and the speaker is given prominence in the typically Hiberno-English predicative structure 'it is myself'.

Consideration of the effects produced by these variants of Lady Gregory leads to the conclusion that her exploitation of Irish forms

common in Hiberno-English usage results in that increased sense of
the concrete, the specific, and the presence of the speaker which has
already been defined in the work of Yeats after 1900.[53] That Synge
followed this same linguistic practice is evident, not only in *Deirdre
of the Sorrows* but in his other plays and his translations. But his
following it was in itself an evolution – an evolution within an
evolution – in which the unfinished *Deirdre* was a culmination. The
play *Deirdre of the Sorrows* was Synge's last literary concern, and
his translation of Andrew MacCurtin's narrative was his first
extended practice of the literary language he evolved. His knowledge of Irish being superior to Lady Gregory's, his exploitation of
the tension between English and Irish in his language was more
dextrous and informed. Since Robin Skelton has shown that 'The
speech that Synge constructed for his translations is very similar to
that of *Deirdre of the Sorrows*',[54] consideration of that speech will be
extended in the context of his translations. Here, those features
which were adopted by Synge other than the language used by Lady
Gregory for her 'Deirdre' should be examined.

First, once the Sons of Uisneach are dead, Lady Gregory gives a
new dramatic prominence to the grave. In accordance with the
oldest version of the tale, she includes in Cathbad's prophecy to
Deirdre at her birth the statement 'you will have a little grave apart
to yourself'.[55] However, the focus she gives to the grave in relation
to Deirdre after the slaughter of Naisi, Ainnle, and Ardan is sharp
and original. She introduces a new sense of the tangible presence of
the open grave and the clay in which the bodies are laid. When
Cuchulain leaves Deirdre, we are told 'After that Deirdre lay down
by the grave, and they were digging earth from it, and she made this
lament . . .'.[56] That lament includes those addresses to the gravedig-
gers seen above, and besides has these further lines on the grave: 'I
was never alone to the day of the making of this grave . . . My sight is
gone from me with looking at the grave of Naoisi'.[57] And there are
two more references to the grave before the final one in which
Deirdre herself is laid in it.

This prominence given to the grave by Lady Gregory alerted
Synge to its dramatic potential on the stage. In his play, Deirdre asks
at her first meeting with Naisi: 'Do many know what is foretold, that
Deirdre will be the ruin of the Sons of Usna, and have a little grave
by herself, and a story will be told forever?'[58] Early in the second act
she has a pre-vision of Naisi's grave before leaving Alba: '. . . it's in
the quiet woods I've seen them digging our grave, throwing out the

clay on leaves are bright and withered'.[59] And a little later, when Owen anticipates death, it is with the concrete image of the grave: 'Dead men, dead men, men who'll die for Deirdre's beauty, I'll be before you in the grave!'.[60]

All of this is preparation for Deirdre's startling discovery of a freshly dug grave behind the tent in which Conchubor lodges her with Naisi and his brothers. Structurally, her discovery is crucial, and relates back to her pre-vision. That Synge intended it to be significant is clear from his note 'make important' in an undated fragment.[61] Before Deirdre's final crescendo, she has the 'stage-business' of throwing clay into the grave, and then has these words: 'Draw a little back from the white bodies I am putting under a mound of clay and grasses that are withered – a mound will have a nook for my own self when the end is come'.[62] Doubtless, had the play been completed, Deirdre's grave apart in the first act would have been synchronized with this final reality of a shared grave. The imposing presence of the grave in Synge's play makes the destination for which the protagonists are bound especially immediate: an effect which poignantly recalls the circumstances in which he made his last attempts to finish it.

The second feature where Synge seems to have followed Lady Gregory is the use of a knife by Deirdre as the means of her own death. Traditionally, Deirdre either dashes her brains out on a stone after a year, or she passively dies on the grave of the Sons of Uisneach after delivering her final lay. Lady Gregory departs from tradition and creates a more realistic situation in which Deirdre goes onto a strand where she sees a carpenter making an oar, using a sharp knife; she secures this knife in exchange for Naisi's valued ring, and then uses it to take her own life.[63]

Synge saw the dramatic potential in Deirdre's securing her own life with something associated with Naisi, but he simplified the situation by supplying his Deirdre directly with Naisi's knife. When his Naisi leaves Deirdre to go to the aid of Ainnle and Ardan, he throws down his belt and cloak before going out. In an earlier draft, he made the following speech at this point: 'There are my sword and knife Deirdre, I will go to Ainnle and Ardan but I have no thought from this out to lift a hand in battle'.[64] Such a speech or action indicating Naisi's knife would doubtless have been integrated in the play, had it been completed, so that when Deirdre later produces 'Naisi's knife' with which to take her life, the audience would have recognized its source.[65]

There is also another knife incident which Yeats reported Synge as wishing to be included in the play. Conchubor was to have used his knife for freeing himself from the threads of Deirdre's embroidery, caught in his brooch in Lavarcham's cottage in the first act. Owen was then to have stolen this knife, and later used it for his suicide.[66] This idea may also have come from Lady Gregory's use of the carpenter's knife for Deirdre. There is much to suggest that Synge had in mind a sub-plot of the kind found in *King Lear*, and this parallel use of a knife would have contributed to it.

From Lady Gregory's narrative, which had a positive influence on Synge's language and provided two features with dramatic potential, we shall now turn to the two plays which were partly responsible for his undertaking a play on the subject of Deirdre: 'I am half inclined to try a play on "Deirdre" – it would be amusing to compare it with Yeats' and Russell's (Æ) – but I am a little afraid that the "Saga" people might loosen my grip on reality', he wrote in 1907.[67] His fear of losing his grip on reality did not arise from lack of such a grip in his own case, but from the example of Russell's play, which had been first performed in 1902, and which he would have seen either then, or when it was performed on the same bill as *Riders to the Sea* in 1903.

Synge broadly followed Russell's plot-structure, using three acts similarly located and including a similar range of characters and action. Up to the revisions of late December 1907, early 1908, he had included Fergus's two sons Iollan and Buinne, as Russell had done.[68] The theme of wisdom and folly, considerably developed by Synge, may have been suggested by Russell's attribution of wisdom to Lavarcham, whose character was traditionally that of a female satirist, feared by all for the power of her tongue. Russell, however, gave her a wisdom based on druidical powers and an affinity with the Sidhe (faeries).

It is precisely this fay quality in his play which most distinguishes it from Synge's. Far from being earthbound and having much of reality about them, both Lavarcham and Russell's other characters move in an uncertain, shadowy world, largely subject to vague powers like the 'blessed Sidhe' and 'the immortal ones'. Accordingly, the quality of the language which conveys this uncertain world is unsubstantial. It carries much innuendo, seen in statements like 'There is a hunger in his eyes for I know not what' and in recurrent references to 'the ever loving ones' and 'the birds of Angus' in the background.[69] Had Synge never seen one of Æ's pictures, this play

alone could have inspired his renowned renunciation of the faery
world in the poem 'The Passing of the Shee: After looking at one of
A.E.'s pictures':

> Adieu, sweet Angus, Maeve and Fand,
> Ye plumed yet skinny Shee,
> That poets played with hand in hand
> To learn their ecstasy.
>
> We'll search in Red Dan Sally's ditch,
> And drink at Tubber fair,
> Or poach with Red Dan Philly's bitch
> The badger and the hare.[70]

It is clear from this poem that Synge hoped for no 'ecstasy' from the
use of faeries, hence the strong contrast between the opening of his
play and Russell's. Whereas Russell's Conchubor wishes that
Deirdre's thoughts would turn to the Sidhe, and asks Lavarcham of
her 'Has she learned to know the beauty of the ever-loving ones,
after which the earth fades and no voice can call us back?', Synge's
high king concerns himself with concrete things such as the mats,
hangings, and silver skillets with which he has provided her; with the
embroidery she is doing; and with her safety abroad in the gathering
storm.[71]

The styles in which the two plays are written are distinct throughout: Synge's is anchored in what is sensible and finite, whereas
Russell's continually fades into the inperceptible, sometimes
through the kind of fanciful references already noted, and sometimes through unsure paradox. In the second act, when Synge's
Deirdre is considering leaving Alba, it is with the following sentiments: 'It's lonesome this place having happiness like ours till I'm
asking each day, will this day match yesterday, and will tomorrow
take a good place beside the same day in the year that's gone, and
wondering all times is it a game worth playing, living on until you're
dried and old, and our joy is gone forever'.[72] This acute sense of the
passing of time corresponds to the following lines in Russell's play:
'How still is the twilight! It is the sunset, not of one, but of many days
– so still, so living! The enchantment of Dana is upon the lakes and
islands and woods, and the Great Father looks down through the
deepening heavens'.[73] Improbable observations such as this, and 'a
light . . . never kindled at the sun' are in strong contrast with those of

Synge's characters, who express a vivid sense of the tangible in images such as 'Orion in the gap of the glen', or 'the moon has her mastery in a dark sky'.[74] Synge's existing preference for a substantivally weighted idiom was augmented by his experience of Russell's vagueness in the context of *Deirdre*.

Finally, from the pens of Synge's contemporaries, we find in Yeats's *Deirdre* a one-act play in blank verse, with the action taking place entirely around the incidents which Synge put in his third act alone. Although Yeats's characters are not peasantish like Synge's, they are more material than Russell's. The blank verse, almost inevitably, has occasional Shakespearean echoes, such as '. . . they are such men / As Kings will gather for a murderous task', and there are Lear-like vibrations in Conchubor's wilfulness, as well as in such phrases as 'My name has still some power', 'What, wilder yet!', and 'empty cage . . . now the bird's gone'.[75]

Yeats's is a ritualistic play based on a tale of treachery, where Naisi and Deirdre are but following a pattern with 'a broken promise and a journey's end'.[76] There is some interest in Conchubor's old age, but this is not at all as developed a theme as the ageing process is in Synge's play, and it has a peculiarly Yeatsian stamp in the description of the old king as 'still strong and vigorous'.[77] A knife is also secured by his Deirdre, with which she presumably takes her life, but this knife belongs to a musician and is only a hovering idea when Deirdre takes her final leave.[78] In this feature, Yeats seems also to be following Lady Gregory.

Viewed together, Yeats's and Synge's plays do not have much in common beyond their subject. The most striking differences are to be seen in structure and language. Synge's idiom affected his entire handling of the material, just as Yeats's choice of blank verse largely shaped his play. Synge's royal personages, with a language based on living speech on their lips, inevitably acquired something of a peasant-like character, whereas Yeats's resounding blank verse gave his a loftier, more courtly aura. This courtliness was probably Yeats's reason for seeking out the experienced actress from the English stage, Mrs Patrick Campbell, to play his Deirdre, rather than relying on the studied naturalness of the Abbey company. In this he was going against Synge's principles for a national theatre, but then Synge did not have a casting problem for his Deirdre since he wrote the part with Molly Allgood in mind.[79] Synge's cultural nationalism, which had informed the development of that psycho-substantial genre discussed in connection with *The Well of the Saints*, was sufficiently assured by the time he wrote his *Deirdre* that he continued to use the same basic language, even for royal personages, thus distinguishing himself from Yeats, who was not entirely committed to this idiom as a basis for his style.

*   *   *

The endeavour to define the kind of use Synge made of the medieval material that is the Early Irish tale of Deirdre has been confounded to some degree by the wealth of intervening renderings of it. It is not the remoteness of that material which makes comparison difficult, it is rather the attempts made by succeeding generations to reduce its remoteness. There is a case to be made for the view that Synge chose such material just because it was remote, not deliberately seeking out the remote but being what in T.S. Eliot's terms is 'a good poet':

> The good poet welds his theft into a whole of feeling which is unique, utterly different from that from which it was torn; the bad poet throws it into something which has no cohesion. A good poet will usually borrow from authors remote in time, or alien in language, or diverse in interest.[80]

Synge's *Deirdre*, though unfinished, has a remarkable degree of cohesion, and is certainly different in its effects from its Early Irish original.

There are two strikingly grotesque aberrations in Synge's Early Irish sources which he does not take up: the unborn child crying out in its mother's womb in the Old Irish version, and the bereaved Deirdre drinking her dead lover's blood in the Glen Masain MS. These omissions are accountable for as according with modern standards of credibility and sensibility, yet we have Yeats's word that Synge intended increasing the grotesque element in his play by developing the character of Owen:

> He read me a version of his play the year before his death, and would have made several more always altering and enriching. He felt that the story, as he told it, required a grotesque element mixed into its lyrical melancholy to give contrast and create an impression of solidity, and had begun this mixing with the character of Owen, who would have had some part in the first act also,

95

where he was to have entered Lavarcham's cottage with Conchubor.[81]

Not only has the character of Owen, even as it stands, grotesque
qualities, but it is in vivid contrast with that of Lavarcham. There is a
fascinating inversion here, in that traditionally it was Lavarcham
who had the sharp tongue and was therefore an outsider, whereas
Eoghan Mac Durrthacht was the upholder of the social code.
Synge's Owen is visionary, sharp-tongued, and regarded as mad,
while Lavarcham is the voice of worldly wisdom rationally based.

By the time that Synge was writing *Deirdre*, he had mastered the
art of energizing his language through the clash of the imperial and
the indigenous, but in excluding certain features found in his original story, and in internalizing choice and motivation, he had lost
some of that story's vigour. The vigour of his 'new' character, Owen,
is already apparent, and even his death is reported in vigorous terms
by Lavarcham: 'It's Owen gone raging mad and he's after splitting
his gullet beyond at the butt of the stone'.[82] The development of
Owen's role would have helped to strengthen the Rabelaisian note.

That note is so muted as to be largely inaudible, because the
degenerative side of the life of the body receives so much emphasis
in this play. Apart from the slaughter of the Sons of Uisneach, which
is a given factor in the story, there are only two charged actions in it:
the suicides of Owen and Deirdre. The development of Owen as a
fool-figure would have reduced the degree of morbidity acquired by
the 'renovated' plot. It would be easy to lapse into speculation about
the regenerative implications of the fool-figure, whose sexuality has
often been exaggerated throughout his history, and whose lewdness
has associations with fertility.[83] It is more pertinent now, however,
to consider that language which Synge used to convey the energy
inherent in a clash of incompatibles.

V TRANSLATION

> The translations are sometimes free, and sometimes almost literal, according as seemed most fitting with the form of language I have used.

It is clear from these words, with which Synge prefaced his Translations, that the touchstone for judgement must be 'the form of language' used and not fidelity to the original poems. That form is grotesque, in the sense that its energy comes from the unresolved clash between implied standard English structures and those which are imposed by thinking in the structures of another tongue. From a standard point of view, this language is therefore unruly, yet it does follow rules which are definable in terms of common Hiberno-English usage.

The linguistic environment into which Synge was born was diglossal in his immediate experience (two dialects of the same language were spoken); while further afield in the west of Ireland it was still bilingual (two different languages operated). A similar diglossal situation prevailed for his contemporaries of equivalent social privilege in England, in areas such as Tyneside or Cornwall, but not that sharper cultural distinction of which Synge became aware at the time he began to learn Irish. The co-existence of the 'standard' English of his family and class with the Hiberno-English spoken by the majority of his compatriots meant that he was early accustomed to 'translation' (the transference of sense from one language to another), and the process of this translation became increasingly intelligible to him as he learned more Irish. The acquisition of the Irish language opened to him the culture which had been driven into an almost unconscious state, demoted to folk level and relegated to antiquarians. As Synge's own consciousness grew, he had to bring two different world-pictures back into a congruence which would satisfy his sense of reality, thus cultivating skills essential to the translator as envisaged by George Steiner:

> In translation the dialectic of unison and of plurality is

dramatically at work. In one sense, each act of translation is an endeavour to abolish multiplicity and to bring different world-pictures back into perfect congruence. In another sense, it is an attempt to reinvent the shape of meaning, to find and justify an alternate statement.[1]

There is a sense in which all of Synge's writing may be viewed as 'an attempt to reinvent the shape of meaning' in Hiberno-English terms, and in a bolder way, his translations are reinventions in those same terms of only those parts of his originals which he felt were consistent with the implied world-picture of that idiom.

After *The Playboy*, Synge declared that he wanted 'a change from Peasant Comedy', and he undertook *Deirdre* as 'an experiment chiefly to change my hand'.[2] At the same time as he was working on *Deirdre*, he made his translations of a series of Petrarch's sonnets 'To Laura in Death'; of a few medieval poems, French and German; and of one nineteenth-century Italian poem. Thus, instead of continuing to reinvent the life and language of the Irish peasant, between 1907 and his death Synge produced only work based on remote material, most of which was medieval, yet he still used the same range of linguistic structures.

The choice of such remote material can be partly explained by the increased objectivity it brought, for although style for Synge was 'a portrait of one's own personality', and although he believed that 'if verse, even great verse is to be alive it must be occupied with the whole of life',[3] he was not on the whole a confessional poet, and also probably feared that he might repeat himself if he were to continue to use subjects from his old sources. Therefore, the poems he chose to translate not only contain ready-made that 'real life' element on which he insisted for great verse, but they also embody certain conventions which their makers inherited from tradition, and which were taken up by some intervening poets. Synge observed these conventions, and adopted this ready-made 'real life', so that his style was freed thereby from much of its expressive function.

The freeing of his style from its function of reinventing peasant life had two evident results. First, no longer having to define his subject, Synge could give full concentration to technical aspects of that style, the salient features of which therefore became more liberated; and not having to seek his text within himself, he was functioning largely as an artisan and writer-craftsman rather than as an artist.

Second, the daring and extravagant phraseology which had helped to express the Rabelaisian note of Irish peasant life became largely redundant. Thus, in *Deirdre* and the Translations, we find few phrases to compare for striking impact with these examples from his last peasant play, *The Playboy*: 'the Holy Father on his sacred seat'; 'a lad with the sense of Solomon to have for a pot-boy'; or 'naked as an ash-tree in the moon of May'. It is arguable that, with this loss and its related loss of humour, a great deal of vitality also disappears. The last works of Synge are, indeed, primarily sombre in tone. Yet the syntactical patterns in the language of *Deirdre* and of the Translations are largely the same as those found in the earlier plays, except that they are less frequent.[4]

Outstanding among the recurrent patterns is, first, the predicative use of the copula 'it's'. This common Hiberno-English structure developed under the influence of the sequential pattern of Irish, in which the sentence begins with a verb, but also from the transferred need to emphasize the noun since Irish is a noun-centred language and English is not. In this structure the 'it's' is never stressed itself, but serves to increase emphasis on what follows. Its lack of stress is reflected in the syncopated spelling. Examples of this structure abound in *Deirdre*, are frequent in the translations of the medieval poems, but are rare in the translations from Petrarch. The following instances are representative:

It's soon you'll have dogs with silver chains
It's in this place we'd be lonesome
It's a hard thing surely we've lost those days forever
It's yourself that bore Jesus
It's that day my youngest will bring me a towel[5]

Synge exploited this structure not only for semantic emphasis, but also for its value as an unstressed particle in creating the stress-rhythms which Robin Skelton noted in both the Translations and *Deirdre*.[6] The predominantly plaintive tone of certain passages of *Deirdre* owes much to the prominence this structure brings to sounds incorporating long open vowels, such as 'It's a poor thing'; 'It's a long while'; and 'It's soon you'll have dogs'.[7]

The second salient feature of Synge's style which recurs frequently in the Translations and in *Deirdre* is the use of 'and' as a connective where standard English would have adverbs of place or time, introducing subordinate clauses. Again, this feature, which is

common in Hiberno-English usage, comes from Irish where the
scarcity of complex sentences, and the stringing together of simple
sentences connected by *agus* (the Irish for 'and'), results from the
dearth of words eligible for use exclusively as adverbs. There is a
subtle effect to be gained by the use of this structure in English, and
that Synge was consciously exploiting it is clear from the notes he
wrote for Max Meyerfeld in connection with *The Well of the Saints*.
'The idiom, of course, is a Gaelic one, and it has shades of meaning
that cannot be rendered in ordinary English', he wrote, indicating
four examples of it.[8] The effect, or the 'shades of meaning' as Synge
put it, is that of maintaining emphasis on the person in question,
rather than dispersing it in precision of time or place. This effect can
be seen in:

1. . . . we old hags do be thinking, of the good times gone away
   from us, and we crouching on our hunkers
2. . . . my youngest will bring me a towel, and she with nice
   manners
3. My flowery and green age was passing away, and I feeling a
   chill in the fires . . .
4. Naisi and his brothers have no match and they chasing in the
   woods
5. It's a strange place he's put us camping and we come back as
   his friends[9]

In addition to the detailed effect of helping to focus on the person,
this structure also contributes to an overall sense of fluency, since
articulation thus becomes unobtrusive and undifferentiating between phrases, rather than manifest and separative.

A third feature of Synge's language is the frequency with which
the emphatic form of the pronoun, with the suffix 'self', is used, such
as myself, yourself, himself, itself, etc., of which examples are too
obvious and numerous to mention. This feature also reflects a
transfer from Irish to Hiberno-English usage, and again it increases
personal prominence. An emergent pattern is evident in these three
features, which is that of a syntactically controlled distribution of
emphasis, both semantic and auditory, which comes from the influence of the Irish language on English. Only four years after Synge's
death, the perceptive Maurice Bourgeois correctly noted: 'The
student who knows Gaelic still thinks in Gaelic as he reads or hears
Synge's plays. This applies not only to the phraseology used by his

characters, but to the syntax of their sentences'.[10] Nowhere is this assertion about syntax more pertinent than where Synge is liberated from any onus of giving direct expression to the lives of those who spoke an English out of Irish thought-structures: in his Translations and *Deirdre*.

The use of the emphatic form of the pronoun by Lady Gregory was noted in the previous chapter, as were some further forms also adopted by Synge. Among these other forms is, first, the substitution of the general pronoun 'that' for the more precise 'who, which', etc. of standard English, seen for example in 'Jesus, that has no end or death'; 'the dread of death or troubles that would tame her like'; and 'you that were my company'.[11] As with the extensive use of 'and' as a connective, this undifferentiating structure contributes to an overall sense of flow. Likewise, a related form, where the relative pronoun is entirely suppressed, contributes to this effect. Such suppression occurs frequently, and the following are but a few examples:

1. The man I had a love for – a great rascal would kick me in the gutter
2. I never set my two eyes on a head was so fine as your head
3. . . . you were a plague . . . to those did hang their life-times on your voice
4. Wasn't there a queen in Tara had to walk out . . .?[12]

These forms, together with the remaining features which will be discussed now, all occurred in the living speech of those whose English still retained an underlying thought-structure from Irish, though not necessarily with the same frequency as in Synge's usage.[13]

The second example above ('I never set my two eyes . . .', from 'Walter Von Der Vogelweide'), also illustrates another phenomenon of Synge's style in his Translations, which is a pronounced sense of duality in relation to parts of the body. In Irish, hands, feet, and so on are referred to in pairs very often: a sense of duality which differs from that seen in Old English, where it is of a social nature as it appears in the dual personal pronoun. Synge uses the form many times in his Translations, where it serves to increase the sense of the concrete and the specific.[14] It appears nowhere in his originals, yet he introduces it three times to Villon's 'An Old Woman's Lamentations' alone – appropriately, since the subject of the poem is physical decay, and the body therefore merits prominence.

Synge also explained the Hiberno-English 'tense of habitude' to Max Meyerfeld, giving him three examples. Of the instances quoted below, the first three are from the Translations, the last two from *Deirdre*:

1. . . . where sinners do be boiled in torment
2. When I do be minding the good days
3. . . . you that do be coming down so often
4. She does be all times straying around
5. . . . the likes of me do be telling the truth[15]

Such a structure also contributes to a sense of the presence of the person, since it expresses a state of being and of actuality.

The following forms seem to have been used primarily for their auditory effects, and are particularly evident in the connected discourse of the play. Sometimes they fulfil a necessary rhythmical function in the stress pattern, and sometimes they reflect the need of the Irish speaker to make the English statement less bald. Kuno Meyer's assertion that 'the half-said thing is dearest to the Celt' is a sensitive intuition, the truth of which can be observed in the failure of the Irish language to develop single words for 'yes' and 'no', so that affirmation or agreement and negation or disagreement must always be expressed in periphrastic verbal forms, and not in monosyllables.[16] The first three pages of *Deirdre* yield these examples: to the Old Woman's question whether Deirdre has returned, Lavarcham replies 'She has not'; then Lavarcham asks whether she is coming from the glen, and the Old Woman replies 'She is not'; and when Conchubor asks whether the tapestry is Deirdre's, Lavarcham replies 'It is, Conchubor'.

There is a series of adverbs which occur frequently, and which are usually placed at the end of a phrase or sentence, so that they ring in the ear and seem to underline what is being stated. They are 'surely', 'only', 'always', 'at all', and 'maybe', as in:

1. Yourself should be wise surely.
2. . . . she's growing too wise to marry a king and she a score only.
3. . . . it's that way I'll be living always.
4. . . . as if you hadn't seen them at all.
5. . . . a man with his hair like the raven maybe[17]

The stress is always trochaic for 'surely', 'only', and 'always'; it is strongly iambic in 'at all'; and 'maybe' can be variously treated in Hiberno-English usage. Synge exploits their possibilities for metrical purposes, as he does inversion in such phrases as 'these two months or three', and 'in two days or three'.[18]

It is noteworthy that, although there were other idiosyncrasies of speech of which he was aware among the Irish-speaking peasants of Aran, Synge did not use them:

> Some of them express themselves more correctly than the ordinary peasant, others use the Gaelic idioms continually and substitute 'he' or 'she' for 'it', as the neuter pronoun is not found in Modern Irish.[19]

Such forms were irrelevant to his purposes, and would have confused some of his audience. He selected from the living dialect only those forms of speech which he found useful for creating literary effects beyond the comic, or for what Yeats called 'noble purpose':

> This use of Irish dialect for noble purpose by Synge, and by Lady Gregory, who had it already in her *Cuchulain of Muirthemne*, and by Dr. Hyde in those first translations he has not equalled since, has done much for national dignity. . . . Synge wrote down words and phrases wherever he went, and with that knowledge of Irish which made all our country idioms easy to his hand, found it so rich a thing that he had begun translating into it fragments of the great literatures of the world . . .[20]

Such use of dialect by Synge was in some respects a parallel to the linguistic practice of those poets who, early during the Latin Middle Ages used the vernacular. Regardless of whether that vernacular was a Romance language, Celtic, Germanic, or other, such practice was an assertion of confidence in the indigenous and popular tongue, and was implicitly a rejection of the imperial one. What was afoot in both cases was a raising of the vulgar tongue to 'monumental' status. In one case it was replacing Latin, in the other, standard English.

Where a language generally accepted as suitable for literary purposes is clearly distinguishable from the language spoken in everyday situations, the registers of these two languages naturally differ. Consequently, the introduction of the everyday language into the literary context has a surprising effect, and where this admixture is extensive and prolonged, it can ultimately alter the literary language fundamentally. The scope for alteration is indeterminate, which is also the case when the vulgar tongue, having become generally adopted for literary purposes, is susceptible to influence from the 'monumental' language which held that status before it.

It is convenient here, because of the historical parallel, to adopt the terms 'monumental' and 'documentary' as they are used by Paul Zumthor when he is dealing with questions of bilingualism in the Latin Middle Ages. Greatly simplified, his view is that each linguistic community primarily uses language for communicative purposes, which function he calls 'documentary'. In addition, there is a secondary use of language, related to the first but surpassing it, whose function is 'monumental'. The language of literature serves a monumental purpose, it is edificative, both in the sense of constructing an edifice and of being uplifting.[21]

Where, in the Middle Ages, the vulgar tongue, hitherto used only for documentary purposes, was brought into use for monumental or literary purposes, the poets, seeing it in this new artificial light, gradually became aware of its vitalizing effect. This monumental use of the vulgar tongue initially brought it into close relationship with Latin, notably in macaronic verse, and for the purposes of *barbarolexis* (using foreign words) and *farciture* (the insertion of passages in another tongue). Eventually, the vulgar tongue became susceptible to external influence from Latin because the two languages appeared in such close proximity, so that artificial syntactical variations and rhythmic combinations taken from Latin were acquired by the vulgar tongue.[22]

Synge's use of non-standard vocabulary in his work, as well as his occasional use of unanglicized words, relates him to the initial attempts to introduce the vernacular in macaronic verse and for *barbarolexis*.[23] However, the syntactical forms which he borrows from Hiberno-English usage, and which reflect Irish thought-structures, represent an advanced development of the use of the vernacular for literary purposes: advanced beyond the comic (where it was connected with the stage-Irishman),[24] and built upon its earlier monumental use, especially by Douglas Hyde and Lady Gregory.

The medieval poems which Synge translated come from the late Middle Ages: too late to provide examples of *barbarolexis*, or for any structural influence from Latin to be perceptible, since it is already so integrated. Yet, through Synge's studies, especially with de Julleville, he was well acquainted with the traditions out of which these poems grew.[25] Besides, the earlier coexistence of two languages, one for communication and one for literature was discussed by de Julleville,[26] as well as the relationship between the conqueror and the conquered in the domain of language.[27]

The 'strong roots among the clay and worms' which Synge thought necessary for enduring poetry indicated a need not only for a real-life source for subject, but also for a living language.[28] That both of these needs were met in those medieval poems which he translated doubtless informed his choice of them, but in addition they were all written by professional poets, a class with which he felt affinity. Maurice Bourgeois noted Synge's consciousness of the role of the professional poet, though lately displaced, in the native Irish tradition.[29] Una Ellis-Fermor, who underestimated his knowledge of that tradition, saw his connection with it only as an affinity of spirit:

> Synge, who thinks less than any of his predecessors about Nationalism or the Gaelic League or the past civilizations of Ireland, is one of the few followers of the movement who, through affinity of spirit, seems to carry on unbroken the tradition of ancient Irish nature poetry.[30]

But it called for far more than 'affinity of spirit' for Synge to be able to draw attention to the extreme technicality of Old Irish verse, as he did when he noted the survival among early Irish MSS of 'une grande quantité de poésies, en vers compliqués, construits avec des assonances extrêmement curieuses' (a great number of poems in complex verse, composed according to extremely meticulous rules of assonance and alliteration).[31]

Before Una Ellis-Fermor, Padraic Colum had seen Synge's relationship with that tradition, also in terms of affinity, but expressed more strongly: 'John Synge's affinities were not with Renaissance, but with medieval art. And being medieval he is in line with the last poets of the Gaelic literary tradition'.[32] Synge himself, characteristically averse to insularity, did not identify himself with the native tradition alone, as is evident in his lines to Ronsard:

> Am I alone in Leinster, Meath and Connaught
>   In Ulster and the south,
> To trace your spirit, Ronsard, in each song and sonnet
>   Shining with wine or drouth?

Here, and in another five of his own poems, Synge relates himself out to a European poetic tradition, primarily a lyric one, and ranging through many countries.[33] He ranged similarly far with the poets he translated.

Robin Skelton has linked the persona assumed by Synge in his own poems with the professional court poet in the medieval tradition, and in particular with the *goliards*.[34] Since the poems Synge translated also hail from that tradition, it is of interest to consider it. In France, it was richly varied, and the poet's function could take a number of forms. Thence came Colin Muset (1210–?1250) and François Villon (1431–?1489), both translated by Synge. Although, for example, troubadours and *jongleurs* were ill-differentiated in practice, we find Guiraut Riquier, himself a troubadour, protesting strongly against any confusion of the two.[35] The distinction between them seems to have been essentially one of class. While the troubadour had ready access to court circles where he was welcomed often as an equal, the *jongleur*'s reputation associated him more with taverns and scurrility. The education of the two classes of poet also differed. The troubadour was a product of a school of poetry, and the less privileged *jongleur* often depended on him for the compositions which he performed.[36]

Goliards, who flourished in France, Germany and England chiefly during the twelfth and thirteenth centuries, displayed their education through their use of Latin, but were apparently very free in their choice of poetic form, and while their position on social issues was more polemic than that of other professional poets, their own behaviour was reputedly libertine. All these professional poets were nomadic, and they all depended on patronage. Despite the differences in the range of their work, their themes often overlapped, and most of them made prominent use of music in their repertoire.

Both the terms minstrel and *trouvère* have been applied to Colin Muset.[37] The *trouvères* were the poets of northern France, whose art, dating from circa 1160, is derived from that of the troubadours. The latter wrote mainly lyric poetry, originally in the *langue d'oc* or Old Provençal, while the *trouvères* used the *langue d'oil* or Old

French, and wrote mainly narrative poetry in the form of *chansons de geste* and *romans*. The term minstrel (*ménestrel*) has in its modern usage a much more elevated and narrowed significance than it had up to the end of the sixteenth century: then it was a general term applicable to any professional entertainer among the various types so far described. Now it signifies a medieval singer of heroic or lyric poetry, composed sometimes by the minstrel himself, sometimes by others, and usually self-accompanied on a stringed instrument. These various terms seem to have been often used loosely and interchangeably during the periods coeval with the persons they designated.

It is not possible to identify a single source for the German lyric tradition from which Walther von der Vogelweide (fl. 1200) came,[38] but there was certainly influence from the *trouvères*, and even from the troubadours.[39] The *Minnesänger* shared certain conventions, topoi, and images with these 'foreign' professional poets. Images of sun, moon, and stars were frequently used, as well as an important complex of images connected with the heart: features all borne out in the poem by Walther which Synge translated.

Despite the rich heritage from *bárd* and *filí* at home, Synge did not officially translate any Old Irish poems: perhaps because translation was a finger exercise for him and their language would have interfered with his freedom in exploiting the tension between Irish and English for its effects.[40] Nevertheless, it was suggested by Robin Skelton that Synge's poem 'Abroad' may be an 'imitation' of an Old Irish poem on the subject of going to Rome.[41] Since this Old Irish poem of two quatrains appeared in 1903 in the same publication as the Old Irish hymn of Saint Patrick which Synge certainly knew, the external evidence concurs.[42]

Synge made two translations of Colin Muset's song of complaint 'Sire cuens, j'ai vïelé', of which only the prose version was published with his consent in the Cuala edition. Despite Synge's doubts about the value of verse translations, there is a certain verve in the movement of the language of the verse rendering which is more in keeping with the spirit of the original than the more melancholy tone of the prose translation. Nevertheless, comparison will be made between the prose version and the original, out of regard for Synge's preference.

The complaint was an established convention of medieval poetry, found not only in French and Latin, but also in English tradition: see for example Chaucer, particularly 'The Complaint of Chaucer to his

Purse'.[43] It thrived in Ireland too, where it could be a fierce weapon in the hands of poets whose satire was a mark of the power and influence they wielded in their society. Eleanor Knott quotes the following sixteenth century source describing the relationship between the Irish poet and his patrons:

> Greedie of praise they be, & fearfull of dishonour, and to this end they esteeme their poets who write Irish learnedlie and pen their sonets heroicall, for which they are bountifullie rewarded, if not they send out libels in dispraise, thereof the lords and gentlemen stand in great awe.[44]

Thus, by translating a medieval complaint, Synge relieved himself of all obligation or temptation to be innovative either in subject or in form, and could thereby concentrate entirely on making Hiberno-English structures serve a pre-ordained purpose.

Muset's complaint turns on the central motif of the purse which can be either full or empty, according to the disposition of the patron. Synge begins, following the original fairly closely, with a complaint to his patron. He then reduces the mockery of the wife in response to an empty purse from a whole stanza to one line, ending like the original again in detailing the pleasures of returning with a full purse. These pleasures, both in the original and in the translation, include the singer wearing a fine grey coat; being welcomed by his wife who puts her arms around his neck; having his son tend his horse, and other members of his household killing two chickens for him and courteously attending him at his toilet.[45] Such features reflect motifs common to the 'good life' register of medieval French lyric poetry, including the gracious young girl, fine clothing, and the display of affection.[46]

There are two questions of a more incidental nature which arise from Synge's translation of Colin Muset's song. First, was he attracted to it initially as a song rather than merely as a poem? His musical interests and training, together with the fact that several editions of Muset's songs which included their musical transcription were current in Paris when Synge first went there, would suggest that he was.[47] The second problem is his translation of *vielé* as 'growing old'. It is unlikely that he would have confused it with the Old French form of *vieilli*, since he would certainly have known from de Julleville that a *jongleur* accompanied himself on a musical instrument called a *vieil*.[48] Therefore he was possibly playing on words for his own amusement and could not resist an opportunity to introduce that favourite theme of ageing. Besides, he may have found the long, stressed, open vowel of 'old' metrically useful, particularly since he was thus avoiding both long-winded expressions for instrumental accompaniment, and a term such as 'fiddle' which would have been too distinctly 'folk' in its connotations.

In addition to this medieval French complaint by Colin Muset Synge chose two poems by François Villon to translate, one religious and one profane. In translating 'Ballade pour prier Nostre Dame', he discards several laudatory, pious lines per stanza without losing the profound sense of religious faith behind this 'prayer'. He drops such commonplace pieties as

> La joie avoir me fais, haute deesse,
> A qui pecheurs doivent tous recourir,
> Comblés de foi, sans feinte ne paresse:
> En cette foi je veuil vivre et mourir.

but retains the concrete images of the following lines:

> Femme je suis pauvrette et ancienne,
> Qui rien ne sais; oncques lettre ne lus.
> Au moutier vois, dont suis paroissienne,
> Paradis peint ou sont harpes et luths,
> Et un enfer ou damnés sont boullus:

translating them as:

> I'm a poor aged woman, was never at school, and is no scholar with letters, but I've seen pictures in the chapel with Paradise on one side, and harps and pipes in it, and the place on the other side, where sinners do be boiled in torment.[49]

The result is an increase in the effect of naïve simplicity found in his original. The fact that Synge was professedly not Christian in belief indicates that he did not choose this poem for the appropriateness of the poet's expression for a sentiment of his own. The choice was rather made in order to increase objectivity, and was almost certainly influenced by reaction to Dante Gabriel Rossetti's translation of it, so full of elevated diction and archaism.[50]

The interest in the disposition of an old woman is retained in Synge's choice of 'Les regrets de la Belle Heaumière' for translation.

This time, however, the sentiments expressed are carnal, not religious. The tone of the poem is distinctive for a greater degree of self-absorption than is usual in the expression of the *carpe diem* theme, where the speaker is normally intent on alerting the audience to such joys of youth as quickly pass. Harsh concrete features, such as 'les sourcils chûs . . . orcilles pendantes, moussues . . . levres peaussues' (fallen eyebrows, lop-ears, frothing skinny lips) are brought into focus. In condensing and re-ordering this material, Synge excludes the first three stanzas of reminiscence, as well as some of the more explicitly sexual references, such as

> Mamelles, quoi? toutes retraites;
> Telles les hanches que les tettes;
> Du sardinet, fi! Quant des cuisses,
> Cuisses ne sont plus, mais cuisettes . . .[51]

(What about my breasts? All shrunken. My hips are the same as my dugs. What a stink! As for the thighs, they no longer exist, and are thighlings instead).

Through such omission, he creates an effect less harrowing in its examination of decay. He also drops the more accusatory tone of his original, and his old woman adopts a more reflective and nostalgic disposition than her medieval counterpart.

Given Synge's knowledge of Old Irish poetry, and the preoccupation in his work with the falling away of the body in old age against a background of youthful physical pleasure, he was doubtless aware that the same theme occurs in several Early Irish lyrics.[52] Because of the striking similarity in point of view between 'Les regrets de la Belle Heaumière' and the ninth-century Irish poem 'Sentainne Bérri' (The Old Woman of Beare), I would suggest that Synge's choice of the Villon poem was influenced by his knowing the Old Irish lament. It had been published, with a translation by Kuno Meyer, with whose scholarship he was familiar, in 1899.[53] Besides, several manuscripts of the poem are to be found in the library of Trinity College Dublin.

Both Villon's poem and 'The Old Woman of Beare' are furnished with the physical evidence of ruin: the Old Woman of Beare is yellow with age, wears a mean veil, and, like La Belle Heaumière, her arms are bony and thin, and her hair grey. La Belle Heaumière describes herself as no longer 'the pick of many' but now relegated to the company of other old hags, crouching together before a miserable fire trying to keep warm. Likewise, the Old Woman of Beare feels the cold, and contrasts her present company with that of her youth: 'I have had my day with kings, drinking mead and wine; now I drink whey-and-water among shrivelled old hags'. The two poems share a forceful expression of sensual frustration, and each reveals an intense emotion arising from the undesirable effects of ageing. Perhaps Synge was struck by the vague and generalized effects achieved by Swinburne when he translated 'Les regrets de la Belle Heaumière', and saw the hard specificity of the Irish tradition as the better manner for rendering such material.[54]

The poem by Walther von der Vogelweide which Synge chose to translate is a conventional lyric in the courtly love tradition, making use of images standard to German practice. It begins: 'Mîn frouwe is ein ungenaedic wîp' (My lady is an ungracious woman), and consists of five stanzas. Of these, Synge translates only one and a half, and the material he drops surprisingly includes the theme of wasted youth and time, as well as a concrete image of *la belle dame sans merci* in ultimate isolation:

> vîent und friunt gemeine,
> der gestêts aleine,
> so si mich und jen unrehte hât.[55]

(She will be alone, without friend or enemy, since she has been so unjust to them and me.)

The contrastive image of the visible head in relief against the unfathomable heart which begins Walther's second stanza is selected by Synge for his opening:

I never set my eyes on a head was so fine as your head, but I'd no way to be looking down into your heart.

Ich gesach nie houbet baz gezogen,
in ir herze kunde iche nie gesehen.

The endeavour to account for Synge's translating so little of this poem raises the question of why he chose it in the first place. The answer would seem to be that the tradition of love poetry in which Walther was partaking is clearly identifiable, and elsewhere

111

Walther expressed his consciousness of such participation.[56] Thus, the poem provides a desirable model for a renewer of tradition. However, the usefulness of convention to Synge was limited by the desire for sincerity introduced into poetry by the Romantics. Therefore he put aside what in Walther's poem seemed to be formal padding, and confined his exercise in linguistic form to the material which had some flavour of 'real life'. It is noteworthy that, among the Minnesänger, Walther is distinguished for his evocative images, fresh feeling, variety, and for being truer to nature than most: for example, in his later work, he replaced the conventional courtly lady with the simple country girl.[57]

The other medieval German work translated by Synge as 'Judaslied 14th Century', seems to have been chosen for its interest in the fate of the betrayer. In one draft Synge had opened his translation with the traditional Irish exclamation of grief and mourning, *ocón*, transcribed as 'Ohone'.[58] Elsewhere, taking notes from *I Fioretti di San Francesco*, Synge shows a further interest in the fate of the betrayer, recording the parallel between one of the twelve followers of St Francis and Judas.[59] Traditionally despised, not only for his act of betrayal but for taking his own life, Judas is grieved over by Synge, who seems to be explicitly identifying himself with him in addressing him as 'our poor Judas' in this translation. It has not been possible to identify an original for this piece, and the addition of 'Fourteenth Century' to the title merely suggests that Synge's inspiration was a work of art of the period (whether painting, sculpture, play or poem) during his stay in Coblenz in the autumn of 1908.

Since that was when his mother died, it is conceivable that the 'sincerity factor' was operating here too, in the choice of a subject which expressed something of the guilt he was feeling for his 'betrayal' of his mother's ideals.[60]

One wonders whether the adoption of this sympathetic attitude towards the betrayer may also owe something to Baudelaire, who in his *Fleurs du Mal* had praised that other betrayer, St Peter: 'Saint Pierre a renié Jésus . . . il a bien fait'. Although Synge disapproved of what he called the morbidity of Baudelaire's mind, that would not necessarily have precluded his appreciation of the dramatic effect of this controversial view of St Peter's denial. Baudelaire shifted the attitude to the betrayer to the opposite position from the traditional one, whereas Synge neither reviles nor praises, but is compassionate.[61]

Besides the medieval French and German poets Synge translated there are two Italian poets who are apparently exceptions to this preference, Francesco Petrarca (1304–1374) and Giacomo Leopardi (1798–1837). Although the Renaissance had begun much earlier in Italy than in France and Germany so that Petrarch is not generally classed as a medieval poet, he was nevertheless the direct inheritor of medieval poetic conventions, which he shares with the poets discussed above; and Leopardi, in certain respects, follows Petrarch in this. Petrarch, as the direct inheritor of the medieval lyric tradition in poetry, has been described as 'the greatest artist of the middle ages'.[62] As Serafino Riva has pointed out, Synge chose to translate the Petrarchan sonnets which had been ignored by the English Petrarchists, that is those which express the greatest intensity.[63] Here again, as with Walther, there is a tension at work between the personal, real-life interest and the poetic convention within which it is expressed, for the Petrarchan sonnets Synge translated retain several of the inherited conventions: four show authorial self-consciousness; affected modesty, occasioned by the poet's feigned lack of technical skill, appears in two; and a conventional nature setting appears in five. Moreover, the poet adopts some of the traditional poses of the courtly lover throughout.[64]

Leopardi, in his poem 'A Silvia' which Synge translates, takes up the same position as Petrarch in relation to the beloved: both Laura and Silvia are addressed in death. The month of May, traditional for amorous dalliance, is chosen for the memories recalled, and the poet pictures himself in the act of writing, though not, strictly speaking, writing poetry. Synge, in his translation, gives us only half the original poem, which falls into two fairly clear divisions: the first, which Synge translates, consists largely of concrete memories, while the second ranges from an address to Silvia on the subject of hope, to a reproach to Nature for the deception she practises in killing the hope which she had raised.[65] While one can assume that the theme of lost youth influenced Synge's choice here as elsewhere, it is clear that the more philosophical and melancholy aspect of Leopardi did not have the same appeal for Synge as did his sense of place and of concrete event.

The comparison of Synge's translations with their medieval originals shows that he was most faithful and literal when the subject of his original was expressed in concrete, evocative images, and when his sense of sincerity, if not actively iterated, was not at any rate offended. He was, on the other hand, free in omission when the material seemed empty, as in the expression of formal pieties or of the berating wife whose impact as a literary type would have been comic for Muset's audience but not necessarily for Synge's. He was also free in omission where the expression was offensive in the terms of an Irish peasantry among whom 'modesty' and 'purity' were established cults. Since his language was based on their living tongue, the grosser references of Villon's whore would have been out of place in it. However, he made additions on occasion, for instance 'two' to qualify hands, eyes, etc.; and he was free in his alteration of tense to the habitual form. The effects he achieved were a marked increase in the sense of the concrete, the specific, and the presence of the person, all of which resulted from following the rules of a language which was substantively weighted. His Translations were a telescoping of the double translation process which he saw as 'the real effort of the artist', that is the translation of life into music, and then from music into literature (p. 23). By beginning with material which coincided sufficiently with his individual world-picture to be regarded as having already been through the initial translation process, he was the better able to concentrate on the inherent form of the language into which he was translating. His choice of a non-standard idiom in the first place could owe something to Victor Hugo who condemned conventional elegance of style and sought only such propriety of language as was rooted in idiom and could thereby hold grammar in tow rather than being bound by its rules. Hugo's denial that French was a fixed language (as the *Académie française* tried to hold it was), and his warning that it would die the day it became so, could have encouraged Synge to employ a living English idiom. Since it was an idiom which had early forced him to recognize clashing world-pictures, in translation he straight away dismissed its suitability for producing a facsimile of his originals and boldly proceeded to the creation of its own integrated, alternative world.[66]

VI FOLLY

Parallel to Synge's use of grotesque realism of the body, which expresses an ongoing need to draw the lofty down to earth, there is in his work a use of folly, which conveys a perennial need to degrade the spirit in order that man should not surpass himself. The spirit with which we are concerned here is that element in man which aspires, which urges him to control life, and to harmonize with his fellows in a social context. As such it is closely affiliated with ideals, order, and social integration. Folly here signifies the thought, attitudes, and behaviour typical of the fool. The fool in question is a literary figure, not that social being whose inadequacies of nature or education cause others to identify him as foolish.

As a literary figure, the history of the fool before the Middle Ages is not directly relevant to the use Synge makes of him, although the range of fool literature with which Synge was familiar is considerable. Among the most pertinent influences is the Pauline notion of the fool as the Christian *par excellence*, the corollary of which is the ultimate futility of worldly wisdom. This view is explicitly articulated in a letter to the Corinthians: 'If any man among you seemeth to be wise in this world, let him become a fool, that he may be wise. For the wisdom of this world is foolishness with God'. This view of folly is reiterated in various forms in St Paul's teaching.[1] It also recurs throughout medieval ascetic writings, among which *The Imitation of Christ* by Thomas à Kempis deserves mention because of Synge's particular interest in this work. The same basic view of folly underlies Desiderius Erasmus's *Praise of Folly*, although there is an additional humanist dimension there in the scepticism and cleverness of the writing, even when Erasmus quotes St Paul to support his argument for the universal nature of folly.[2] Synge was sufficiently familiar with Erasmus to quote him in Latin.[3] François Rabelais, also admired by Synge, was greatly influenced by Erasmus, so that his Panurge appears to be a fool for wanting to be worldly wise.[4] Worldly wisdom, in accordance with the Pauline view, is portrayed unfavourably in Synge's plays, but the view is not simply Pauline in that the alternative suggested to it is not a Christian wisdom, but rather an individual, imaginative conception of values which are in harmony with nature. Such values are embodied in

Nora and the tramp in *The Shadow*, and in Martin and Mary in *The Well*.

A second form of folly to be found in Synge's plays is that where a certain illusion is pursued. The literary fool who most readily comes to mind in this connection is Don Quixote. Synge himself made the association between *Don Quixote* and *The Playboy* in an interview following the first performance of his play.[5] Don Quixote's folly results from allowing fantasy complete sway, so that chivalric ideals are pursued to the point of madness, yet these values often appear preferable to their 'sane' alternative.

Madness in the form of unreason constitutes one of the qualities attributed to the Renaissance court fool, who is a third influence on Synge's use of folly, in his conception of Owen in *Deirdre*. The court fool, through his unreason, is paradoxically wise and has an increased capacity for perceiving 'the truth'. He is the sage fool who becomes a licensed critic. His most important literary occurrence in relation to Synge's Owen is in *King Lear*, a play which Synge once considered 'the only readable play in the world'.[6]

In addition to the fool who is the opposite of worldly wise, to folly based on illusion, and to the sage fool, there is also a fool in Synge's work who inverts received values, and places himself outside established social structures, rejecting their restraint. This energetic figure is descended from the fool of the Middle Ages, especially in France, and it is once again to Petit de Julleville that Synge's debt of introduction goes. The 'Festival of Fools' had already come into being by 1190 as one of a series of revels in the days following Christmas. Although chiefly known in France, there are records of it from Lincoln, Beverley, Salisbury, and St Paul's in England too. It was forbidden in France in 1212, and was eventually banned by canon law in 1234 by Pope Gregory IX.

During the festival, behaviour was riotous. It began during the regular ritual in church, at the line in the Magnificat 'He hath put down the mighty from their seat, and hath exalted the humble'. The deacons continued to chant this line repeatedly, interrupting the normal sequence of the ceremony, while the subdeacons (who were repressed, secondary figures in the regular ritual) took over the staff of office, and profaned the sacred things which they had revered, or were obliged to revere during the rest of the ecclesiastical year. Documents of 1222 from Beauvais tell of an ass ridden by a pretty girl with a baby being taken into the church and up to the altar, and each ritual portion of the Mass being concluded with a bray. Also, the *Precentor Stultorum* (the leader of the fools) would be 'baptized' with several buckets of water, while some revelling deacons dressed up as women, and others had their clothes removed.[7]

When the church eventually banished this event from its precincts, it was carried on in other public places, in various transmutations, by societies which grew up in order to take over the tradition. Such societies were attached, sometimes only tenuously, to institutions like the Cathedral Schools or the law faculties of the universities, in relation to which they invariably represented a reaction to restriction by authority and a periodic inversion of the pervading rule. The *Basochiens*, *Mère Folle* and 'her' troupe at Dijon, and the *Enfants-sans-souci* are all examples of these societies which fostered the tradition of the clever, licensed fool since their members were educated critics who, outside their performances, knuckled under the general social and ecclesiastical rule.

This medieval version of folly emerges as a social and intellectual reaction, expressed in an outburst of energy from the confines of rule and ongoing restriction. Suffocating, all-pervading piety and rigid rules of thought evoke a contrary response from man's vital instincts, so that under the guise of folly the sacred is mocked and aspirations to order and harmony are degraded. It will be seen that Synge's fool-figures take up this tradition, and express the vitality which he sought in great writing, which he declared was read of old by 'strong men, and thieves, and deacons, not by little cliques only'.[8] The deacons he had in mind were no modern, minor ecclesiastics upholding the dilute and dwindling state of an anachronistic institution. They were rather the full-blooded deacons of the flourishing church of the Middle Ages, inverting the established order during a time of license under their chosen 'Lord of Misrule'.

The nature of the literary fool is not such that he suffers from any inherent defect of mind to make him incapable of leading a full life in relation to his fellow-men. Rather, a defect of mind is attributed to him for certain of his actions and ideas which are perceived as aberrations. Thus his position in relation to society is not favourable, so that he is treated as an outcast, a butt, or a laughing-stock.

The literary fool, behaving as if he were independent of society, represents 'natural man', that is man as he was before the foundation of organized society. In this he is clearly an invention, a figure created in order to arrive at some hidden truth.[9] The freedom attributed to him from law and custom allows him a special perception of what the truth is, because the spectator sees most of the game. The truth which he speaks is arrived at, however, not by rationalization, but by inspired intuition.[10] Because his *modus operandi* is non-rational, he is hunted by the rational element of society, which perceives him as someone who 'transgresses or ignores the code of reasoned self-restraint under which society attempts to exist, is unmeasured in his hilarity or in his melancholy, disregards the logic of cause and effect and conducts himself in ways which seem rash and shocking to normal mortals'.[11]

Three aspects of the literary fool as Synge uses him are important: first, his relationship to nature is markedly closer than the non-fool in that he does not allow imposed structures to separate him from it. Also, in the realm of the psyche, he remains in touch with the unconscious so that his instinctive responses and impulses remain vital. This leads to the second aspect, which is his irrationality. There are two sides to this: the positive one causes the fool to be viewed as inspired visionary, which relates him to the poet and the truth-teller, while the negative one leads others to see him as mad. The third aspect is that the fool remains an outsider.

An early interest in the nature of the outsider is shown in an entry in one of Synge's notebooks for 1889. It consists of a definition of the term idiot, with the word entered in Greek as well as in English. This definition appears among many others, of which it is by far the longest. The notes are from R.C. Trench's *On the Study of Words* and are mainly of one line, while this runs as follows:

> Idiot = private man, as contradistinguished from one clothed with office and taking his share in the management of public affairs. In this its primary use it is occasionally used in English; thus Jeremy Taylor – 'humility is a duty in great ones, as well as in idiots'. Thence it soon signified a rude intellectually unexercised person, this second sense bearing witness to a conviction in the Greek mind of the indispensableness of public life, even to the right development of the mind. Thus pushed farther gives our tertiary meaning – an imbecile.[12]

Although 'fool' and 'idiot' have different meanings, they overlap in that traditionally neither has a place within organized society. It is noteworthy that Synge lived very much as a 'private man' himself, and repeatedly used the figure of the outsider in his work.

Turning now to Synge's plays, *The Shadow of the Glen* is the first in which he makes use of the fool-figure. There he creates a strong dramatic conflict between the worldly wisdom of Dan Burke and Mike Dara on the one hand, and the folly of the tramp and Nora on the other. These two figures stand out clearly against their foil, and their social and material vulnerability is underlined by their common attachment to Patch Darcy. It is curious how the spirit of this dead man pervades a play in which he never appears. Soon after meeting, the tramp and Nora talk about fear, and it transpires that neither of them is easily frightened. Talk of fear reminds the tramp of Patch Darcy's madness and his frightful end, running up into the back hills, clad only in an old shirt, and being eaten by the crows.[13] Darcy is brought even closer to the audience when the tramp reveals that he himself was the last person to have heard his voice.

Synge viewed the tramps he met in county Wicklow as a healthy expression of vitality, and wrote of them:

A few of these people have been on the road for generations; but fairly often they seem to have merely drifted out from the ordinary people of the villages, and do not differ greatly from the class they come from. Their abundance has often been regretted; yet in one sense it is an interesting sign, for wherever the labourer of a country has preserved his vitality, and begets an occasional temperament of distinction, a certain number of vagrants are to be looked for. In the middle classes the gifted son of a family is always the poorest – usually a writer or artist with no sense for speculation – and in a family of peasants, where the average comfort is just over penury, the gifted son sinks also, and is soon a tramp on the roadside.

In this life, however, there are many privileges. The tramp in Ireland is little troubled by the laws, and lives in out-of-door conditions that keep him in good humour and fine bodily health.[14]

In Synge's view of the real-life tramps he knew we find the clue to how the tramp in his play is meant to be seen. He is not a good-for-nothing unfortunate, but someone privileged with sound bodily health and good humour, enjoying a degree of freedom and license from the law. He is probably a tramp because of his distinction of temperament, in which he is related to the artist. Above all, he is acceptable because he is vital, and he encourages those he

encounters to be so. He has, in short, many salient characteristics of
the literary fool.

In contrast with such buoyancy in the nature of the tramp there
was a certain desolation noted by Synge in the climate and landscape of Wicklow, which had negative effects on those who lived in
the glens:

> This peculiar climate, acting on a population that is already
> lonely and dwindling, has caused or increased a tendency to
> nervous depression among the people, and every degree of sad-
> ness, from that of the man who is merely mournful to that of the
> man who has spent half his life in the mad-house, is common
> among these hills.[15]

This was the landscape which harboured the proto-type for Patch
Darcy. The true story of the man eaten by the crows was recounted
to Synge by an old man on a Wicklow road.[16]

Sociological research into the mental health records of Synge's
day would doubtless reveal the basis for his statement to Stephen
MacKenna that 'blessed unripeness is sometimes akin to damned
rottenness, see percentage of lunatics in Ireland & causes thereof',
as well as for the declaration he attributed to Jameson in his
scenario for 'National Drama: A Farce': 'There are 27 lunatics per
thousand in Ireland, the highest figure on earth'.[17] What is relevant
to a consideration of folly in Synge's plays is that madness is neither
portrayed sentimentally nor in proscriptive terms. The fate of his
madman in *The Shadow* is, true to fact, to be eaten by crows.
Nevertheless, it is portrayed sympathetically in that the fool figures
convey a sense of its pathos to the audience, while at the same time
they recognize their own bond with the madman. Nora praises
Patch in terms which relate him to Christ (the Good Shepherd), thus
suggesting the Pauline connection between the fool and Christian
values: '. . . Patch Darcy, God spare his soul, who would walk
through five hundred sheep and miss one of them, and he not
reckoning them at all'.[18] Predictably, mundane Michael replies with
a query as to whether that was the man who 'went queer in his head'.
But the more sympathetic tramp takes up the praise of Patch, thereby increasing his bond with Nora. From this point on these two fool
figures are united in their conflict with worldly values.

The inspired vision of the fool in *The Shadow* belongs mainly to
the tramp. His lyrical and optimistic speeches, where he views

nature as kind, distinguish him sharply from those around him. While Dan depends on ironical repetition of various kinds (such as 'a man that's dead can do no hurt', and 'Your teeth'll be falling and your head'll be the like of a bush where sheep do be leaping a gap'), the tramp's speech is conciliating: 'the rain is falling but the air is kind, and maybe it'll be a grand morning by the grace of God'. Besides, he consoles Nora with the view that one does not grow old so long as one lives a life close to the seasons: 'The time you'll be feeling the cold and the frost, and the great rain, and the sun again, and the south wind blowing in the glens, you'll not be sitting in this place, making yourself old with looking on each day and it passing you by'. Dan considers that 'it's to much talk' the tramp has, and refers disparagingly to it as 'blathering'. But Nora, who had earlier been seen by the tramp as 'a grand woman to talk' (conversation being an honoured art in Irish tradition), although she is still un-practised in the fool's vision, finally declares to the tramp 'you've a fine bit of talk, stranger, and it's with yourself I'll go'.[19]

When the two 'fools' leave the stage at the end of *The Shadow* for their life of freedom and hardship close to nature, they carry the sympathy of the audience with them in a similar way to Martin and Mary Doul in their departure at the end of *The Well of the Saints*. Martin, when they are being chased off the stage, asserts the right of Mary and himself to be outsiders:

> We're going surely, for if it's a right some of you have to be working and sweating the like of Timmy the smith, and a right some of you have to be fasting and praying and talking holy talk the like of yourself, I'm thinking it's a good right ourselves have to be sitting blind, hearing a soft wind turning round the little leaves of the spring and feeling the sun, and we not tormenting our souls with the sight of the grey days, and the holy men, and the dirty feet is trampling the world.[20]

Here he divides the world they are leaving behind into the workers (the worldly wise) and the pious (the heavenly wise, perhaps); and he anticipates a kindness from nature which is in contrast with the treatment these two groups, both of whom regard him as mad, have shown him. While Martin had been working for Timmy, the smith who represents the worldly wise had called him a 'lazy, basking fool' and 'a raggy-looking fool'; and it was only despite his finding Martin to be a 'foolish man' that he asked the saint to cure him a second time.[21]

Molly also calls Martin a fool a couple of times, and twice attributes madness to him. The other characters who are worldly wise call him mad too, notably Timmy and Patch. But what is most striking among the various accusations of folly and madness is that the saint, who is the official representative of Christianity, is ironically lacking in its appropriate folly, and is bent instead on imposing a vision of the world which is highly selective. After Martin refuses the cure, the saint enquires of him: 'Is his mind gone that he's no wish to be cured this day, and looking out on the wonders of the world?'. But when asked to confound Martin in the argument about wonders and fine sights, the saint can only think of examples which are generated out of things as they are, whereas the 'finer sights' Martin claims for the blind are generated within the mind also:

> Isn't it finer sights ourselves had a while since and we sitting dark smelling the sweet beautiful smells do be rising in the warm nights and hearing the swift flying things racing in the air (SAINT *draws back from him*), till we'd be looking up in our own minds into a grand sky, and seeing lakes, and broadening rivers, and hills are waiting for the spade and plough.[22]

The vision expressed here is that of the artist. Martin 'tells us of realities, but he knows that art has never taken more than its symbols from anything that the eye can see or the hand measure', which are the words Yeats wrote of Synge in his preface to *The Well of the Saints*.[23] The vision of the worldly wise, on the other hand, views what the eye can see and the hand measure as of primary importance, hence they have long connected the lunatic, the lover, and the poet with folly. It is folly, not reason, which urges men to obey their vital, creative instincts (physical and otherwise); and in the zone of the irrational they create images of a world which is imaginary, rather than actual.[24] In *The Well* the fool/artist expounds an imaginary world which appears preferable to the audience to the actual world in which he had lived as a seeing man, and which is an acceptable secular alternative to the weak religious vision of the saint.

At the end of *The Shadow* and *The Well* the fool figures who leave the stage do so for a healthier life, reflecting Synge's observations on the Wicklow tramps. At the beginning of *The Tinker's Wedding* we meet another nomadic type, the tinkers, who are already collectively living such a life: Michael remarks that Sara is thriving, in good health, and has a lot of children. Because the movement of these characters in relation to established society is the opposite of the movement in the other two plays, and the number of outsiders is greater than that of the establishment, there is no fool-figure as such in *The Tinker's Wedding* since the fool is essentially a solitary figure. There is, however, much talk of folly, but since that is presented as universal, it is not a particularly dramatic theme.

Yet there is some dramatic conflict between the instinctual wisdom of the tinkers and a temporary drive towards social conformity. Sara is the leader of this drive, Michael her reluctant follower, and old Mary never budges from the position which her son expects her to hold. Knowing that she would consider it folly for Sara and himself to get married, he says 'She'll be . . . saying it's fools we are surely'. And sure enough, Mary guesses and asks 'It's at marriage you're fooling again, maybe?', and when Sara ignores her, she insists 'Is it at marriage you're fooling again?'. The admission makes her deride her son: 'I never knew till this day it was a black born fool I had for a son'. Michael's excuse that Sara might otherwise leave him brings the instinctual pointer to truth from Mary: 'And you're thinking it's paying gold to his reverence would make a woman stop when she's a mind to go?'.[25]

Sara had attributed the stirrings within her to spring, but Mary said to Michael of her 'Didn't you hear me telling you she's flighty a while back since the change of the moon?', and later she explained Sara's ill-temper with 'Oh! isn't she a terror since the moon did change?'. The traditional connection between the moon and lunacy indicates that Mary, herself 'as wise as a March hare', views Sara as temporarily mad. At the end of the play, when Sara tells the priest '. . . my heart's scalded with your fooling; and it'll be a long day till I go making talk of marriage or the like of that', she has returned to her right mind in Mary's view.[26]

Money is always a problem for the fool, since he lives close to nature and there is no economy in the law of nature.[27] Hence the tinkers' ongoing struggle and concern with money. Michael tells Sara to 'leave your fooling and not be wasting our gold', but when at the end he expresses his delight at having been prevented from 'fooling our gold', ironically the gold is destined for a purpose without material benefit, for Michael declares '. . . we'll have a great time drinking that bit with the trampers on the green of Clash'.[28]

Twice the priest thinks he might be a fool in relation to the tinkers, but as the curtain goes down he is 'master of the situation', so he cannot be regarded as a fool figure. The tinkers are not a minority, much less solitary, which deprives them of the pathetic dimension this might have brought. They enjoy an established independence from settled society, and are at no great personal risk at any point in the play. In effect they have their own sub-culture. What they forgo proves to be superfluous to them, whereas the literary fool suffers for his role as outsider.[29]

The history of the title of *The Playboy of the Western World* is interesting because before Christy became the 'playboy' (distinctly not with its current meaning of a man given to idle amusement and amorous dalliance[30]), he had been called 'The Fool of Farnham' and 'The Fool of the Family' in the titles of earlier drafts.[31] Thus it is evident that from the beginning Synge conceived of Christy as some kind of fool. However, at the outset the conception seems to have been more of a natural fool than a literary one, a social subject rather than a metaphor, whereas in the published play the only clear remnants of this conception are Christy's statement 'I'm slow at learning', and old Mahon's that he had been a dunce at school.[32] Otherwise the references to Christy's folly are ambiguous, or else they are made by old Mahon who has a case to make against him and is therefore bent on disparagement.

Christy, as the playboy who entertains, has many of the characteristics traditional to the literary fool. First, he lacks a fully established personal and social identity. He is unknown to everyone on stage at his arrival, and his own unverifiable word is the only evidence that his father is a well-off farmer 'with wide and windy acres of rich Munster land'.[33] Second, as a borderline figure moving into a defined society from an uncertain outer zone he can hold the social world up to values which transcend it. While the heroic values Christy initially represents for the people of Mayo are based on illusion they are later borne out, but ultimately the audience is unable to penetrate and rationally grasp what, precisely, the values are which Christy represents.[34] Then Christy's failure to marry Pegeen at the end relates him to the tradition that the fool is left outside the rush of weddings which brings comedy to a close: the borderline existence has to be maintained. And finally, Christy is accompanied into this uncertain zone by another fool figure, thus falling into the category of fools who come in pairs.[35]

The relationship with old Mahon as Christy insists on it before his final departure is of 'a gallant captain with his heathen slave', which is reminiscent of that between the noble knight whom

124

Don Quixote imagines himself to be and his 'squire' Sancho Panza. In order to provide one exception to an otherwise incredulous world, Cervantes has to supply his fool with an unquestioning companion to share his illusion. Old Mahon complies with his son's demand for service, but he does so under the impression that he has gone 'crazy again'. It is, of course anti-rational and socially untraditional for a father to serve his son, but as old Mahon had earlier declared: It's maybe out of reason that man's himself'. By contrast, the yokel Sancho Panza 'without much salt in his brainpan' is beguiled by Don Quixote's illusory promises into serving him as 'squire', and he trustingly agrees with the knight's admonition that he should not be content with any worldly title less than Captain General. There is an ironical dimension to old Mahon's accepting his role which is absent in the case of Sancho Panza.[36]

The uncertain nature of the identity of both Don Quixote and Christy is dependent on illusion. In the case of Don Quixote, his illusory identity is born of books in his own mind, and it is treated as the fictive thing it is by the other characters closely connected with him, barring Sancho Panza. At the end, before he dies, the self-styled knight abandons his illusion and resumes his true identity: according to his epitaph, he dies wise having lived a fool. Christy's identity as a hero is born of a real deed and a psychic need among the people of Mayo for a hero. Only the outcome of Christy's deed is illusory, and as soon as he sets about altering that by trying to make fact of the fiction, the people of Mayo reject him. This very rejection helps to realize for him that side of his identity which is a gallant hero capable of 'romancing through a romping lifetime'. Synge's play ends, one might argue, where Cervantes begins, but since Christy's relationship to his own folly is more balanced and realistic than Don Quixote's (before whose death the pendulum swings violently, so that he tries to exclude folly from the next generation in his will), there is more hope for his heroism.

Because of the thin borderline between courage and foolhardiness, the relationship between the fool and the hero is close: a degree of folly is necessary to the hero. Christy, in order to assert his adult status in the face of his father, gives rein to his folly which carries him to violence, but this violence ultimately has a redemptive effect. William Willeford writes of the need for the hero to become an individual by wresting the line of his destiny from the unknown so that when

... the larger form of his action emerges to view, it is often clear that he has redeemed some part of chaos and some part of his own folly. That folly is negatively the possibility that he will foolishly fail in his role as hero. But positively it consists of qualities essential to his heroic purpose, such as his openness to the queer and unforeseen and his mockery of conventional opinions when they are shortsighted. He redeems his folly by finding the right relationship to it, by allowing it expression without letting it possess him completely.[37]

Retrospectively Christy turns his folly to narrative purpose by envisaging himself the subject of ballad or story, whereas Don Quixote fails to distinguish between romance and reality and becomes the victim of folly as romance.

Where Christy as a fool figure with a heroic dimension owes some of his ancestry to Don Quixote, Owen in *Deirdre of the Sorrows* owes some of his to Lear's fool. Synge's intention to develop the character of Owen is well known, and Ann Saddlemyer has suggested that in that development he 'would perhaps have taken on also more of the Elizabethan fool'.[38] The early historic setting of the tale and the play can be seen as an Irish parallel to that in *King Lear*, and Owen as a variation on that particular court fool. We can see the embryo of such a licensed critic in, for example, the familiar tone which Owen adopts to Deirdre and Naisi, and in the degrading images he uses in reference to Naisi and Conchubor.

Besides, Owen suffers misery and loneliness, to the point of suicide, in a manner comparable to Lear's fool pining for Cordelia. His attempt to usurp the positions of Naisi and Conchubor in relation to Deirdre is a possible variation on the conventional fool's usurpation of the ruler's position, seen in the mock trial in *King Lear*.[39] Owen has no material power, only the power of his words; and his little material wealth, represented by the money he received from his spying, he scatters over Fergus. This gesture links him with the feckless and dependent fool. Conchubor, who by contrast does have material power, squanders it as Lear did his through folly. Owen's part in the play ends early like that of Lear's fool, leaving behind an old king vainly trying to retrieve the young woman whom he had wanted to hoard for himself in his endeavour to deny the reality of time. In the case of Lear, it is his daughter that he tries to hoard; Conchubor wants his foster-daughter for his wife.[40]

The thwarted love of Owen for Deirdre echoes a feature of the traditional court fool:

> The yearning of the fool for a woman is often ill-defined: he blindly gropes after an inchoate something, often hoping that it will serve as an object of his random and diffuse sexuality. Yet the fool often suffers painfully acute yearnings for a woman who would be, like the morning star, above the urgent mess of his inarticulate will. In the tradition of kingship she is sometimes the queen, but more often she is the king's daughter, destined for the hero.[41]

That Owen is beneath Deirdre is made explicit to him in her question 'Are there no women like yourself could be your friends in Emain?'[42]

Owen is different from Synge's other fool figures in having a sharp tongue, which relates him to the sage fool. He gives impudent retorts right from the beginning of his existence, but it was only later on that Synge emphasized his madness.[43] After his first entry in the play as it stands he gives the following reply to Deirdre's question 'what brought you from Ulster?'

> The full moon I'm thinking and it squeezing the crack in my skull. Was there ever a man crossed nine waves after a fool's wife and he not away in his head?[44]

Owen is wise enough to acknowledge his own folly, and when he has killed himself and Fergus dismisses him as 'a fool and raver', Ainnle recognizes the wisdom of the fool saying 'It's many times there's more sense in madmen than the wise'.[45] The same notion of the wisdom of the fool is to be found in another version of a speech of Owen's to Deirdre: 'Though I play the fool I'm no fool'.[46]

In the play's exploration of the relationship between folly and wisdom, the embryonic character of Owen stands in stark opposition to Lavarcham, whom Synge introduces as 'a wise woman and servant of Conchubor, about fifty'. At his first entry Owen gets rid of Lavarcham by telling her that Fergus's men are looking for her, because he wants to be alone with Deirdre. Lavarcham's dislike of him is explicit at this encounter, and she accuses him of bringing ill-luck as well as of being a spy. When he makes his final hysterical exit everyone on stage runs out after him except Lavarcham, who looks on at his suicide with her hands clasped and is thus able to report his ugly death to Deirdre. Yet she finally recognizes that 'he knew a power if he'd said it all'. Lavarcham is beyond the turmoil of love (Owen recalls her youthful frolics with his father) and she is opposed to the chaos which the fool, Owen, threatens.[47]

Lavarcham's wisdom is not that worldly wisdom which is in opposition to Christian values, or to what could be called nature-values in the case of Synge's alternative. It is rather the wisdom of age. It is life-orientated and her judgements are earth-bound. Her age associates her most closely with unwise Conchubor, and she gains the sympathy of the audience primarily through her intimacy with Deirdre. At the beginning of the third act there is a telling exchange between herself and Conchubor when he says 'You think I'm old and wise, but I tell you the wise know the old must die, and they'll leave no chance for a thing slipping from them, they've set their blood to win'. Seeing this folly of Conchubor in trying to separate his age from his wisdom by holding onto the young Deirdre, she points out that she too is old and wise, and warns that there are things that even a king cannot have. She is of course proved right in this. Her gift for perceiving 'the truth' is also displayed when she detects Conchubor's dishonesty in claiming to be well pleased that Deirdre is light and airy. With a snort of irony she says 'Well pleased is it? It's a queer thing the way the likes of me do be telling the truth and the wise are lying all times'. Her capacity to see the truth is not, however, the inspired vision of the fool, nor is her's the harsh truth that the social outcast sees, for she is peculiarly privileged in being acceptable and integrated in all circles.[48]

In the relationship between Lavarcham and Deirdre folly and wisdom play a prominent role. After Conchubor's first visit she reproaches Deirdre for 'not heeding those are wiser than yourself', but Deirdre lapses further into folly in her eyes by asking her to hide in the hills. Lavarcham is earth-bound enough to know that Conchubor would have them tracked in half-a-day, and she is life-orientated enough to want to avoid having herself and all belonging to her 'destroyed forever'. She knows too that 'In the end there is none can go against Conchubor, and it's only folly that we're talking'. But these are wasted words on Deirdre, who ignores them without being ignorant of their truth.[49]

Seven years later, in the second act when Lavarcham sees Deirdre refuse to 'stir stick or straw' to save Naisi, she momentarily poses as a fool in order to move Deirdre: 'Maybe I was a big fool thinking his dangers, and this day, would fill you up with dread'. This pose angers Deirdre, who is now older and wiser herself, so that she chastises Lavarcham for playing the fool: 'Let you end such talking is a fool's only'. At one stage Synge considered attributing the suggestion that Deirdre may have grown tired of Naisi after seven years to Lavarcham at this point in the play, but he later realized that this notion rather belonged with Owen because of his wishful thinking than with Lavarcham who knew Deirdre so well, and who can honestly admit some lines further on that Deirdre is indeed in her 'hour of joy'. What distresses the old and wise Lavarcham is seeing the young she loves 'breaking up their hearts with folly'.[50]

In the exploration of the complex inter-relationship between youth, age, folly, and wisdom in this play, Lavarcham almost consistently merits her natural or appropriate grouping of old and wise, whereas Conchubor is the embodiment of the maxim 'there's no fool like an old fool'. Throughout the play Lavarcham's primary role is to protect Deirdre, both from her own youthful folly and from Conchubor. But of course each person must bear the burden of his own folly, so that eventually Lavarcham fails in this role. The old cannot protect the young beyond their childhood, and wisdom has to be dearly bought anew in each individual life.

At the first confrontation between youth and age in the play, Deirdre in her naïveté says to Conchubor about his worldly knowledge 'Yourself should be wise surely'. But by the time she has lived seven years in love with Naisi and witnessed the murder of him and his brothers at Conchubor's command, she dismisses the old king as a fool. Conchubor at this stage can only see the madness of others and suggests that Deirdre is growing crazy: 'Let you rise up and come along with me in place of growing crazy with your wailings here'. But Deirdre dismisses Conchubor from the world of lovers: 'It's yourself has made a crazy story, and let you go back to your arms, Conchubor, and to councils where your name is great, for in this place you are an old man and a fool only'. His reply reveals his desperation, and his enduring commitment to possessions, and not to love: 'If I've folly I've sense left not to lose the thing I've bought with sorrow and the deaths of many'. Fergus then comes between Conchubor and his 'possession' Deirdre, but she orders them all to 'draw a little back with the squabbling of fools'. Fergus then warns Conchubor of the shame of capturing a queen 'who is out of her wits', and only this evokes the following realization from him: 'It is I am out of my wits', so that Deirdre can once again refer to him as 'Conchubor who was wise' in her speech of final reckoning.[51]

Two categories of folly can be distinguished in *Deirdre of the Sorrows*: the folly of the lover, and that of the old. The lovers include Deirdre, Naisi (with his brothers), and Owen, and they are fools for denying certain material realities. In addition, Deirdre ceases to be Time's fool only by escaping into death. The old fool Conchubor tries to deny that he is caught in the cycle of time, and is redeemed only by becoming the old man he actually is at the very end of the play, when he is led off by Lavarcham and the nameless Old Woman.

Taking an all-round view of Synge's use of folly, its function in the four plays preceding *Deirdre* can be defined as a metaphor for an alternative vision to the collective one. The laudatory attitude to the fool-artist and the sage fool is favourably presented, whereas any proscriptive social view of the mad fool is not. The tension between the fool's values and those of society is ongoing. In *Deirdre* it is resolved only in death, or in the acceptance of time's havoc. To this extent folly in all the plays is a metaphor for the energy which arises from the clash between the inspired vision and the collective one; between man's 'natural', individual instincts and his social ones; and between the rational and the irrational in him.

VII INCONGRUITY

Synge explored the clash between man's individual and social needs through his use of the fool figure. The fool's drive to pursue an individual eccentric vision supersedes his need for social integration, so that he becomes a social incongruity. But Synge also makes use of other forms of incongruity besides folly.

The term incongruity is used in two ways here. First, it signifies a want of accordance with what is fitting or reasonable, which is an external relationship: and second, it indicates a disagreement of character or qualities within a given phenomenon. In all cases of the grotesque as incongruity the effect is disturbing or disconcerting. When incongruity has a simple or harmless effect, such as when a child puts on one red and one green sock, the emotions are not engaged, therefore there is nothing grotesque about it. The moment this same incongruity is related to a blind person the emotions are engaged and it becomes grotesque. This emotional engagement arises from our feeling that something vital is at stake. Lack of sight threatens man's whole existence, whereas the child's failure to pair his socks merely tells us that his sense of accord has not yet developed in that respect.

To perceive the incongruity which depends on an external relationship requires an existing preconception of what that relationship should be. An education based on 'enlightened' principles, such as Synge had, cultivates many preconceptions concerning what is fitting or reasonable, and eventually these preconceptions become emotionally charged, notably where they involve matters which are vital or sacred. Such preconceptions caused Synge to perceive many incongruities in rural Ireland among people who were themselves quite unaware of them because of their different culture and education. He records with equanimity many examples of incongruity in his prose, which in his plays and poems he uses for their disturbing or disconcerting effects.

There are three instances in his prose where the suckling of infants receives public attention – something quite discordant with the ideas of what might be fitting in circles such as those from which

131

Synge came. However, on Aran he both witnessed it and heard it included in a story told by Pat Dirane. He records that the infant of the cottage where he lodged was wet-nursed in the absence of its mother by two different women in the space of a few hours.[1] Elsewhere he records that the sister of a recently drowned island-man keened while she suckled her infant, which Synge thought made her like 'a type of the women's life upon the islands'.[2] And finally he heard the tale of the woman who died a little while after the birth of her child, but returned to suckle it. It transpired that she had been taken by the fairies, and was not dead at all.[3] The suckling in the last instance is not simply discordant with what is fitting, but also belongs to the second type of incongruity, that is presents an internal disagreement of character or qualities. What appears to be a dead mother, or perhaps a fairy, gives suck to a living human child. This raises the question of the relationship between the living and the dead, between the supernatural world and the natural. Can a dead mother give suck? Can a fairy nourish a human? Not according to the rules of reason, yet the imagination does envisage such things, as the folk-tale shows. Reason does not hinder the folk-imagination from bringing in a supernatural solution to the problem of nourishing a famished child.

Mikhail Bakhtin tells us that in the grotesque concept of the body it is not separated from the rest of the world. It is not a closed, completed unit; it is unfinished, outgrows itself, transgresses its own limits. The stress is laid on the body going out to meet the world, ever unfinished, forming a link in the chain of development, or two links at the point where they enter each other. This is what we have in the image of the suckling child, which, Bakhtin says, is preserved in an individualized and closed manner, only a pale reflection of its former dual nature, in modern art, that is art after the early Renaissance.[4] Individualized and closed here means that the collective and continual nature of nourishment is lost, which would not be the case as the image is perceived in a primitive culture still close to nature without and within.

From the folk background of Aran Synge borrowed two images of suckling for *The Playboy*. They are disturbing for the incongruity of their pairing. The Widow Casey, who was chosen as a wife for Christy by his father was rejected because 'all know she did suckle me for six weeks when I came into the world'.[5] This puts the relationship between man and wife in a light where its essentials are questioned. Can the same woman be wife and mother to one man?

Society has tabooed the possibility, and yet literature has repeatedly envisaged it.

Also, Pegeen accuses the Widow Quin in the following terms: 'Doesn't the world know you reared a black ram at your own breast, so that the Lord Bishop of Connaught felt the elements of a Christian, and he eating it after in a kidney stew?'[6] Here the black ram seems to have diabolical connections, which are enhanced by its religious associations. Not only is Synge exploring the relationship between human and animal in this grotesque image, but also he is introducing a supernatural dimension. There is a double incongruity: first, that of human suckling animal, and second, that of human eating human. In French medieval literature Synge could have found an instance of human eating human in the fabliau of 'Ignaurès', the chevalier who is lover to twelve women. When their husbands discover what is going on, they have the lover killed and mutilated, and then serve a portion of his sexual member to each of their unsuspecting wives to eat.[7] There is extravagant exaggeration, seen for example in the prowess of the lover who can satisfy twelve women and the corresponding proportions of his member, yet the connotations of the husbands' solution are relatively limited, relating only to the sexual realm, and having a clearly comic effect. In Synge's incident, on the other hand, there is a more complex mesh of connotations, involving those which are human, animal, and sacred, so that the question seems to be posed whether human can by nature suckle animal, and whether by nature he can also eat human.

It is normal that Synge should use animal imagery since he portrays in his work the lives of people who live close to the animal world. The manner in which he uses these images has the effect of heightening the brutal side of man's nature at the same time as his higher nature seems to be dominating. When the noble nature of the love between Naisi and Deirdre is well established, Owen comes along to talk of the harshness in Naisi's 'two sheep's eyes', and to describe Deirdre as 'seven years spancelled with Naisi and the pair'. Noticing the incongruous manner in which Owen had addressed her, Deirdre had remarked: 'It should be a long time since you left Emain, where there's civility in speech with queens'. Owen's speech would indeed be unfitting at court, yet as the subsequent events show, there is a reductive sequel to this high love, and the royal house is brought low because of the king's brutality.[8]

Pegeen's discovery that Christy is a fine lad with great savagery, a mighty spirit, and a gamey heart is preceded by Christy's image of himself 'going in strange places with a dog nosing before you and a dog nosing behind.'[9] And after Christy has established his gallantry, his father describes him to the Widow Quin as 'a dunce never reached his second book, the way he'd come from school, many's the day, with his legs lamed under him and he blackened with his beatings like a tinker's ass'; and later as 'the fool of men, the way from this out he'll know the orphan's lot with old and young making game of him and they swearing, raging, kicking at him like a mangy cur'.[10] Likewise the 'decent Christian' that Michael Flaherty has chosen for his daughter is seen by her as more evocative of 'a bullock's liver' than a lily or a rose. The incongruity between what Molly Byrne calls Martin Doul's 'great romancing' and the harsh reality of his physical abode 'lying down in a little rickety shed . . . across a sop of straw', is brought out in Martin's own image of the children dreaming 'that it's in grand houses of gold they are, with speckled horses to ride' and waking to find they are 'destroyed with the cold, and the thatch dripping maybe, and the starved ass braying in the yard'.[11] Repeatedly the animal imagery serves to emphasize the disagreement between the aspirations man has on the one hand, and the low level of his existence on the other. The result is that the animal side of man's nature, so carefully supressed by his reason, is reinstated.

According to rational assumption, only animals bite each other in aggression, but Synge knew otherwise. He recorded that after the races on the sand in West Kerry when the men had got drunk, one of them said to him 'There was great sport after you left', and went on to describe the drunken men beating and cutting each other, including one red-head who had his finger bitten through.[12] Whereas in real life the brutality surfaced only when the men were drunk, no such cause is offered for brutality on the three occasions when Synge uses this motif in his poetry and drama. In the poem 'Danny', the finger bitten becomes a thumb:

> Then Danny smashed the nose on Byrne,
> He split the lips on three
> And bit across the right hand thumb
> Of one Red Shawn Magee.[13]

Here it is not the merely animal side of man's nature which is explored, but a more sinister brutality which will be further discussed in the context of ugliness. In *The Playboy* the finger which is bitten through is replaced by a nostril, and later a leg. Sara Tansey is reported by Susan Brady to have yoked the ass and cart and driven ten miles to set her eyes on the man who 'bit the yellow lady's nostril on the northern shore'. It is striking that the interest is in the biter, not the bitten: it is he who raises the question of what the nature of man is, and no sentiment is wasted in feeling for his unfortunate victim. In the length that Susan was prepared to travel to see the marvel, the same need for dramatic relief is evident as was responsible for Christy being perceived as a hero. Later in the play when Christy bites Shawn's leg under the threat of torture, Shawn shrieks 'He's the like of a mad dog', thus crystallizing the animal nature of the behaviour.[14]

We are told of Michael in *The Tinker's Wedding* that he tells the priest to hold up 'as if speaking to a horse'. Besides, he remarks 'with contempt' to Sarah at the outset of the play that 'the Beauty of Ballinacree' is the kind of name one would give to a horse, after she has proclaimed her delight at receiving that name from Jaunting Jim, a man who had 'a grand eye for a fine horse, and a grand eye for a woman'. In the case of Sarah, the incongruous use of the horse-image is a reminder that the animal element in man can be over-played, whereas in the case of the priest it is underplayed.[15]

God and godly people might reasonably be expected to be linked with goodness and order in the lives of men, yet Synge prefers to place them in dubious positions. Christy, in reference to having killed his father admits: 'With the help of God I did surely, and that the Holy Immaculate Mother may intercede for his soul.'[16] This want of accord between the deed referred to and the common idea of God is also present in Mary Doul's prayer 'The Lord protect us from the saints of God!'[17] There is a similar effect when Martin accuses the saint of 'making a great mess with the holy water', and when Mary talks of washing 'a naggin bottle' as a container for the holy water.[18] The water which embodies such supernatural and God-given power would normally be treated with awe and respect by people of faith such as Synge protrays. Yet because of the material limitations within which they live, as well as the want of the kind of social education which might inculcate certain notions of propriety and thereby preclude the use of a liquor-bottle for holy water, they readily mix the sacred and the profane.

We see this mixture in Mary Byrne's threat to tell everyone that Sarah Casey had 'put down a head of the parson's cabbage to boil in the pot with your clothes', as well as in Philly's account, in *The Playboy*, of his Sunday entertainment as a young lad:

> ... when I was a young lad, there was a graveyard beyond the house with the remnants of a man who had thighs as long as your arm. He was a horrid man, I'm telling you, and there was many a fine Sunday I'd put him together for fun, and he with shiny bones you wouldn't meet the like of these days in the cities of the world.[19]

In addition to exemplifying the juxtaposition of sacred and profane, this is one of many instances of death in the midst of life to be found in Synge's plays. He had been struck by this co-presence in rural Ireland, both in life and in story. Recording a dark rainy night in a Wicklow town, he writes:

> Many cars and gigs were collected at the door of the public house, and the bar was filled with men who were drinking and making a noise. Everything was dark and confused yet on one car I was able to make out the shadow of a coffin, strapped in the rain, with the body of Mary Kinsella.[20]

Such a scene is macabre to the sophisticated sensibility, but it passes unnoticed in a setting where life is rude. Only when there is real pathos does the peasant remark on the mingling of life and death, such as in the story told to Synge of a Sligo man during the potato famine. This man's wife caught the plague; he reported it to the authorities and she was taken away to the hospital. Later he heard she had died and was to be buried the following day. He had an uneasy feeling, and went to the mortuary where she had been put. He found her alive among fifty corpses; he took her home and she recovered.[21] As the story was told to Synge, the emphasis was not on the macabre aspect of it but on the pathos and on the mystery of the borderline between life and death. For historical and cultural reasons death was ever present in the memory and the consciousness of the rural Irish, Synge found. It had not been tidied away, therefore it lost some of its terror, though not its mystery.

Using the skeleton as a plaything – putting it together for fun as Philly did – is a natural outcome to such familiarity, but the playwright knew that his audiences would not generally share such familiarity, and so expected them to respond to the incongruity.

Likewise, this is the response evoked when Jimmy asks 'Did you never hear tell of the skulls they have in the city of Dublin, ranged out like blue jugs in a cabin of Connaught?'.[22] The audience would not attribute a decorative quality to human skulls because they would have conceptually separated the dead from the living and the decorative from the decayed. The attention to detail in the rest of Jimmy's speech creates an impression as immediate as the representations we have from the Middle Ages of the dance of death, in which death, depicted as a skeleton, is hand in hand with the living: 'White skulls and black skulls and yellow skulls, and some with full teeth and some haven't only but one'.[23]

In a modified way the immediacy of death is also suggested when old Mahon, who is supposed to be dead, gets up and displays his 'splintered crown'. It is there too in Dan's 'corpse' being on the stage at the opening of *The Shadow*, as it is in the grave replete with newly dead bodies at the end of *Deirdre*. In *Deirdre*, however, the effect is tragic, as it is in that singular play *Riders to the Sea*, where Bartley's corpse is brought in and laid on the table.

There are two poems where death is present in the midst of life: in 'Rendez-vous Manqué dans la rue Racine' the poet 'met two creaking coffins that passed'; and in 'Patch-Shaneen' we are told of the protagonist and his wife that 'He found her perished, stiff and stark,/Beside him in the bed'. Besides the skeleton and skulls already mentioned, a 'stock of thigh-bones, jaws and shins' appears in the poem 'In Kerry', and we have Edward Stephens's word about Synge that 'The significance of the remains of the unnamed dead always impressed his mind'.[24]

So far we have seen three primary aspects of man's nature asserted through Synge's use of incongruity: first, his need for nourishment, seen in the image of suckling. An extension of this fundamental need occurs in the primitive behaviour of Christy when he begins 'gnawing a turnip', and of Owen when he 'finds a loaf and sits down eating greedily'.[25] Second is the presence of brutality suggested through the widespread animal imagery. And third is man's eschatological interest, betrayed by the presence of death in the midst of life. All three of these aspects of man's nature are refined and played down in sophisticated town life, but remain strongly evident among people who live a rudimentary existence.

Two further features generally obscured by sophistication are reasserted through Synge's use of incongruity: man's artistic urge and his sense of dignity. Crafts were not highly evolved for want of continuity of tradition and materials in the rural Ireland Synge knew, and although there was a tradition of folk song, it was above all in their storytelling that he found the people expressed themselves artistically. Consequently he attributes a marked capacity for linguistic flourish to the characters of his plays. It is scarcely necessary to illustrate such a renowned phenomenon, but three consecutive speeches of Michael Flaherty in *The Playboy* provide ready examples: he refers to Christy as a 'young gaffer who'd capsize the stars', and as 'wet and crusted with his father's blood'; and he describes himself as 'swamped and drownded with the weight of drink'.[26]

The incongruity of such hyperbolic expression arises partly from the banal environment against which it is uttered. The usual expectation is not that the peasant, worn with hardship and lacking in formal education, is likely to express himself with flourish and flair. Synge, however, gladly acknowledges his debt to the country people in this respect in his preface to *The Playboy*:

> I am glad to acknowledge how much I owe to the folk-imagination of these fine people. Anyone who has lived in real intimacy with the Irish peasantry will know that the wildest sayings and ideas in this play are tame indeed compared with the fancies one may hear in any little hillside cabin in Geesala, or Carraroe, or Dingle bay . . . in countries where the imagination of the people, and the language they use, is rich and living, it is possible for a writer to be rich and copious in his words, and at the same time to give the reality which is the root of all poetry, in a comprehensive and natural form. In the modern literature of towns, however, richness is found only in sonnets, or prose poems, or in one or two elaborate books that are far away from the profound and common interests of life.[27]

The wildest sayings and ideas, then, are the natural and comprehensive form in which Synge sought to express some of the reality and the profound interests of life which he considered to be the root of all poetry. Here we are arriving at what is essentially a grotesque aesthetic, an acceptance of incongruity.

According to this aesthetic there is a veracity to the wild sayings. Their exuberant exaggeration conveys a richness which is part of reality, but which co-exists with extreme simplicity and poverty on another level. Christy Mahon's rhapsodic language co-exists with the uncouth behaviour of his father as he describes him:

> . . . rising up in the red dawn, or before it maybe, and going out
> into the yard as naked as an ash tree in the moon of May, and
> shying clods against the visage of the stars till he'd put the fear of
> death into the banbhs and the screeching sows.[28]

The clash inherent in such a speech between its manner and its
matter reflects the inclusive nature of Synge's vision of life, It is also
the solution he found to the artistic problem of creating 'a romance
of reality'.[29]

There are three instances in the poems and plays of Synge where,
through the use of incongruity, he questions the basis for attributed
social dignity, which is ephemeral, and asserts an inherent human
dignity, which endures. This is first seen in the poem entitled
'Queens', which is a variation on Villon's celebration of royal ladies
of the past in his 'Ballade des dames du temps jadis'.[20] Whereas the
French poet's queens are historical or legendary women with
European and largely French associations, Synge replaces both the
ladies and the locations which are French with Irish ones. The tone
of Villon's poem is melancholy both because of its concern with
death and its rhetorical refrain 'Mais ou sont les neiges d'antan?'
(Where are the snows of yester-year?). Synge does not make use of
the rhetorical question in his poem, although it is common in
Hiberno-English usage and was extensively exploited by Yeats, but
rather makes a declarative statement in answer to Villon: the
queens are rotten.

That the dirt and decay to which queens are subject as human
beings should be brought into prominence through references to
wormy sheepskins, fleas, and vermin, is incongruous with the dignity
usually attributed to them. So is it that they should put the knowledge and learning to which they have access to evil purpose (slaying
with drugs and learned sin); and also that they should have to do
such menial tasks as cutting turf and driving an ass-cart. Yet all of
this Synge specifies in 'Queens', and besides he increases consciousness of the queens' bodies through reference to hand, foot,
finger, belly, and shin. Thus he undermines the notion of a queen's
dignity – she has a body which rots – while at the same time, by the
very naming of them, he pays them tribute. Finally the tribute turns
into the naming of a living unnamed woman as queen, so that

139

something living, perceived by the poet, endures which warrants such dignity.

The queen who drove an ass-cart in this poem was a 'tinker's doxy', and elsewhere too Synge makes this incongruous connection between tinkers and queens. In *The Tinker's Wedding* drunken Mary Byrne professes to be the possessor of 'the finest story you'd hear any place from Dundalk to Ballinacree, with great queens in it, making themselves matches from the start to the end, and they with shiny silks on them the length of the day, and white shifts for the night'.[31] The incongruities here are multiple: matchmaking, a practice actively operated by tinkers is also necessary to the survival of royal houses; and queens and their opulent way of life are accessible to tinkers as the subject of stories. Mary goes on to draw a direct connection between Sarah and the queens of Ireland: 'I've a grand story of the queens of Ireland with white necks on them the like of Sarah Casey, and fine arms would hit you a slap the way Sarah Casey would hit you'. Although Mary's first-hand experience of queens is non-existent, she has experienced the queenly assertion of Sarah, and recognizes a regal feature in her white neck.

Deirdre, for all her natural dignity, has to listen to the degrading addresses of Owen, and her princely consort realizes that there are nights when 'queens will stick their tongues out at the rising moon'. Among Owen's derisive remarks about Deirdre's ongoing fidelity to Naisi is the reminder of 'a queen in Tara had to walk out every morning till she'd meet a stranger and see the flame of courtship leaping up within his eye'. Such lustful behaviour, incongruous in a queen, may have been suggested to Synge by Villon's poem mentioned above, where the reference to the scholar Buridan is to his legendary capture by the Queen of Burgundy, who is supposed to have lain in wait for passing males who pleased her fancy.[32]

Although 'natural man' is merely a conception, there is behind Synge's use of incongruity a traceable desire to strip away both social and conceptual convention so as to arrive at something like 'essential man'. The drive towards the primary satisfactions together with the ineluctable fact of death contradict the kind of dignity and spirituality for which aspiring man reaches. Synge's art reflects both sides of this antithetical vision.

It is noteworthy that, where the incongruities he came across in life did not pertain to vital issues and were without emotional content, he did not make use of them in his art. For instance, there was the weird conglomeration of objects stocked in the shops in Connemara:

> Inside many of the shops and in the windows one could see an extraordinary collection of objects – saddles, fiddles, rosaries, rat-traps, the Shorter Catechism, castor-oil, rings, razors, rhyme-books, fashion plates, nit-killer, and fine tooth combs.[33]

Also, the hospitality which Synge received in West Kerry took a surprising form: the candle for lighting Synge to bed was stuck on the bedpost with a few drops of candle-grease; the hostess removed her apron and fastened it to the window as a blind, and laid another apron on the floor as a mat. An old hairbrush propped the window open, and a spoon served to lift the door-latch. His host came home in the middle of the night, asked whether he might stretch out in the second bed in Synge's room, lit his pipe, and talked at length. When eventually they settled down to sleep, the son of the house came in, clambered over his father and also stretched out in that bed. At about six o'clock the following morning, the daughter of the house served whiskey to the three men in bed, from the same glass.[34] Such entertainment scarcely accords with Ascendancy expectations, yet it did not blind Synge to the true courtesy of these people. However, since neither the lack of domestic amenities nor the absence of a sense of order in shop display are of fundamental human importance, and cause no immediate emotional effect, these instances of incongruity could not be put to significant artistic use and therefore remained anecdotal material.

The incongruities which have been principally discussed in this chapter are not purely comic in effect. Since they reflect the coexistence of the animal and the divine or diabolical elements in man, they give rise to conflicting emotions of repulsion and fascination. There is something about suckling and violence which evokes this dual response; and death and dignity can appear both strange and familiar. The detachment which is a pre-requisite for the purely comic effect is not present for the grotesque as incongruity.[35] Such incongruity is often the basis for Synge's irony, as T.R. Henn pointed out, 'particularly when he wishes to emphasize the humanity of his characters'.[36] It is an irony in which the divine or diabolical element in man is forcefully implied behind the evident animal.

141

VIII   UGLINESS

Whereas incongruity used for grotesque effect disturbs or disconcerts, ugliness used in the same way has a sharper, more immediate effect: it gives rise to repulsion or disgust. The feelings roused by Synge's use of ugliness do not remain simple, however, for behind that ugliness lies some idea of beauty or of the sublime, so that there can be no thoughtless turning away.

Ugliness considered as the opposite of beauty appears as a deformity of some norm, offending against rules or order and proportion based on an ideal. Ideals of beauty developed on the Romantic principles to which Synge was heir centred on organic, natural form at its optimum. Thus, in terms of physical beauty the human ideal cannot be maintained beyond its prime. In terms of beauty of the soul or spirit the ideal is the supremacy of the higher instincts.

Yeats records a revealing statement which Synge made to him on the subject of beauty: 'a dramatist has to express his subject and to find as much beauty as is compatible with that, and if he does more he is an aesthete'.[1] Two important views should be noted here: first, that whatever beauty appears in a play depends on its subject and must be compatible with that; and second, that Synge here dissociates himself from the Aesthetic Movement. It is scarcely news that Synge was no aesthete, but his dissociation from the principles put forward by those who were has some bearing on his use of ugliness in his work. One might say that he uses ugliness to balance the beauty of his subject. Occasionally, where he feels that the beauty is already self-evident, he presents ugliness undilute.

In the last chapter, consideration of incongruity yielded one example of human biting human in the poem 'Danny'. In this poem there is also much ugliness. It is an ugliness of the spirit conveyed by the subject of physical cruelty expressed in earthy language. The protagonist, Danny, is first presented as a social menace, responsible for acts of cruelty, some connected with sexual assault. The retaliation planned on him for this cruelty is itself cruel both in the vast outnumbering by the assailants, and in the precise nature of the conceived attack:

> Ten will quench his bloody eyes,
> And ten will choke his gullet.[2]

The cruelty contemplated here is comparable on one level to that behind the blinding of Gloucester in *King Lear*. True, the play's evocation of horror and disgust is sustained, whereas the ballad form, with its rapid movement and distracting jingle precludes that. Yet there is the same barbaric lack of feeling for that ultra-sensitive organ, the eye.

In the poem reference to the eyes is confined to anticipation of the attack; they are not mentioned in description of the attack proper, possibly to suggest that man feels more cruelty than he dare show. In a version of the poem which Robin Skelton regards as later, it is interesting to note that the 'eyes' have been changed to 'sight' – perhaps in an attempt to make the poem more acceptable to Miss Yeats for publication by the Cuala Press. The abstract 'sight' is decidedly less strong than the concrete 'eyes', which hold instant emotional value in the context.

In the description of the attack cruelty is rife:

> Then Danny smashed the nose on Byrne,
> He split the lips on three,
> And bit across the right hand thumb
> Of one Red Shawn Magee.
>
> But seven tripped him up behind
> And seven kicked before,
> And seven squeezed around his throat
> Till Danny kicked no more.
>
> Then some destroyed him with their heels,
> Some tramped him in the mud,
> Some stole his purse and timber pipe,
> And some washed off his blood.

Eyes, nose, lips, thumb, throat, heels, and blood all form, together with their accompanying savage verbs, part of an accurate and detailed picture of brutality, while the mass assault and the wanton continuation of Danny's punishment after he had ceased to kick reveals the base nature of the assailants. Clearly, man's higher instincts are not supreme here.

In the Introduction (p. 17) we saw Synge's opinion that the 'crimeless virtuous side of Irish life' was well known, whereas the wilder side was so wild as to be unacceptable in books meant for Irish readers. The problem which 'Danny' presented for Miss Yeats bears this out. In it he had endeavoured to redress the balance and bring to consciousness some of the ugliness which was the necessary corollary to the beauty already recognized. Thereby he was putting into practice the recommendation for Irish writers which he had written to Stephen MacKenna: 'I think squeamishness is a disease, and that Ireland will gain if Irish writers deal manfully, directly and decently with the entire reality of life'.[3] The beauty is taken for granted; he did not wish to add more than would be compatible with his subject.

The plays, apart from *Riders to the Sea*, juxtapose ugliness and beauty. In *The Playboy*, for example, physical cruelty is used to convey a degradation of spirit, while there is much imaginative beauty of speech in the love-scenes between Christy and Pegeen. Ugliness, however, predominates. When Christy turns his 'gallous story' into a 'dirty deed', it causes the ugly side of Pegeen's nature to surface, so that she burns his leg with a sod of turf. Christy needs no instrument to express his cruelty: he simply uses his teeth and bites Shawn's leg. This instinctive and defiant act follows hot on his realization that violent deeds will make him the subject of songs and ballads, and his final triumphant speeches take full account of the necessity of fighting for his championship.

Synge attempted in the plays to deal with 'the entire reality of life' as he perceived it. His reality included both bodily and spiritual ugliness, and it was against this spiritual ugliness above all that his audience reacted with squeamishness. The nature of the champion contains a necessary measure of violence, and it is because Christy Mahon is the only character who becomes conscious of that and is prepared to face it that he becomes the champion. Synge was insistent that healthy art is in harmony with nature, and nature was for him not only the external natural world, but also man's inner nature. In the reality which he expresses in his art, therefore, both inner and external nature are fearlessly accomodated. 'The thin and sickly artist fears nature', he wrote. 'The art we call decadent, or at least the more unholy portion of the art we call decadent, is not the fruit of disordered minds but rather the life of a people far from the real fount of all artistic inspiration'.[4] Nature, reality, life: that is the inspiration for his art, and as he discovered early, 'Nature is cruel to living things'.[5] As he observed human nature, it too was cruel.

The mindless cruelty of the human crowd is shown in the mass rejection of Christy after he has given them immediate evidence of his capacity for violence. Similarly, at the end of *The Well* when the crowd throws things at the blind couple, there is a movement as one against them. Dan Burke's satisfaction at putting Nora out on the road also bears witness to his cruelty, and is in accordance with Nora's image of him 'with no teeth in him and a rough word in his mouth, and his chin the way it would take the bark from the edge of an oak board'.[6] And Molly, whom Martin had thought of as a 'fine soft, rounded woman' with a 'sweet beautiful voice you'd never tire hearing' turns out ironically to have the sting of cruelty in her voice when she rebuffs him with the words 'Let you keep away from me, and not be soiling my chin'.[7] Timmy too, in contrast with the kind heart he claims for himself, orders Martin to strip off his coat, to which Martin replies:

> Oh, God help me! ... I've heard tell you stripped the sheet from your wife and you putting her down into the grave, and that there isn't the like of you for plucking your living ducks, the short days, and leaving them running round in their skins, in the great rains and the cold.[8]

Synge creates a design in which pity and cruelty, beauty and ugliness flow in and out of each other in a contrasting coexistence such as is crystallized in Martin's accusation 'Well, there's cruel hardship in the pity of your like'.[9]

This contrasting coexistence of ugliness and beauty in Synge's work is in keeping with the view in some jottings in his notebook for 1901:

> Contrast gives wonder of life. It is found in
> a) Misery of earth consciously set against Heaven, see pious writing. Happy other World, Hearn, etc.
> b) Wonder of world set against the misery of age and death (see Villon).[10]

Such an aesthetic led to the deliberate juxtaposing of the misery of actual life with the imagined bliss of some dream-world, and the wonder of poetry and present beauty with the misery of age and death.

The coexistence of beauty and pitilessness, and the impossibility of reconciling beauty and pity is a central theme in *Deirdre*. It reaches its climax at the point where Deirdre sends Naisi to his death. She asks the rhetorical question 'isn't it a poor thing we should miss the safety of the grave, and we trampling its edge?' because she knows that their love and her beauty have reached their prime. Were they to live on, the fading would ask for pity, and that is alien to beauty: pity distorts the beautiful face, and it is the haggard face, not the beautiful one, that evokes pity. Thus the grave is the only safe place, for 'In a little while we've lived too long'.[11]

The following exchanges between Deirdre and Conchubor immediately after Naisi's death trace the stand of beauty against pity:

> CONCHUBOR. Make your lamentation a short while if you will, but it isn't long till a day'll come when you'll be pitying a man is old and desolate and High King also. . . . Let you not fear me for it's I'm well pleased you have a store of pity for the three that were your friends in Alban.

> DEIRDRE. I have pity surely. . . . It's the way pity has me this night, when I think of Naisi, that I could set my teeth into the heart of a king.

> CONCHUBOR. I know well that pity's cruel, when it was my pity for my own self destroyed Naisi.

> DEIRDRE (*more wildly*). It was my words without pity gave Naisi a death will have no match until the ends of life and time. (*Breaking out into a keen*.) But who'll pity Deirdre has lost the lips of Naisi from her neck, and from her cheek forever: who'll pity Deirdre has lost the twilight in the woods with Naisi, when beech-trees were silver and copper, and ash-trees were fine gold?

> CONCHUBOR (*bewildered*). It's I'll know the way to pity and care you, and I with a share of troubles has me thinking this night, it would be a good bargain if it was I was in the grave, and Deirdre crying over me, and it was Naisi who was old and desolate.

> (*A keen rises loudly over the grave*.)

146

DEIRDRE (*wild with sorrow*). It is I who am desolate, I, Deirdre that will not live till I am old.

Here Conchubor appeals for Deirdre's pity, thereby evoking her cruelty since her attachment is to the dead Naisi. This then makes Conchubor recognize how pity in one direction means cruelty in another. Deirdre recalls her pitiless dispatch of Naisi, and then asks another rhetorical question 'who'll pity Deirdre?'. The question is rhetorical because the only valid source of pity for her is now in the grave. The advantage of the grave in such circumstances becomes apparent to Conchubor, who would therefore be prepared to exhange his age and desolation for the pity Naisi has. This gives rise to Deirdre's final rejection of old age, of life without beauty and with pity.[12]

Old age is rejected in the play for its ugliness, which is repeatedly envisaged in concrete bodily terms. As Alan Price observed, Synge has shifted the emphasis in the Deirdre tale 'from the destructiveness of an individual ruler to the destructiveness of Time'.[13] The ugliness that results from time's destructiveness is offset by Deirdre's renowned beauty and by the 'life that will be envied by great companies' and the 'joy and triumph to the ends of life and time'. Deirdre's seven years with Naisi – 'the choice of lives we had in the clear woods' – is outside the scope of time now, and the deliberate choice of the grave saves Deirdre from unbearable ugliness: 'it is not a small thing to be rid of grey hairs and the loosening of the teeth'. The state here envisaged by Deirdre at the end of the play had been expressed in related terms by Owen, who also emphasized the beauty that would be lost: 'Queens get old Deirdre, with their white and long arms going from them, and their backs hooping. I tell you it's a poor thing to see a queen's nose reaching down to scrape her chin'.[14] Owen, the fool with special access to truth, is given an echo of Villon's 'La Belle Heaumière', but with an additional exaggeration in the gargoyle-image of the nose reaching down to scrape the chin.

Elsewhere, Owen uses the emotive verb 'to rot' in his attempt at suggesting to Deirdre the deterioration which time would bring, and he harshly describes the effects of time on Conchubor's body, saying he has 'a swelling belly, and eyes falling down from his shining crown'. But he is only giving word to fears which Deirdre had earlier expressed to Lavarcham, admitting that she was 'wondering all times is it a game worth playing, living on until you're dried and old, and your joy is gone forever'. Owen finds a further example of ugly old age in Lavarcham, saying that she would 'scare a raven from a carcass on a hill'. And he implies the solution to this ignominious fate by putting a riddle to Deirdre concerning his father, who used to be Lavarcham's lover: 'I'll give you a riddle, Deirdre. Why isn't my father as ugly and as old as Conchubor? You've no answer? . . . It's because Naisi killed him'. Thus Owen acts as a catalyst in directing Deirdre's mind towards death, not least in his dramatic announcement 'Dead men, dead men, men who'll die for Deirdre's beauty, I'll be before you in the grave!' – because he carries out his intention.[15]

The sight of Owen's corpse makes Deirdre realize that 'death should be a poor untidy thing, though it's a queen that dies'. This view is in direct opposition to her denial of the terror of death at the beginning of the play, when she tells Naisi: 'I'm in little dread of death, and it earned with richness would make the sun red with envy and he going up the heavens, and the moon pale and lonesome and she wasting away . . . Isn't it a small thing is foretold about the ruin of ourselves, Naisi, when all men have age coming and ruin in the end'. Naisi's response then had something of her later reaction to actual, as opposed to remote, imagined death: 'Yet it's a poor thing it's I should bring you to a tale of blood, and broken bodies and the filth of the grave'. When finally Deirdre is faced with Naisi in his grave, the full impact of its ugliness hits her, and while she recognizes that the night is 'pitiful for the want of pity', she is prompted to make her most moving speeches, of which the following is an example:

> What are crowns and Emain Macha when the head that gave them glory is this place Conchubor, and it stretched upon the gravel will be my bed tonight?[16]

Here, in musically controlled language, Synge expresses an ugly truth about a lofty character, using an earthy image. Starting with a crown, he moves to the head that has the power to give that crown glory, but which has, alas, been brought low upon the gravel. One can, of course, quibble as to whether a head can literally be stretched, but imagination and feeling readily connect it with the stretched body of Naisi. In the association of crown/Emain/glory on the one hand with head/gravel/stretched on the other, ugliness serves a rhetorical purpose through contrast.

According to T.R. Henn, it is a serious criticism that Synge at times strains after his rhetorical effects, and that his fondness for violently colliding images often leads to failure. While the claim that he strains after his rhetorical effects is true, that this should be a serious criticism depends on whether he achieves the effect after which he is straining. Since there is a demonstrable interest in contrastive effects, only very rarely is there failure. The 'sun red with envy' (above) is not felicitous, and to make 'the moon pale and lonesome and she wasting away' is scarcely flattering, but the play is unfinished.

In his straining Synge might be compared to another over-reacher, Christopher Marlowe, although in most other respects these two dramatists are in strong contrast. For the most part Marlowe uses language which is resounding, has a relatively regular rhythm, and consists of a wide variety of figures of speech. Synge, on the other hand, uses language which is sometimes plaintive, sometimes vigorous, is periphrastic and depends mainly on simile and earthy images, as well as on delicate cadence for its effects. To illustrate the comparison, some lines from Marlowe's *Edward II* serve well:

> But what are kings, when regiment is gone,
> But perfect shadowes in a sun-shine day?
> My nobles rule, I beare the name of king,
> I wear the crowne, but am contrould by them . . .[17]

Here the crown also has glorious associations, but these are of an external nature, connected with power and regiment. The tension arises from the temporary separation of the crown from these externals, and it could be dispelled through the reunion of these factors. Nothing earthy or ugly is introduced to balance the exaltation. There is an implicit faith in the value of the crown in Marlowe's attitude, whereas in Synge's its only glory arises from the bearer, who is now brought irrevocably low. The Renaissance dramatist reaches from the crown to the sun, whereas Synge enforces the collision between crown and gravel.

The contrastive use of ugliness arising from age, besides its use in *Deirdre*, is also to be found in *The Shadow* and *The Well*, though it is less extensively explored in these earlier plays. In both of them it is juxtaposed with the beauty of the dream-life into which the protagonists escape. Nora first points out the horrors of ageing to Michael, using Dan as evidence:

149

> Why should I marry you, Mike Dara? You'll be getting old, and I'll be getting old, and in a little while, I'm telling you, you'll be sitting up in your bed – the way himself was sitting – with a shake in your face, and your teeth falling and the white hair sticking out round you like an old bush where sheep do be leaping a gap.[18]

Dan is clearly smitten by her image, for he repeats it when he throws her out:

> Walk out now, Nora Burke, and it's soon you'll be getting old with that life, I'm telling you; it's soon your teeth'll be falling and your head'll be the like of a bush where the sheep do be leaping a gap.

He goes on to envisage her death in terms devoid of human dignity: '. . . hiding herself away till the end will come, and they find her stretched like a dead sheep with the frost on her, or the big spiders, maybe, and they putting their webs on her, in the butt of a ditch'.[19]

In *The Well*, Mary in her dream envisages herself as a beautiful, white-haired old woman, which is in direct conflict with what the audience sees her to be, described by Martin when he first sees her as follows:

> Your hair, and your big eyes, is it? . . . I'm telling you there isn't a wisp on any grey mare on the ridge of the world isn't finer than the dirty twist on your head. There isn't two eyes in any starving sow, isn't finer than the eyes you were calling blue like the sea.[20]

When Martin tries to share Mary's dream of beautiful white hair, she excludes him by anticipating his repulsiveness: 'In a short while you'll have a head on you as bald as an old turnip you'd see rolling around in the muck'. Martin is discomfited by this, so that Mary, seeing her advantage, continues with details of his ugliness – rat's eyes, big ears, griseldy chin, slouching feet, hooky neck, and knock knees – but Martin escapes from this into his own dream of 'a beautiful, long, white, silken, streamy beard'.

From the above examples it can be seen that Synge frequently uses animal images for the purpose of conveying man's physical ugliness. This use differs from that seen in the discussion of incongruity in the explicitness of the connection made between animal and man. Whereas the animal images were introduced obliquely for

150

incongruous effect, here they are proferred in direct confrontation with the beauty of the dream-life.

The victory of death in *Deirdre* is also conveyed through reference to animals taking over the human dwelling-place. Lavarcham, when she sees that she cannot stay Conchubor's hand, prophesies that Emain will be destroyed and overrun with deer, goats, and sheep; when Deirdre sees Emain in flames she acknowledges that because of her the royal palace will be the home of weasels and wild cats. Besides, the victory of death over Owen's body is conveyed by Lavarcham in terms of the live worms inside his corpse. The presence of the grave causes Naisi to resort to animal associations when he considers the stirring of desire in Deirdre after he is dead:

> If a day comes in the west that the larks are cocking their crests on the edge of the clouds, and the cuckoos making a stir, and there's a man you'd fancy, let you not be thinking that day, I'd be well pleased you'd go on keening always.

Likewise, it drives him to call the high king a 'knacky fancier' (a good judge of a horse), and to threaten him with an animal fate: 'I've got ten fingers will squeeze your mottled goose neck though you're king itself'.[21]

In *The Well* and *The Playboy* there are occasional instances of ugliness being used without any associations with cruelty, age, or death. These instances might be regarded as accidents of nature, but they are not part of any fundamental, vital conflict as the others are. When Martin recounts the ugliness he finds in the world when he can see, he refers to the saint's 'bleeding feet and they cut with the stones'; and he forcefully expresses the repulsiveness of the results of asceticism: 'Let you walk on now with your worn feet, and your welted knees, and your fasting, holy ways have left you with a big head on you and a thin pitiful arm'.[22] Likewise, the unattractive, abnormal nature of the possible suitors, apart from mousy Shawn, for the fine Pegeen is conveyed by reference to 'Red Linahan, has a squint in his eye and Patcheen is lame in his heel, or the mad Mulrannies were driven from California and they lost in their wits'.[23] Such ugliness is incidental only; it is freakish, and is therefore not central to Synge's philosophy of using only variations of vigorous life as a basis for art.[24]

There is no morbid concentration on ugliness in the work of Synge, simply an insistence on its co-presence with beauty throughout the plays. It is at its most Rabelaisian in *The Playboy* where the comic note is loudest. But by the time Synge was writing *Deirdre*, death in life had crept distressingly close, which perhaps accounts for why the sense of ugliness there is strong. An examination of the drafts of *Deirdre* shows that his earlier conception of Owen, who acts as a messenger of death, allotted him a grosser manner of expression. Earlier drafts have him telling Deirdre of having loafed around for two weeks 'in the wet muck of the bogs till I've ague and asthma, and water in my guts'; and asking in his next speech 'Was ever a man pewked out the inside of himself crossing the sea after a woman that wasn't away in his head?'.[25] But Synge realized that such coarseness was gratuitous and considerably reduced it as his revisions progressed.

Yet we have Yeats's word in his preface to the Cuala edition in 1910 that Synge felt that the grotesque element in *Deirdre* should be increased: 'He felt that the story, as he told it, required a grotesque element mixed into its lyrical melancholy to give contrast and create an impression of solidity, and had begun this mixing with the character of Owen'.[26] This is Yeats's considered opinion after he had examined the final drafts in detail and recalled Synge's most recent remarks. In April 1908 he had written to John Quin, when Synge was still alive: 'There is, however, nothing grotesque in it, and an astonishing amount of sheer lyrical beauty';[27] and this view is also recorded in Yeats's preface to Synge's poems in April 1909. The variation in Yeats's views over that year reflect the problems which Synge was having with the character of Owen. The grotesque element was not simply a matter of increasing the ugliness, it was a much more complex balancing involving contrast and movement. Above all, humour was necessary for equilibrium in approaching what was wild and coarse in life:

> Certain portions of life, wild and coarse in a sense, that we can never get away from can only be looked at safely when they are seen with the humour which makes them human for no vice is humorous (bestial is opposed to the very idea of humour and as far as the person is concerned we may say also almost that) and whatever can be done gaily is not criminal.[28]

How was he to increase the grotesque element without humour, and how could he have reconciled humour with the tragedy of Deirdre?

The 'lyrical melancholy' of *Deirdre* comes from the beauty and

sublimity of the characters of Deirdre and the sons of Uisneach. But
the sublime, according to Victor Hugo, palled without the contrast
of the grotesque:

> comme objectif auprès du sublime, comme moyen de contraste,
> le grotesque est, selon nous, la plus riche source que la nature
> puisse ouvrir à l'art. Rubens le comprenait sans doute ainsi,
> lorsqu'il se plaisait à mêler à des déroulements de pompes
> royales, à des couronnements, à d'éclatantes cérémonies, quel-
> que hideuse figure de nain de cour. Cette beauté universelle que
> l'antiquité répandait solennellement sur tout n'était pas sans
> monotonie ; la même impression, toujours répétée, peut fatiguer
> à la longue. Le sublime sur le sublime produit malaisément un
> contraste, et l'on a besoin de se reposer de tout, même du beau. Il
> semble, au contraire, que le grotesque soit un temps d'arrêt, un
> terme de comparaison, un point de départ d'ou l'on s'élève vers
> le beau avec une perception plus fraîche et plus excitée.[29]

> (the grotesque, as an object beside the sublime, as a means of
> contrast, is in my view the richest source which nature can offer
> art. Rubens certainly saw it in this way since he chose to mingle
> some hideous form of court dwarf in his depictions of royal
> pomp, coronations, and dazzling ceremonies. The universal
> beauty solemnly spread over all in antiquity was not without
> monotony. The same impression repeated over and over can tire
> in the end. The sublime added to the sublime does not easily
> create a contrast, and one needs a rest from everything, even
> from beauty. It seems that the grotesque, on the contrary, pro-
> vides a stopping-time, a term of comparison, a point of departure
> from which one can approach beauty with a fresher and more
> animated perception.)

Synge could, on the basis of the example put forward by Hugo, have
been endeavouring to further integrate the hideous Owen in his
particular court tableau in order to achieve the contrast which he
saw as capable of giving 'the wonder of life' to art. He had not
managed in *Deirdre* that counterpointing of pity and gaiety which
operated in the previous four plays where he might well have been
attempting to fulfil the expectations of Hugo for Romantic drama:

> . . . le drame romantique . . . ferait passer à chaque instant

l'auditoire du sérieux au rire, des excitations bouffonnes aux émotions déchirantes, *du grave au doux, du plaisant au sévère*. Car ainsi que nous l'avons déjà établi, le drame, c'est le grotesque avec le sublime, l'âme sous le corps, c'est une tragédie sous une comédie.[30]

(the Romantic drama would take the audience from gravity to laughter; from farcical excitation to harrowing emotion; *from the serious to the light*; and *from the amusing to the harsh*. For as we have already established, the drama is the grotesque with the sublime, the soul beneath the body, it is a tragedy beneath a comedy.)

Being one of 'The Three Sorrows of Storytelling', *Deirdre* in its received form belonged with tragedy, therefore such a contrastive aesthetic was not readily applicable to it. However, Synge hoped, through the admixture of the grotesque as ugliness to alter the form so as to give it contemporary significance.

IX THE COMIC

Because of the inclusive nature of Synge's vision there is little in his drama which is purely comic in effect. 'Purely comic' here means that for which indifference is a prerequisite, the comic with which Henri Bergson is concerned when he writes:

> Il semble que le comique ne puisse produire son ébranlement qu'à la condition de tomber sur une surface d'âme bien calme, bien unie. L'indifférence est son milieu naturel.

> (It seems that the comic can only take effect providing it falls on a state of feeling which is quite calm and at one with itself. Indifference is its natural medium.)[1]

Typical of this kind of comic effect is that achieved by a dramatist like Oscar Wilde. When Lady Bracknell says 'To lose one parent, Mr Worthing, may be regarded as a misfortune; to lose both looks like carelessness', we laugh freely. The emotional implications of loss of kin are so remote from the situation Wilde presents, from the rigidity of character in Lady Bracknell, and above all from the epigrammatic wit, that no feeling is discharged. The loss of his daughters has, by contrast, unhinged King Lear's mind so that there are resounding emotional consequences, therefore the comic element in the fool's remarks has quite a different effect. When Lear in anguish tears off his clothes in the storm and the fool says 'Prithee, Nuncle, be contented; 'tis a naughty night to swim in' we laugh, but we do so to release tension. It is a guilty, forced laughter which offsets the pathos.[2]

Comic characterization presupposes a social perception of character, a view from the outside, whereas Synge also looks into the souls of his characters so that a degree of emotional involvement on the part of the audience results, which precludes detachment. Situational comedy is rare in his plays too, and what there is does not give rise to easy laughter: the revival of Dan, and the arrival of 'dead' Mahon raise serious problems of sympathy in addition to

155

laughter, as is the case when the priest discovers old bottles where he expected a tin can, and when Martin and Mary 'hide' themselves in full view. Besides, Synge's use of language is not witty since his humour does not appeal primarily to the intellect.

In his Preface to *The Tinker's Wedding* Synge cautions: 'Of the things which nourish the imagination humour is one of the most needful, and it is dangerous to limit or destroy it'. In early drafts of this preface, the danger he sees is identified with morbidity and insanity, and he also states that the dramatist's duty is to provide healthy fare for the minds of his audience. In trying to fulfil this duty he attempts in *The Tinker's Wedding* 'to catch some of the humour and freshness which is in all life'. Humour, then, formed part of Synge's 'entire reality of life' and is therefore included in his dramatist's brief. Without it he believed, as we saw at the end of the last chapter, that it was impossible to face certain wild and coarse aspects of life.[3]

Humour, according to Vivian Mercier in *The Irish Comic Tradition*, is the simplest form of the comic. It is something sensed rather than apprehended with the intellect, and it is not dependent on words.[4] Pirandello sees the humorist as a singularly perceptive individual whose vision penetrates custom and conventional order: he has a special capacity for reflection which typically generates a sense of contradiction.[5] In Synge's case the contradiction which he senses is not something to be eliminated; rather, it is accepted. The disposition is clearly not that of the satirist who wants to improve and correct, and who therefore uses his art for didactic purposes. Synge's declaration that the drama does not teach anything precludes such a disposition. The acceptance of contradiction is essentially an ambivalent attitude, and Synge's humour is accordingly ambivalent.

By implication, then, such ambivalence is conducive to health since it allows man to live with irreconcilables by laughing at them. Synge took exception to Baudelaire's view that laughter is the 'greatest mark of the Satanic element in man', and he noted the poet's morbidity in hating the laugh of the healthy man. In his exploration of the contradiction between man's earthbound existence and his exaltation, he made the counter-statement 'Gaiety is a divine impulse peculiar to humanity'.[6] Here he was evidently working out his own view of laughter in response to Rabelais's statement:

rire est le propre de l'homme
(laughter is man's peculiar property).

Besides, his views on the value of laughter to health are also germane to those of Rabelais.[7]

Petit de Julleville, who frequently discusses the role of laughter in comedy, quotes Rabelais's lines in the course of concluding that the sole object of medieval comedy was to amuse, to provoke laughter, not to correct morals. Elsewhere, he twice quotes the same passage from Desiré Nisard on the distinction between 'le gros rire' (the belly-laugh) and the laugh which carries a sad afterthought.[8] Once again the influence of de Julleville in raising issues which were to be of central importance to the practising dramatist can be seen.

Yet influence must not be thought of as unfiltered in the case of Synge, for his mind was strong and independent, as Yeats recorded of him:

> In one thing he and Lady Gregory are the strongest souls I have ever known. He and she alike have never for an instant spoken to me the thoughts of their inferiors as their own thoughts. I have never known them to lose the self-possession of their intellects.[9]

Thus, the Rabelaisian element, important though Synge considered it, is only one side of his work, and the Romantic extension of sensibility which he inherited tempers the humour of his work. However, it tempers it without exaggerating feeling. He had partaken in, and admired, the hardness of the physical life of the rural Irish when the absence of modern technology and medicine meant that pain was common-place. He recorded that where the person who felt pain was in no danger, the reaction of those who looked on was amusement.[10]

That he had full confidence in the humour of the country people is clear from his preface to *The Tinker's Wedding*:

> In the greater part of Ireland, however, the whole people, from the tinkers to the clergy, have still a life, and a view of life, that are rich and genial and humorous. I do not think that these country people, who have so much humour themselves, will mind being laughed at without malice, as the people in every country have been laughed at in their own comedies.[11]

But it was not the country people who generally constituted his audiences, which on occasion proved anything but humorous in their responses. In an earlier draft for this preface he wrote that 'the clergy in every Roman Catholic country were laughed at through the ages that had real religion'.[12] Here 'the ages that had real religion' evidently allude to the Middle Ages, a period when, as de Julleville took pains to point out, genuine religious feeling and piety coexisted with irreverence.[13] Besides, de Julleville attested that the clergy of the Middle Ages tolerated being used as a butt for mockery very well.[14]

Because Synge made these remarks about the clergy in his Preface to *The Tinker's Wedding*, it is likely that he was consciously renewing a tradition with the priest of this play. T. R. Henn is of the opinion that this priest is a 'traditional comic figure, and a medieval audience would have recognized him at once'.[15] Yet although he shares many of the characteristics of the secular clergy in medieval French farces and fabliaux, he also differs from them in several ways. He is avaricious, over-fed, and neglects his official duties, but he is not lecherous and debauched as were most of the priests in medieval comic literature – including one in *La Farce du Meunier* by André de la Vigne, written and played at the same time as *La Moralité de l'aveugle et du boiteux*.[16] On the contrary, his celibacy, which is offset by the freedom and fecundity of the tinkers, appears pathetic. The audience, through the understanding which squalid, bawdy Mary Byrne shows for the priest, feels some pity for him. Mary, to console him for the restrictions of his life says to him, patting him on the knee: 'Let you rouse up, now, if it's a poor, single man you are itself, and I'll be singing you songs unto the dawn of day'.[17]

This is not to say that a clear sympathy for him is roused. There is fluctuation. At first he appears frightened, disdainful, and suspicious, but his hard heart softens a little when Sarah Casey sobs in front of him. There is a contradiction between the conventional expectation of what a priest should be – magnanimous, generous, merciful – and the reality which Synge puts before us. The priest's humanity peeps through only because of a basic weakness which he shares with Mary Byrne and which is mentioned several times in the play: a fondness for drink. Mary arrives drunk, singing the following lines of 'The Night Before Larry Was Stretched', which convey the superfluity of the clergy for those reduced to the simplest state:

And when we asked him what way he'd die,
And he hanging unrepented,
'Begob', says Larry, 'That's all in my eye,
By the clergy first invented'.[18]

Superfluous though Mary finds the clergy, even when she is sober, she nevertheless warmly offers him the jug of porter she is carrying, partly, of course, to save her own skin from Michael and Sarah for having drunk so much of it. Only when the priest drinks does he unbend a little, to reveal the gloom and despondence behind his official exterior. Yet because of the hardness which he ultimately shows, the audience takes satisfaction in seeing him trussed.[19]

The play sometimes rouses easy laughter, for example when Mary, for the thrill of hearing Latin which she doesn't understand, asks the priest to say a prayer for her entertainment:

Stop till you say a prayer, your reverence; stop till you say a little prayer, I'm telling you, and I'll give you my blessing and the last sup from the jug.[20]

The irreverence is so benign, and the *insouciance* of the 'flagrant heathen' in the face of the sacred is so spontaneous that there is no residue of feeling. But the spectacle of the priest failing to cope in his personal dealings with the tinkers, and being at bottom a man oppressed by his chosen way of life, does not coincide with the criteria for a purely comic character.

So as to make clear how the laughter at Synge's priest is tinged with sympathy, it will be useful to make a comparison with Ben Jonson, a writer much admired by Synge. The putting of Zeal-of-the-Land Busy in the stocks in *Bartholomew Fair* might be compared with the tying up of the priest in the sack in *The Tinker's Wedding*. Both plays bring a man of God into contact with earthy and unruly members of society, who protect themselves from this supposedly spiritual force as best they can. The contact between these opposites illuminates the ambiguities in the position of the man of God in each case. Jonson resolves the ambiguity by having Busy, who is 'zealous for the cause – as a dog for a bone' converted, in the end, to the side of the players: 'I am changed and will become a beholder with you'.[21] Synge, however, retains the ambiguity in his priest's position, and at no time is his character as clear-cut as Jonson's elder, who is patently hypocritical, pompous, gluttonous, mercenary and repressive, and who, accordingly, does not evoke an emotional engagement in the audience.

The Tinker's Wedding does not give us a caricature of a priest, but the portrayal of a man who has a religious role to play and is trapped by the rules laid down for it. Rules are inadequate for coping with ordinary human needs which require instinct, feeling, and flexibility. Mary is describing the real state of things when she says to the priest at the end of the play 'it's little need we ever had of the like of you to get us our bit to eat, and our bit to drink, and our time of love when we were young men and women, and were fine to look at'.[22] In this she is in line with the other mother-figures of Synge's plays. Maurya, in *Riders to the Sea*, when Nora reminds her that the priest had said she would not be left without a son, responds: 'It's little the like of him knows of the sea';[23] and Mary Costello, in one of the drafts for *When the Moon Has Set*, says: 'give no heed to the priests or the bishops or the angels of God, for it's little the like of them, I was saying, knows about women or the seven sorrows of the earth'.[24]

Besides, in *The Well of the Saints* Martin Doul voices the feeling of Mary concerning the saint/friar's insistence on curing them when he tells him 'let you not be taking my rest from me in the darkness of my wife. . . . What call have the like of you to be coming in where you're not wanted at all'.[25] This interference of the priest between man and wife is reminiscent of a feature often found in farces and fabliaux, though there the interference is usually for the priest's own benefit since he becomes the wife's lover.[26] In Synge's play it is the result of his inability to step outside his role.

The asceticism of the friar in *The Well* is, like the celibacy of the priest in *The Tinker's Wedding*, treated as an impediment which is recognized primarily by the women in the play. Molly reports him as saying that young girls 'are the cleanest holy people you'd see walking the world' as he imparted his holy water, bell, and cloak to the girls. The report is made ironically, and Mary Doul picks up the irony and laughingly says 'Well, the saint's a simple fellow, and it's no lie'. Later, Molly shows her vanity by saying of him 'He'd walk by the finest woman in Ireland, I'm thinking and not trouble to raise his two eyes to look upon her face . . .'.[27]

In *The Playboy of the Western World* likewise, Pegeen identifies Shawn's timidity as a lover with the clergy when she says to him: 'Go on then to Father Reilly, and let him put you in the holy brotherhoods and leave that lad to me'. Although Father Reilly never appears on stage in this play, there are about a dozen references to him, always in close association with Shawn, whose will is completely subject to him – in the matter of dispensation to marry Pegeen; in his choice of heroes; and in the question of whether to keep Pegeen company himself of allow Christy to stay alone in the house with her. At Michael James's suggestion that he keep Pegeen company alone, he runs away leaving Michael holding his coat, which the latter indicates saying 'Well there's the coat of a Christian man'.[28]

The overall impression of the clergy which emerges from *The Playboy* is of a repressive force unable to cope with the vitality which Christy represents. Without the actual presence of a priest, there is no question of direct sympathy. However, the final incident in which Father Reilly's legate, Shawn, takes part suggests a rejection, for Pegeen, unimpressed by the dispensation, retains her independence of the clergy in the matter of coupling:

SHAWN (*going up to her*). It's a miracle Father Reilly can wed us in the end of all, and we'll have none to trouble us when his vicious bite is healed.

PEGEEN (*hitting him a box on the ear*). Quit my sight.[29]

Ultimately, the priest has no place in the presence of lovers, and is thereby both comic and pathetic.

Insofar as Synge saw the church as a human institution created by man to fulfil a religious need, he did not satirize it. The clergy, as its official representatives, rather took their place in literary tradition, yet they were not simply comic figures. Although the law, another human institution, does not have a personal representative in his plays, it is nevertheless something of a background presence in two plays, *The Tinker's Wedding* and *The Playboy*. Since the law of the people to whose lives Synge was giving expression was still a foreign one in his day, the attitude to it is highly ambivalent.

Were the law in Ireland then native and supported by the majority, it might have been eligible for comic treatment since, according to Bergson social forms tend to become fixed and therefore comic, and human laws become mechanical substitutes for natural laws.[30] But this was not the case, so that in the west there was widespread resistance to the law, as Synge knew:

This impulse to protect the criminal is universal in the west. It seems partly due to the association between justice and the hated English jurisdiction, but more directly to the primitive feeling of these people, who are never criminals yet always capable of crime, that a man will not do wrong unless he is under the influence of a passion which is as irresponsible as a storm on the sea. If a man has killed his father, and is already sick and broken with remorse, they can see no reason why he should be dragged away and killed by the law. [31]

He recorded these remarks in connection with the story of the real-life parricide on which he had based the central incident of *The Playboy*. In this play we find various instances of an interest in the letter of the law so as to be able to exploit it.

Christy, under the impression that he is guilty of a crime, wishes to ascertain his chances of avoiding the law, and soon after his entry is reassured to this effect by Michael James. In his reply to Pegeen's question as to whether he had shot his father – 'I never used weapons. I've no license, and I'm a law-fearing man' – it is evident that his only interest is in the letter of the law, not in its spirit. That same interest can be seen both in Michael's earlier proud boast of a licence for the sale of beer and spirits, and in the story of Jimmy Farrel who 'hanged his dog from the licence and had it screeching and wriggling three hours at the butt of a string, and himself swearing it was a dead dog, and the peelers swearing it had life'.[32]

The notion of an even-handed justice is given the lie by Pegeen when she warns Christy 'I've heard the Circuit Judges in this place is a heartless crew'; and again by Sara in her toast to the wonders of the western world, which include 'jobbing peelers, and the juries fill their stomachs, selling judgements of the English law'. The ease with which the officers of the law can be diverted from their duty is conveyed in Philly's speech, after the discovery that they failed to follow Christy: 'The peelers is fearing him, and if you'd that lad in the house there isn't one of them would come smelling around if the dogs itself were lapping poteen from the dung-pit of the yard'. It is with approbation rather than disapproval that Michael describes their ineffectiveness: 'the peelers in this place is decent droughty poor fellows, wouldn't touch a cur dog and not give warning in the dead of night'. And one of Pegeen's heroes is 'Daneen Sullivan knocked the eye from a peeler'. The most palpable absurdity is apparent the only time the people have recourse to the law: Christy replies to his father's question as to why he is tied up 'They're taking me to the peelers to have me hanged for slaying you'; and paradox matches paradox in Michael's explanation 'It is the will of God that all should guard their little cabins from the treachery of the law'.[33]

Synge's consciousness of the discordance between the people of Aran and their imposed law can also be seen in the following comment:

> The mere fact that it is impossible to get reliable evidence in the island – not because the people are dishonest, but because they think the claim of kinship more sacred than the claims of abstract truth – turns the whole system of sworn evidence into a demoralizing farce, and it is easy to believe that law dealings on this false basis must lead to every sort of injustice.[34]

The claim of kinship is more primitive than that of 'objective' law, and it is possible that Synge noticed this because of de Jubainville's teaching on Old Irish law. A distinction was made in Old Irish law between a necessary and an unnecessary crime, and complicated laws governed the price paid to the family for the body of a murdered man as well as for his honour. The penalty for the murder of a compatriot was merely exile, whereas it was death for that of a foreigner because of the danger of provoking war.[35]

Besides the clergy and the law, which are traditional subjects for comic treatment, there are several motifs which Synge introduces into his plays that are also commonly treated thus in medieval and folk literature. The feigned death motif which Synge uses in *The Shadow* is particularly common in French and Italian medieval literature;[36] and the motif of the faithless wife which accompanies it in *The Shadow* appears with remarkable frequency in French medieval literature. Petit de Julleville stresses this in a long chapter on 'The Satire of Love, Women and Marriage', and he takes the view that this satirical approach to women and love was a reaction to the idealization of woman in the chivalric tradition.[37]

That Synge is not satirizing the woman of *The Shadow* is evident, but what is of interest here is the question of the source he used for this play. Much discussion has centred around this question, beginning with that first notorious furore about the supposed slight on Irish womanhood. The source on that occasion was conveniently traced to a foreign literature, but Synge strongly denied the suggestion of 'The Widow of Ephesus'. His immediate source was undoubtedly a story he heard from Pat Dirane;[38] and as Lady Gregory pointed out, the same story had already been given in Jeremiah Curtin's edition of Irish folk-tales.[39] Yeats wrote in a letter of defence:

> I can remember several Irish poems and stories in which the husband feigns death for precisely the reason the husband does in Mr. Synge's play.[40]

And the matter was taken up again in 1947 by David Greene when he noted that the central incident of the Aran tale is common to the folk literature of many nations. Nevertheless he pointed out that

> Synge himself always had the suspicion that the tale might have been originally European. He was always puzzled to know how the word *gallery* got into the story. 'You don't find galleries in Irish cottages, but might find something of the sort in a peasant's house in the south of Europe'.[41]

On the basis that the word 'gallery' is commonly used in reference to Irish churches, Greene concludes that a foreign origin for the tale is not necessarily indicated because of its use. However, Synge's conviction is telling: he had recorded specific connections with medieval European literature in the case of the story of Lady O'Connor.[42] Here he could not make such a specific connection precisely because no one instance in that literature provides quite the same combination of features as *The Shadow*. Subconsciously, he was making the connection for individual aspects of the combination with countless parallels in French farces and fabliaux, and perhaps also with their analogues among *exempla, contes*, and *novelle*. Probably unconsciously, Synge had taken up literary tradition in his use of the motifs of the faithless wife and feigned death under the stimulus of their occurrence in Irish folk-tale. Whereas in the middle ages they had been treated in a comic manner, Synge penetrates psychologically and finds undeniable needs whose neglect is not possible without pathos.

The January/May motif, where an old man is paired with a young woman, and which is perhaps most familiar in English literature from Chaucer's use of it in 'The Merchant's Tale' and 'The Miller's Tale', is also widespread in the same range of literature as the feigned death and the faithless wife motifs. Viewed from a certain angle, this motif brings into focus the degenerating aspect of bodily life, and this is the angle which Synge adopts when he uses it, whereas the comic angle is taken in medieval literature. Besides occurring in *The Shadow*, it also appears in *Deirdre*, and is tentatively there in Martin's lust for Molly in *The Well*. It can also be seen germinating in the scenario for 'The Lady O'Connor', although it is not present in the prose account of the folk-tale as Synge published it, nor in Boccaccio nor the medieval German tale of which he had been reminded by it.

In his attempts at dramatizing 'The Lady O'Connor', which Synge began after *The Shadow* was written, he changes the disposition of Lady O'Connor so that she is in certain ways reminiscent of Nora Burke. Both women are lonely and desolate in their surroundings and see life slipping by; Nora goes with the tramp taking pleasure in his fine talk, but Lady O'Connor's husband, although described by the captain as a 'gallous talker', is seen by her as 'half a monk'. Lady O'Connor, like Nora, is younger than her husband, as can be seen from the captain's words on arrival:

CAPTAIN. We thank you kindly Lord and this your daughter –
O'CONNOR. My wife, good friends –
CAPTAIN (*bowing low*). Then the more honour to her.[43]

The unequal pairing draws attention to neglected instinctual needs, but without any comic resolution. There is no suggestion that this neglect is repaired, as it is in medieval literature where the motif occurs.

In the folk context, humour tends to centre on the body and is often connected with sex, death or violence of a harmless kind. It is generally spontaneous and vacuous, whereas when a writer takes that same humour and uses it, this is no longer the case. Synge, in his endeavour to put 'the entire reality' of the life of the rural Irish on the stage did so including their humour, which shares with other folk humour its ambivalence.[44] The humour is not aimed particularly at an elite or learned audience, as can be inferred from the following remarks of Synge:

I think that while Tolstoy is wrong in claiming that art should be intelligible to the peasant, he is right in seeking a criterion for the arts, and I think this is to be found in testing art by its compatibility with the outside world and the peasants or people who live near it.[45]

Through its ambivalence, then, his humour is in harmony with his folk subject. To have sought a purely comic effect would have been incompatible with his inclusive theory, for that would have called for an emphasis which would have been exclusive. Whereas Chaucer creates a purely comic effect with the burning of Nicholas's buttocks through presenting an outlandish situation and an unsympathetic character in the Miller's Tale, Synge makes Christy's plight too credible and immediate and his character sympathetic so that the comic effect is strongly qualified with feeling when Pegeen burns his leg.

We find a heightening of ambiguities in the four plays which Nicholas Grene calls 'unhappy comedies',[46] that is *The Shadow, The Tinker's Wedding, The Well of the Saints* and *The Playboy*. In the other two plays there is a resolution, so that we have endings with 'all passion spent'. At the end of *Riders to the Sea* Maurya says 'They're all gone now, and there isn't anything more the sea can do to me'; and at the end of *Deirdre*, Fergus tells us that 'The flames of Emain have gone out: Deirdre is dead and there is none to keen her'.

The combination of a lack of resolution in the endings of these four plays with the widespread presence of the grotesque in them makes them tragi-comedies of a peculiarly modern kind. Writing of a 'comic-grotesque' tradition, Thomas Mann had occasion to remark:

> The striking feature of modern art is that it has ceased to recognize the categories of tragic and comic, or the dramatic classification tragedy and comedy. It sees life as a tragi-comedy, with the result that the grotesque is its most genuine style.[47]

Although Mann probably has more recent writers in mind here, what he writes is true of the four of Synge's plays which defy classification as either tragedy or comedy.

As in life disparate elements occur side by side, so in tragi-comedy and the grotesque we find that the writer does not sift and segregate so as to create a clear-cut effect. Yet these elements do not merge and lose their individual identities in their collateral presentation. Rather, the clash or contrast is exaggerated, and this is what causes the disturbed response. In the Classical tradition, part of the cathartic effect of the drama was achieved through the resolution at the end, but since the unconscious has been released 'from

166

the cramping bonds of logic', this resolution no longer seems imperative, and Synge was early in his change of mode.[48]

This lack of resolution applies not only to the endings of these four plays, but also to each category of the grotesque as it appears in Synge's work. Incongruity ceases to exist if it is resolved; the repellant nature of ugliness is reduced in the absence of ideals of beauty or the sublime; and folly becomes imperceptible when the fool is integrated into society. Synge's work in this respect bears out Wolfgang Kayser's view that 'tragicomedy and the grotesque are conceptually related and the history of the grotesque in the field of drama is largely one with that of tragicomedy'.[49]

The emphasis which Synge gives to ambiguities heightens them to a degree which makes laughter uneasy. Thus the clergy, the law, and traditionally comic motifs such as feigned death, the faithless wife, and January/May do not evoke the disengaged laughter of their medieval counterparts.

X CONCLUSION

Synge's pre-conscious vision was comfortably accommodated in the medieval literature with which he was intimate, but that literature was not responsible for the vision. The deep structure of his thought may have been reinforced by the acceptance of imperfection, incompleteness, and disharmony which he found in the medieval literature which he used, but its basic cast preceded his experience of that literature and was also reinforced by other factors. Important among those other factors were his reaction to his inherited culture, his response to the richer, more liberal cultural life of continental Europe, and his participation in the primitive life of rural Ireland. The imposition of the unresolved clash which can be detected in his work between reason and folly, between ugliness and beauty, and in a great number of incongruities, reflects the deep structure of his thought as being both antithetical and kinetic. While according to his own brief for the writer he should 'deal manfully, directly and decently with the entire reality of life', the reality which he perceived had to be integrated into his own vision (see p. 144). That vision focused on contrast and motion, thereby investing them with prominence in the process of translating or reinventing the 'entire reality'.

The first literary source-material which Synge consciously used (for *The Well of the Saints*) was both medieval and grotesque, but by making the grotesque the structural basis for his play he entirely altered his source and through his new emphasis exposed the cruelty in pity. Deliberately avoiding a 'Cuchulanoid' hero in *The Playboy* he asserted the necessary violence in the nature of the hero, thus giving prominence to an unresolved clash between the heroic and the despicable sides of the nature of 'the only playboy of the western world' who is the central character of the play. Staging the clashing needs of the old man and his young wife in *The Shadow*, he also realized the tension between man's imaginative existence and that imposed by material necessity, as well as between his individual and social urges. Adopting the literary fool, he exploited anew the clash between the rational and the irrational in man, and between the

168

collective and the inspired, individual vision, while adding a Romantic note of pathos. He chose remote, medieval poems to translate, only some of which contained a grotesque element, but on all of which he exercised that idiom which reflected the tensions inherent to his vision and which contained the plaintive note which he had recognized in Lady Gregory's use of it. To strengthen the lyrical sweetness with which he had overlaid the tragic tale of Deirdre, he was in the process of increasing the grotesque element, having already established the pitilessness of beauty. In short, Synge carried the use of the grotesque as a structural principle to a new pass: whatever clash of incompatibles he found in medieval material he intensified and modified in terms which were both directly rooted in external nature and nurtured by his own vision.

Such practice on Synge's part coincides with that theory which he expressed in the arch-Romantic metaphor of tree and roots: 'In these days poetry is usually a flower of evil or good, but it is the timber of poetry that wears most surely, and there is no timber that has not strong roots among the clay and worms'.[1] This metaphor conveys the necessity for the artist to look beyond the surface of life, and to find those deeper levels which, although dark and forbidding, are nevertheless vital. The clay and worms are not confined to external nature but also form part of the inner life of the artist where Synge thought he should live, 'in the half sub-conscious faculties by which all creation is performed' and not in the bright light of the intellect.[2]

In his use of the tree/roots metaphor to express his theory of the relationship between life and art, Synge is echoing Victor Hugo:

Le poëte, insistons sur ce point, ne doit donc prendre conseil que de la nature, de la verité, et de l'inspiration qui est aussi une vérité et une nature ... Il faut puiser aux sources primitives. C'est la même sève, répandue dans le sol, qui produit tous les arbres de la forêt, si divers de port, de fruits, de feuillage. C'est la même nature qui féconde et nourrit les génies les plus différents. Le vrai poëte est un arbre qui peut être battu de tous les vents et abreuvé de toutes les rosées, qui porte ses ouvrages comme ses fruits, comme le *fablier* portait ses fables.[3]

(The poet, let me emphasize, should take counsel only from nature, from truth, and from his inspiration which is also an aspect of truth and of nature ... He must draw on primary

sources. It is the same sap, diffused in the ground, which produces all the trees of the forest, so varied in their bearing, fruit,
and foliage. The same nature fertilizes and nourishes the most
diverse geniuses. The true poet is a tree which can be blown by all
winds, watered by all dews; he bears his works as if they were
fruit, as the fable-tree bore its fables.)

Hugo here recognizes 'inspiration' as the inner aspect of nature and
truth, and besides he goes on to stress the importance of the
individual artist's vision. It is because Synge shared this belief in the
role of 'inner truth' in addition to an external one that he did not
'care a rap' about those criticisms of *The Playboy* which arose
essentially from demands for some one-to-one surface veri-
similitude. While he had indeed used the life of the rural Irish as a
primary source (=external nature) for his drama, whatever he
found there that was in itself grotesque was intensified in the light of
his vision. While he drew sustenance and nourishment from that
external source as the tree does from the soil, the work he bore was
informed by his individual vision. A distinction can be expected
between the fruit and the soil, although it would not make sense to
claim absolute autonomy for the fruit. Such autonomy Synge never
claimed for his work: he was ever ready to acknowledge both his
linguistic debt and that for his subject material.

Publicly, he defended *The Playboy* against charges of libel with
concrete examples from the west of Ireland, yet in a private context,
in a letter to Stephen MacKenna, he communicated the complex
'truth' of the parricide-hero and reaction to him:

> It isn't accurate to say, I think, that the thing is a generalization
> from a single case. *If* the idea had occurred to me I could and
> would just as readily have written the thing, as it stands, without
> the Lanchehaun case or the Aran case. The story – in its *essence* –
> is probable given the psychic state of the locality. I used the cases
> afterwards to controvert critics who said it was *impossible*.[4]

Two important points should be noted here: first, Synge's strong
sense of fact and his ability to use it when appropriate; and second,
the phrase 'the psychic state of the locality', which throws light on
his particular interests. The phrase was used not by someone given
to fairies or theosophy, or to interests conflicting with science, but
by a man who combined a strong sense of fact with an intuitive

intelligence and an interest in psychic truth.

In *The Playboy* and elsewhere in Synge's work, psychic truth is conveyed in terms of the unresolved clash of incompatibles. To this extent the work is anti-rational, and reflects the author's still being carried on the wave of reaction against rationalism, that is against exaggeration of the importance of reason. It presents the sublime only in the presence of the grotesque, and in a variety of ways shows incompatibles side by side. Its exposure and acceptance of certain of the darker aspects of human nature, for instance the capacity to accept ugliness and folly as both repulsive and fascinating at the same time, was at least partly responsible for its disturbing effects on the audiences of Synge's own time.

Those audiences expected certain kinds of 'truths' to be excluded from art, so that comparison of Synge's work with that of the Pre-Raphaelites who fulfilled such expectations is revealing. In addition to his close historical relation to this group, Synge shared their predilection for peasants and their backward look to the Middle Ages. Also, there is little that he would have quarrelled with in their aims: to have genuine ideas to express; to study directly from nature; and to envisage events as they must have happened rather than as the rules of design required.[5] However, Pre-Raphaelite practice was disappointing beside these avowed principles, because in envisaging events as they must have happened their imagination stopped at the decorative level, and failed to penetrate with an inner vision.

Pre-Raphaelite emphasis on the decorative, with consequent exclusion of ugliness, can be clearly seen in the treatment of the beggar-maid in Edward Burne-Jones's 'King Cophetua and the Beggar Maid' (Tate Gallery, London). Although the beggar-maid is barefoot, she is depicted in a comfortable interior; she wears an elegant dress; and she looks well fed. There is nothing here to disturb the dominant note of opulence, and even according to Burne-Jones's own admission he sought to represent his beggar-maid as convincingly poverty-stricken 'without introducing the ugliness of poverty'.[6] Such exclusion inevitably falsifies in the direction of a spurious beauty which was unpalatable to Synge, who believed only in expressing as much beauty as would be consistent with his subject (see p. 142 above), and who disliked the reproductions of Burne-Jones which hung in his rooms in Paris, at the Hôtel Corneille.[7]

Synge does not hesitate to include the ugliness of poverty in *The*

Shadow, The Well, and *The Playboy* where it is appropriate to his subject, but it coexists with much that is beautiful and lofty. In *Dierdre* too he presents a noble and beautiful heroine who is securely anchored in the senses and is acutely aware of the harsh realities of bodily life, so that she goes to join her dead lover with this acknowledgement: 'it is a cold place I must go to be with you, Naisi, and it's cold your arms will be this night that were warm about my neck so often'.[8] Thus Synge avoids the effect of dreamy vagueness which Rossetti achieves in his 'Blessèd Damozel' where the lady waits in heaven for her lover to join her, with these reflections:

> When round his head the aureole clings,
> And he is clothed in white,
> I'll take his hand and go with him
> To the deep wells of light . . .
>
> He shall fear, haply, and be dumb:
> Then will I lay my cheek
> To his, and tell about our love,
> Not once abash'd or weak . . .[9]

The choice of the after-life point of view contributes to the dreaminess here through the reduction of the body to emblematic features of head, hand, and cheek, and it is in contrast with Deirdre who contemplates death from the graveside, physically. But whatever point of view he adopted, Synge remained conscious of the body. This counteracted the remoteness which he saw as a danger in the Deirdre tale: 'I am a little afraid that the "Saga" people might loosen my grip on reality', he wrote in one letter, and in another: 'These saga people, when one comes to deal with them, seem very remote; one does not know what they thought or what they are or where they went to sleep, so one is apt to fall into rhetoric'. (One might perhaps read 'ate' for 'are' here, since this avoids the illogical change of tense and coincides with the subsequent physical detail of sleep.)[10] This consciousness of the body, then, prevented Synge from retreating into medievalism, unlike the Pre-Raphaelites,[11] in particular Rossetti, who in his watercolours created a 'dream-world of moody medieval romance entirely remote from the original Pre-Raphaelite concepts'.[12]

In an article contrasting Synge's account of island life in *The Aran Islands* with that in three books by native islanders, Malcolm Kelsall suggests a similarity between Synge and the Pre-Raphaelites:

> None of the islanders (ignorant of pre-Raphaelitism) write of that 'something of the artistic beauty of medieval life' that Synge sees about their life. (58–59) But Synge turns continually from the thing itself to the picturesque image, and, like the pre-Raphaelites, misses the spirit for the decorative exterior . . .[13]

Since the present work is concerned with the medieval and the grotesque primarily in Synge's plays and poems, a claim for distinction between him and the Pre-Raphaelites would not necessarily be invalidated by allowing a similarity in his prose. However, while Synge did emphasize certain decorative, attractive aspects of life on the Aran islands as he described it, he neither concealed nor ignored what was harsh, cruel, and ugly. Because Malcolm Kelsall can identify the subjective colouring of Synge's prose, he denies all its objective value beyond topographical detail. Yet he accepts as *true* the spirit he divines from the narratives of the three native islanders, and he assumes a one-to-one correspondence between their depicted heroic spirit and that of the actual life led on the islands.

But the apparently transparent narrative style of the islanders has deceived him, and he has failed to reckon with the lively tradition of storytelling from which they came – a tradition which valued the impact of the image as highly as Synge, if not more so, but presented it in a different manner. Also, Malcolm Kelsall makes no allowance for the view that heroic literature develops when a heroic age is past or in decline; and he does not consider the pride which would forbid the islanders to include the kind of unheroic incidents which the outsider felt free to place beside heroic ones. In this case for Synge's missing the true spirit of the Aran islands in his prose, it is only by recognizing the legitimate lies of the native writers that the illegitimate truth of the vision of the outsider can be perceived. And in Synge's plays the presence of the grotesque distinguishes them from the work of the Pre-Raphaelites where it is excluded.

The nature of Synge's grotesque involves not only a clash of incompatibles (arising from the antithetical nature of his vision), but also a downward movement towards the body (its kinetic aspect). This direction of emphasis towards the body serves to relate his work to that of other artists in the grotesque tradition, though it functions in a variety of ways. The tension maintained in Synge's work between 'the half sub-conscious faculties' and external reality restrains the fantastic treatment of the body. This restraint distinguishes it from much grotesque writing in the Irish tradition. The Early Irish literature of which he made use has recurrent instances of the fantastic bodily grotesque. There are, for example, the huge protruding yellow eyes of the challenging boor in *Bricriu's Feast*; the distortions frequently ascribed to Cuchullain's face when he was moved to anger; and Loigaire's hair, described by Findabair to her mother as he was approaching Cruachan: of three different colours – brown near the scalp, like gold at the tip, and red as blood in the middle, so that it looked like three circles round his head. Such extraordinary attributes were a mark of the exceptional nature of the heroes in a heroic literary tradition, but Synge created a world of ambiguous heroes where fantasy remains primarily an internal process. Such internalization is determined to some extent by the absence of narrator in the dramatic form, but even the conceptions of Synge's individual characters do not extend to such unbounded fantasy.

Swift, particularly in *Gulliver's Travels*, makes extensive use of another kind of bodily grotesque, but here too the fantasy operates without restraint, notably in the realm of proportion. The human body is held up with some distaste to the hard, cold frame of reason, and the Dean's satiric intent informs all. Although Synge lowers the sight to the body in the presence of some aspiration or illusion, he does so with some compassion.

Samuel Beckett's exploitation of the irrational and his concentration on the degenerative processes of the body are more radical than Synge's, and his vision is far darker. He admitted much when he described *Endgame* as 'more inhuman than *Godot*'.[14] He had recourse to another language and culture in order to feel free enough to progressively reduce the body in its degenerative state, and to use language against itself so as to reveal its inadequacy as an instrument of communication. Although Synge too deserted his mother tongue (for another dialect but not another language), and according to Yeats's view 'only through dialect could he escape self-expression' (meaning subjective dreaming), there is nevertheless a certain faith and confidence behind the way his characters use their language which is lacking in Beckett's.[15] The exaggerated attention to the body in Beckett is part of the darker vision which excludes, or cannot see, what might be called 'nobility' in human nature, or at least cannot see enough to balance what is ignoble, whereas Synge's vision, as we have seen, is inclusive and compassionate.

174

The degenerative side of the life of the body is prominent in the work of artists whom Synge admired and is most readily seen in the visual arts. Rembrandt is a case in point, and Kenneth Clark relates this aspect of the Dutch painter to the Middle Ages:

> To Rembrandt . . . ugliness, poverty and other misfortunes of our physical life were not absurd, but inevitable, perhaps he might have said 'natural', and capable of receiving some radiance of the spirit because emptied of all pride. It is curious how this medieval view of our bodily estate led him to see the nude in the same shape as the artists of the middle ages . . .[16]

Here the misfortunes of the physical life coexist with a radiance of spirit. Rodin offers a related combination, and he like Synge was inspired to use Villon's 'La Belle Heaumière' as a subject. The statue to which he gave that title is seen by Kenneth Clark, in the context of his definition of the Gothic as opposed to the idealizing approach to the human body, in the following terms:

> Rodin's old woman is a final image of decrepitude, a *memento mori*, reminding us of certain Gothic figures with exactly this intention. . . . Rodin's Heaulmière, although conceived in a graver spirit than the old courtesan of Villon's poem, is still bound to the body, and brooding on its deficiencies. Yet she is far from those pitiless figures of late Hellenistic art in which the worn-out body is represented as contemptible or derisory, for Rodin has seen in her shrunken members a Gothic grandeur of construction.[17]

Here the deficiencies of the body coexist with a certain grandeur. Whereas the same individual terms as those applicable to the work of these two admired artists may not be eligible to describe what Synge combines with the deficiencies or misfortunes of the body, the nature of the combination is similar.

The treatment of the body in the work of Rabelais clearly puts the emphasis on its regenerative aspect, which is an evident difference from that of Synge, where the emphasis is on degeneration. There is no contrasting factor to accompany the frank grossness of *Gargantua and Pantagruel* either. One wonders whether the exuberant imagination, seen especially in its floods of epithets, could owe anything to the special liking Rabelais is reported to have had for fantastic Celtic tales.[18] Such continual exuberance precludes the pathos of the ageing body which accompanies the Rabelaisian note in Synge's work.

Deficiencies of the body acquire the status which leads to brooding only when the body is of vital importance, as it is in the case of Synge's work. That he wished to root his art in 'real life' we know. The aspect of that 'real life' he found most useful for the nourishment of these roots was the body. Concerned about the absence of bodily life from much writing of his own day, he wrote: 'When the body dies the soul goes to Heaven or to Hell. So our modern art is – must be – either divine or satanic'.[19] In order to avoid such ethereal alternatives he concentrated on the movement, energy and conflict inherent in physical life. However, the effect of this concentration is not simple since the conception is essentially dualist: the body is presented always in coexistence with some non-physical opposing factor. Synge's practice in this is in accord with the little literary comment and theory which he has left.[20] The antithetical cast of mind can be seen throughout.

When he considers poetry, it is as 'poetry of exaltation' and 'poetry of ordinary things'; and where he sees the eighteenth century putting ordinary life into 'verse that was not poetry', he sees Coleridge and Shelley putting poetry into 'verse that was not always human'.[21] On the stage, he insists 'one must have reality, and one must have joy';[22] and in *The Playboy* the Romantic note and the Rabelaisian note must each have its climax. Immersed in the natural world of Aran he reflects 'Once men sought in art to make natural things beautiful. Now we seek to make beautiful things natural'.[23] by time. It fulfils the hope of Victor Hugo that modern poetry

The process of making beautiful things natural in his own art results in the inclusion of what is low, base, irregular or grotesque, and it is incompatible with selection only on the basis of some notion of sublimity. Above all it allows for the degeneration brought about by time. It fulfils the hope of Victor Hugo that modern poetry would adopt the opposing forces of nature unresolved:

> . . . la poésie fera un grand pas, un pas décisif, un pas qui, pareil à la secousse d'un tremblement de terre, changera toute la face du monde intellectuel. Elle se mettra à faire comme la nature, à mêler dans ses créations, sans pourtant les confondre, l'ombre à la lumière, le grotesque au sublime, en d'autres termes, le corps à l'âme, la bête à l'esprit . . .[24]

Conclusion

(. . . poetry will take a great step which will be a decisive one, and
which will change the entire face of the world of the intellect like
the shock of an earthquake. It will begin to do as nature does: in
what it creates it will mix shade with light, the grotesque with the
sublime, in other words the body with the soul, the beast with the
spirit – without, however, confusing them . . .)

If it was from Hugo that Synge adopted the dualist aesthetic on
which his work is based, then Hugo too could have been responsible
for alerting him to the wealth of grotesque in the art of the Middle
Ages.[25]

NOTES

Throughout the notes, references to Synge's published works are to *J.M. Synge: Collected Works*, General ed. Robin Skelton (London: Oxford University Press, 1962–68; republished, Gerrards Cross: Colin Smythe; and Washington, D.C.: The Catholic University of America Press, 1982), abbreviated as *Works*. I *Poems*, ed. Robin Skelton; II *Prose*, ed. Alan Price; III and IV *Plays*, Ann Saddlemyer.

Chapter I

1. Maurice Bourgeois, *John Millington Synge and the Irish Theatre* (London, 1913), pp. 53 and 217.
2. Of those writers who have commented on specific connections between medieval literature and Synge's work, the most notable are:
   - Una Ellis-Fermor, who sees Synge as carrying on, through affinity of spirit, the tradition of ancient Irish nature poetry. See *The Irish Dramatic Movement* (London, 1939), p. 164.
   - Adelaide Duncan Estill, who identifies some of the medieval sources used by Synge, but does not attempt to relate them. See *The Sources of Synge* (Philadelphia, 1939).
   - Paul N. Robinson, who in an unpublished thesis (University of Wisconsin, Madison, 1971) entitled 'Medieval Aspects in the Plays of J.M. Synge' indicates some medieval attitudes on the part of the peasants in the plays: their religiosity, a dualistic concept of man, and the notion of man as *homo viator*. Literary parallels are noted only in passing.
   - Gertrude Schoepperle, who identifies the source for *The Well of the Saints* in her article 'John Synge and his Old French Farce', *North American Review*, October 1921, pp. 503–513.
   - Robin Skelton, who relates the persona adopted by Synge as poet, to the goliards. See *The Writings of J.M. Synge* (London, 1971), p. 164.
   - Following M.J. Sidnell and T.R. Henn, Declan Kiberd takes up the connection between Christy Mahon and Cuchulain: *Synge and the Irish Language* (London, 1979), Chapter 4. See also Chapter III, n. 41 of the present work.
3. Victor Hugo, *Théâtre Complet I* (Paris, 1963), 'Préface du Cromwell' pp. 409–454. First published 1827. See especially pp. 416, 419, 423, 425, and 450 for pertinent references.
4. Philip Thomson, *The Grotesque* (London, 1972), p. 27.
5. The concept of grotesque realism centred on the body is developed by Mikhail Bakhtin in *Rabelais and His World*, translated by Helen Iswolski (Boston, 1968).

6. Wolfgang Kayser, *The Grotesque in Art and Literature*, translated by Ulrich Weisstein (Indiana, 1963), p. 188.
7. *Works* IV, p. xxv.
8. See Clive Williams, 'Pestalozzi and John Synge' *Hermathena*, Dublin, Spring 1968, pp. 23–32.
9. Edward Stephens, *My Uncle John*, ed. Andrew Carpenter (Oxford, 1974), p. 37.
10. Ibid., p. 51.
11. *Works* II, p. 13.
12. See Edward Stephens, *My Uncle John*, p. 67.
13. *Works* II, p. 11.
14. Edward Stephens, *My Uncle John*, p. 85.
15. Ibid., p. 84.
16. Ibid., pp. 92–93.
17. David Greene & Edward Stephens, *J.M. Synge 1871–1909* (New York, 1959), p. 65.
18. Petit de Julleville, *Histoire de la langue et de la littérature Française* (Paris, 1896), III, p. 2. The biographical information on de Julleville comes from *La Grande encyclopédie des sciences, des lettres et des arts.*
19. *La Moralité de l'aveugle et du boiteux* is treated at length in *La Comédie et les moeurs*, pp. 99–103; *Le Théâtre en France*, pp. 39–41 repeats this material verbatim, except that the spelling of the quotations from André de la Vigne has been modernized; and *Répertoire du théâtre comique au moyen âge*, pp. 37–39 gives details of MSS and publications, as well as a synopsis of the play.
20. See Bourgeois, *Synge and the Irish Theatre*, p. 51.
21. Synge MS 4424, No. 44d in the Library of Trinity College Dublin, which is de Julleville's certificate, states that 'M. Synge a suivi avec assiduité mes cours et conférences . . .'. Greene and Stephens, pp. 58 and 69, tell us that Synge attended de Julleville's lectures both in summer 1895 and winter 1896.
22. Greene and Stephens, pp. 80 and 131.
23. Ibid., p. 125.
24. Bourgeois, *Synge and the Irish Theatre*, p. 53.
25. Ann Saddlemyer (ed.), *Some Letters of J.M. Synge to Lady Gregory and W.B. Yeats* (Dublin, 1971), p. 65.
26. The biographical data on de Jubainville come from the *Dictionnaire de biographie française.*
27. *Works* II, p. 384.
28. Ibid., p. 113.
29. Ann Saddlemyer, 'Synge to MacKenna: The Mature Years', in *Irish Renaissance* (Dublin, 1968), p. 65.
30. Edward Stephens, *My Uncle John*, p. 105.
31. E.R. Dodds (ed.), *Journal and Letters of Stephen MacKenna* (London, 1936), p. 66.
32. Quoted by Ann Saddlemyer, 'Synge to MacKenna', p. 67.
33. E.R. Dodds, *Journal and Letters of Stephen MacKenna*, p. 122.
34. Edward Stephens, *My Uncle John*, p. 138.
35. Greene and Stephens, p. 73.
36. Robin Skelton, *J.M. Synge and His World* (New York, 1971), p. 62.
37. 'A Celtic Theatre'.
38. Ann Saddlemyer (ed.), *Letters to Molly* (Cambridge, Mass., 1971), p. 192.

39. 'Celtic Mythology' and 'Irish Heroic Romance'.
40. Such a list, begun by Edward Stephens (Synge MS 6188), suggests many fascinating possibilities for further investigation, but in the light of Synge's avowed eclecticism it is also intimidating.
41. On Synge's reading while in Paris see Bourgeois, *Synge and the Irish Theatre*, p. 53.
42. *Works* II, pp. 30, 65 and 363.
43. Ibid., pp. 65 and 347.
44. Edward Stephens, *My Uncle John*, p. 98. It may be that Stephens was himself unclear about periods.
45. Bourgeois, *Synge and the Irish Theatre*, pp. 15 and 16.
46. Gottfried von Strassburg, *Tristan*, translated by A.T. Hatto (Harmondsworth, 1960), p. 107.
47. Ann Saddlemyer, *Letters to Molly*, p. 293.
48. 'An Epic of Ulster'.
49. *Works* II, p. 371.
50. Ann Saddlemyer, *Letters to Molly*, p. 46.
51. Ibid., p. 16.
52. Ibid., p. 22. I have been unable to identify the particular editions known to Synge, or any individual features in Synge's work for which he is evidently indebted to Malory.
53. *Works* II, pp. 347f.
54. Ibid., pp. 32f.
55. Synge used the term 'the prepared personality' in his Autobiography (*Works* II, p. 10), and Ann Saddlemyer discusses the concept in her essay 'Art, Nature, and "the Prepared Personality" ' in *Sunshine and the Moon's Delight*, ed. S.B. Bushrui (Gerrards Cross and Beirut, 1972), p. 107.
56. *Works* II, p. 116.
57. Ibid., p. 127.
58. Ibid., p. 199.
59. Ibid., p. 140.
60. Ibid. I am indebted to Ann Saddlemyer for suggesting the connection with folly.
61. *Works* II, p. 58.
62. Ibid., p. 65.
63. Ibid., p. 270.
64. Ibid., p. 259.
65. Ibid., p. 56.
66. Ibid., p. 57.
67. Ibid., p. 266.
68. *Works* IV, p. 53.
69. Style for Synge was a 'portrait of one's own personality, of the colour of one's own thought.': quoted by Ann Saddlemyer in ' "A Share in the Dignity of the World": J.M. Synge's Aesthetic Theory' in *The World of W.B. Yeats: Essays in Perspective*, ed. Robin Skelton and Ann Saddlemyer (Dublin, 1965), p. 245.
70. *Works* IV, p. xxv.
71. *Works* II, p. 265.
72. *Works* III, p. 185.
73. Ronald Gaskell, 'The Realism of J.M. Synge' in *Critical Quarterly*, London, Autumn 1963, pp. 242–248.

74. Bakhtin, *Rabelais*, p. 18.
75. See Ann Saddlemyer, ' "A Share in the Dignity of the World": J.M. Synge's Aesthetic Theory'.
76. Bakhtin, *Rabelais*, pp. 18–23.
77. For examples of the fair as a background event in Synge's plays, see *Works* III, pp. 38, 47, 51, 71, and 77; *Works* IV, pp. 11, 27, 29, 31, 37, 39, and 49; and an August fair is also mentioned in *The Playboy*, *Works* IV, p. 87. For Synge's remarks on fairs he attended see *Works* II, pp. 225–229 and 264–268. The circus reference is ibid., pp. 242–244.
78. Allan Wade (ed.) *The Letters of W.B. Yeats* (London, 1954), p. 671.
79. *Works* II, p. 124.
80. Ibid., p. 92.
81. Ibid., pp. 59.
82. *Works* III, p. 174.
83. *Works* II, p. 135.
84. Ibid., p. 117.
85. Synge MS 4384, f.42.
86. *Works* II, p. 24.
87. Ibid., p. 74.
88. Ibid., p. 75. Padraic Colum too remarked on the keen being a lament, not for one man dead but for the dead generally, and noted that the voices of the keening women became remote and unfamiliar: see *The Road Round Ireland* (New York, 1926), pp. 180f.
89. *Works* II, pp. 74–76. For details of wake festivities see Vivian Mercier, *The Irish Comic Tradition* (Oxford, 1962), pp. 51–53; also, see W.G. Wood-Martin, *Traces of the Elder Faiths in Ireland* (London, 1902).
90. *Works* II, p. x.
91. *Works* III, p. 183.
92. *Works* III, p. 174.
93. *Works* IV, p. xxv.
94. *Works* III, p. 223.
95. Ann Saddlemyer, 'Synge to MacKenna', p. 66.
96. *Works* IV, p. xxv, Synge writes of *The Playboy*: '. . . the romantic note and a Rabelaisian note are working to a climax through a great part of the play'.
97. *Works* III, p. 186.
98. *Works* II, p. 38.
99. Ibid.
100. Synge's early morbidity was such as to make him decide against having children: 'But I will never create beings to suffer as I am suffering'; and again in the poem in Vita Vecchia we find:

>   Cold, joyless I will live, though clean,
>   Nor, by my marriage, mould to earth
>   Young lives to see what I have seen,
>   To curse – as I have cursed – their birth.

    Works II, pp. 9 and 19.
101. Compare Pierre de Ronsard, *Poésies Choisies*, ed. Françoise Jankovsky (Paris, 1969), pp. 422–424 with Synge, *Works* I, p. 19. (If nature should engender something from a corpse lying rotten, and if generation occurs from corruption, then a vine will spring from the stomach and from the paunch of the good Rabelais . . .)

102. *Works* IV, pp. 296f.
103. Ibid., p. 301.
104. Ibid., p. 121.
105. Cf. François Rabelais, *Gargantua and Pantagruel* I, translated by Thomas Urquhart (London, 1929), pp. 148f.
106. Quoted by Ann Saddlemyer in ' "A Share in the Dignity of the World": J.M. Synge's Aesthetic Theory', p. 245; 'A Letter About J.M. Synge by Jack B. Yeats', *Works* II, p. 402.
107. *Works* II, p. 349.

Chapter II

1. See Gertrude Schoepperle, 'John Synge and his Old French Farce', pp. 503–513.
2. See P.L. Jacob, *Recueil de Farces, Sotties et Moralités*, (Paris, 1882), pp. 211–230. Petit de Julleville writes of de la Vigne's *mystère* that it was still unpublished, and that it consisted of 10,000 lines, in his *Mystères II*, p. 539; in *Le Théâtre en France*, however, he writes that it consisted of 20,000 lines; and his description of the MS in *Répertoire du Théâtre*, p. 37, says that it fills 233 of the 264 pages. What is pertinent is that the *mystère* was long.
3. See P.L. Jacob, *Recueil de Farces* p. 212.
4. Ibid., p. 214, and de Julleville, *Théâtre en France*, p. 31.
5. De Julleville, *Mystères II*, p. 535.
6. Gertrude Schoepperle, p. 504.
7. Greene and Stephens, p. 79.
8. See P.L. Jacob, ibid., and Edouard Fournier, *Le Théâtre français avant la Renaissance* (Paris, 1872), pp. 155ff.
9. Greene and Stephens, p. 79.
10. All these issues are raised in the Introduction to *La Comédie et les Moeurs*, pp. 1–13. They recur throughout this work, as well as elsewhere in the corpus.
11. De Julleville, *Répertoire du théâtre comique*, p. 38; *La Comédie et les Moeurs*, p. 102; and *Mystères II*, p. 537.
12. Edouard Fournier, p. 155.
13. P.L. Jacob, p. 211. Translations are my own unless otherwise indicated.
14. De Julleville, *Théâtre en France*, p. 36f.
15. De Julleville, *La Comédie et les Moeurs*, pp. 350–353, and *Théâtre en France*, p. 47. Synge, *Works* IV, p. 3.
16. See P.L. Jacob, pp. 228–230.
17. De Julleville, *Théâtre en France*, p. 47.
18. In the plastic arts this tendency is particularly evident, e.g. human and animal combinations in Gothic and Celtic MSS, and the carvings of the medieval cathedrals.
19. Although there is an emotional interdependence between Pozzo and Lucky, there is also a physical interdependence brought about by their respective blindness and dumbness in the second act. See Samuel Beckett, *Waiting for Godot* (London, 1979), pp. 77 and 89.
20. *Works* III, p. 151.
21. Ibid.

22. See Mario Roques (ed.) *Le Garçon et l'Aveugle* (Paris, 1912), p. iii.
23. P.L. Jacob, p. 216.
24. *Works* III, p. 264.
25. Ibid. Synge was using the term 'current' in a musical sense, in accordance with 'crescendo' in his analysis of the first act.
26. Ibid.
27. *Works* III, p. 151.
28. Ibid. p. 265.
29. P.L. Jacob, *Recueil de Farces* p. 222. It is noteworthy that de Julleville did not use this edition of the play. Although he has retained the Old French spellings in *La Comédie et les Moeurs*, they differ in many cases from P.L. Jacob's. We can tell that Synge made his transcriptions from *La Comédie et les Moeurs* because his quotations from the play correspond with that and not with those in Modern French which appear in the otherwise identical passage in de Julleville's *Théâtre en France*, the work where Synge's biographers suggest he found it (Greene and Stephens, p. 139).
30. *Works* III, p. 103.
31. Ibid.
32. Ibid., p. 266.
33. P.L. Jacob, p. 221.
34. *Works* III, p. 89.
35. Ibid., p. 135.
36. *Works* II, p. 386.
37. *Works* III, p. xxvii.
38. *Works* II, p. 349.
39. Ibid., p. 393.
40. *Works* III, p. xxviii.
41. *Works* IV, p. xxxi.
42. See de Julleville, *La Comédie et les Moeurs*, p. 99.
43. *Works* III, p. 69.
44. Ibid., p. 145.
45. Ibid., p. xxvii. It is interesting to note that de Julleville complained that many contemporary plays did not stand up to reading: *Théâtre en France*, p. 425.
46. *Works* II, p. 398.
47. *Works* IV, pp. 49 and 173.
48. De Julleville, *Répertoire du théâtre comique*, p. 24.
49. Lady Gregory records that Synge was 'most enthusiastic' about her rendering of *Les Fourberies de Scapin* in Kiltartanese: *Seventy Years: Being the Autobiography of Lady Gregory*, ed. Colin Smythe, (Gerrards Cross, 1973), p. 420.
50. De Julleville, *La Comédie et les Moeurs*, p. 2, and *Théâtre en France*, p. 419.
51. De Julleville, *Théâtre en France*, pp. 426f and 413.
52. Ibid., pp. 427–429.
53. Ibid., p. 431.
54. See *Works* III, pp. xxviiif.
55. De Julleville, *La Comédie et les Moeurs*, p. 305.
56. Ibid., pp. 304f. The same passage appears *verbatim* in *Les Mystères I*, p. 277.
57. An examination of Synge's notebooks with this connection in mind could reveal notes from Hugo's Preface. Declan Kiberd has kindly indicated to me that Synge MS 4416 (Combridges Diary 1895) contains the entry 'Victor Hugo: Odes' for March 18th.

58. Victor Hugo, *Théâtre Complet* I, p. 426.
59. Ibid.
60. Ibid.
61. Ibid., p. 427.
62. Ibid., p. 429.
63. Ibid., p. 437.
64. *Works* II, p. 349.
65. Victor Hugo, *Théâtre Complet* I, p. 437.
66. Quoted by Ann Saddlemyer, *Works* IV, p. xxvi.

Chapter III

1. See Gerard Murphy, *Saga and Myth in Ancient Ireland* (Cork, 1961, reprint 1971), pp. 41f.
2. See M.A. O'Brien in *Irish Sagas*, ed. Myles Dillon (Cork, 1968) pp. 68f.
3. *Works* II, p. 367.
4. Eleanor Hull, *The Cuchullin Saga in Irish Literature* (London, 1898), p. xxvi; de Jubainville, *L'Epopée celtique en Irlande* (Paris, 1892), pp. 81–147.
5. De Jubainville, *Introduction à l'étude de la littérature celtique*, pp. 301f.
6. Ernst Windisch, *Irische Texte I* (Leipzig, 1880), pp. 235ff.
7. *Works* II, p. 354.
8. Ibid., p. 360.
9. George Henderson, *Fled Bricrend: The Feast of Bricriu* (Dublin, 1899), p. xviii.
10. See Lady Gregory, *Cuchulain of Muirthemne* (Gerrards Cross, 1973), p. 271.
11. *Works* II, p. 370.
12. Ibid., p. 95.
13. *Works* IV, p. 99.
14. Ibid., pp. 125 and 139.
15. Ibid., p. 169.
16. Ibid., p. 171.
17. Ibid., p. 173.
18. Ibid., pp. 71 and 73.
19. Ibid., pp. 73, 85, 103, and 119.
20. De Jubainville, *L'Epopée celtique*, p. 107; George Henderson, *Fled Bricrend*, pp. 42f; Thomas Kinsella, *The Táin* (Dublin, 1969), p. 120.
21. *Works* IV, pp. 143 and 161.
22. George Henderson, *Fled Bricrend*, pp. 99f.
23. *Works* IV, pp. 119, 125, 161, and 171.
24. Ibid., p. 75; cf de Jubainville, *L'Epopée celtique*, p. 99.
25. *Works* IV, pp. 75, 67, and 69.
26. Ibid., p. 85; de Jubainville, *L'Epopée celtique*, p. 106.
27. *Works* IV, p. 89.
28. Ibid., p. 97.
29. George Henderson, *Fled Bricrend*, p. 199.
30. Ibid.
31. Eleanor Hull, *The Cuchullin Saga*, p. xxviii.

32. *Sir Gawain and the Green Knight*, eds. J.R.R. Tolkein and E.V. Gordon, 2nd edition revised by Norman Davis (Oxford, 1968), 11.2509–2512.
33. *Works* IV, p. 173. Christy's refusal to accept the petticoat and shawl in which the widow Quin and Sara wish to save him might be contrasted with Gawain's acceptance of the green girdle to save himself.
34. See *Works* IV, pp. 271f.
35. Ibid., pp. 281f.
36. Robin Skelton, *The writings of J.M. Synge*, p. 70.
37. *Works* IV, p. 102.
38. Ibid.
39. See ibid., p. 169.
40. T.S. Eliot, 'Tradition and the Individual Talent', *The Sacred Wood* (London, Reprint 1976), p. 49.
41. T.R. Henn, in his Introduction to *The Playboy* writes of it in terms of mock-heroic and half parody: *The Plays and Poems of J.M. Synge* (London, 1973), pp. 57f; and in *Hermathena* CXII, Dublin Autumn 1971, p. 16 he describes it as a 'semi-parody of the Celtic heroic cycles'. M.J. Sidnell, in his article 'Synge's Playboy and the Champion of Ulster', *Dalhousie Review* XLV Spring, 1965, p. 58 sees Christy as 'Synge's ironic comment on the concept of the hero and heroic virtues'. More recently, Declan Kiberd has written of 'The Playboy as Heroic Parody' in his book *Synge and the Irish Language*, pp. 109–121.
42. *Works* II, pp. 59 and 66.
43. Quoted by Ann Saddlemyer in 'A Share in the Dignity of the World', p. 247.

Chapter IV

1. Lady Gregory, *Seventy Years*, p. 403.
2. For a detailed introduction to the tale, see Vernam Hull (ed.), *Longes Mac N-Uislenn: The Exile of the Sons of Uisliu* (New York, 1949), pp. 1–60.
3. *Works* II, p. 353.
4. De Jubainville, *L'Epopée celtique en Irlande*, pp. 217–236.
5. *Works* II, pp. 352 and 354.
6. See, for example, Eleanor Hull, *The Cuchullin Saga*, p. 22.
7. See *Irische Texte* II, (Leipzig, 1887), pp. 109–122 for Whitley Stokes's introduction to this version, and ibid. pp. 153–178 for his English translation of it.
8. See *L'Epopée celtique en Irlande*, pp. 219f for de Jubainville's introduction to this version, and pp. 220–236 for Georges Dottin's French translation.
9. *Works* II, p. 367.
10. Ibid.
11. Ibid., p. 372.
12. Ibid., p. 373.
13. See *Oidhe Chloinne Uisnigh: The Fate of the Children of Uisneach* by Andrew MacCurtin, (Dublin, 1898), Introduction, p. v.
14. See Ann Saddlemyer, in *Works* IV, p. 368.
15. Andrew MacCurtin, *Oidhe Chloinne Uisnigh*, p. 9.
16. *Works* II, p. 368.
17. Compare Andrew MacCurtin, *Oidhe Chloinne Uisnigh*, pp. 9 and 12.

18. *Works* IV, p. 183.
19. Ibid., p. 187.
20. Ibid., p. 211.
21. Ibid., p. 189.
22. Andrew MacCurtin, *Oidhe Chloinne Uisnigh*, p. 17.
23. *Works* IV, pp. 235 and 225.
24. See *Works* IV, p. 253, where Deirdre comes between Naisi and Conchubor using the grave as a force of reconciliation; and pp. 255–257 where she insists that Naisi face his loyalty to Ainnle and Ardan.
25. *Works* IV, p. 241.
26. Andrew MacCurtin, *Oidhe Chloinne Uisnigh*, p. 27.
27. Compare *Works* IV, p. 207, and Andrew MacCurtin, *Oidhe Chloinne Uisnigh*, p. 15.
28. *Works* IV, p. 205.
29. Examples of colour-imagery can be found in *Works* IV, pp. 187, 191, 209, 221, and 231. Animal imagery is treated on p. 91 of the present work.
30. *Works* II, pp. 367f.
31. Synge MS 4341.
32. *Works* II, p. 359.
33. Andrew MacCurtin, *Oidhe Chloinne Uisnigh*, p. 73. The present work was near its final form when Declan Kiberd's book *Synge and the Irish Language* appeared. There a more detailed discussion of Synge's translation of MacCurtin's text is given on pp. 81–84.
34. Synge MS 4341, f.54.
35. E.R. Dodds, *Journal and Letters of Stephen MacKenna*, p. 39.
36. *Works* II, pp. 360 and 363.
37. Geoffrey Keating, *Foras Feasa ar Éirinn: The History of Ireland*, Vol. II, ed. David Comyn (Dublin, 1905), pp. 190–197.
38. *Works* II, pp. 352, 358, and 361.
39. Ibid., p. 362.
40. Ibid., p. 358.
41. Cf. Keating, *Foras Feasa ar Éirinn* p. 192 'agus ris an bhfáilte cuiris sáthadh sleighe thríd' (and with the welcome he gave a stab of his spear through him); and *Works* IV, p. 235.
42. Keating, *Foras Feasa ar Éirinn*, p. 196.
43. *Works* IV, p. 223.
44. Ibid., p. 209.
45. See Vernam Hull, *Longes Mac N-Uislenn*, p. 63.
46. Douglas Hyde, *A Literary History of Ireland* (London, 1967), p. 303, fn 2.
47. *Works* II, pp. 385f.
48. Compare *Works* II, p. 361 and Douglas Hyde, *Literary History of Ireland*, p. 556.
49. See p. 00 and note 32 above; compare Douglas Hyde, *Literary History of Ireland*, p. 319.
50. See Douglas Hyde, *The Three Sorrows of Storytelling* (London, 1895), text of *Deirdre* pp. 1–39; note on variant endings p. 150. Examples of Hyde's linguistic influence on Synge are given by Bourgeois in *Synge and the Irish Theatre*, p. 277, and these are taken up and expanded on by Michael O h-Aodha in his Introduction to the reprint of Douglas Hyde's *Love Songs of Connacht* (Shannon, 1969), pp. viif.

51. *Works* II, pp. 369f.
52. Compare ibid. with *Oidhe Chloinne Uisnigh*, pp. 85f.
53. See Colin Meir, *The Ballads and Songs of W.B. Yeats: The Anglo-Irish Heritage in Subject and Style* (London, 1974), 'Yeats's Debt to Anglo-Irish Dialect' pp. 65–90.
54. Robin Skelton, *The Writings of J.M. Synge*, p. 135.
55. Lady Gregory, *Cuchulain of Muirthemne*, p. 93. It is interesting to note that de Jubainville had translated the relevant line from Cathbad's prophecy as 'Tu auras une petite tombe quelque part', thus not stressing Deirdre's separation from the sons of Uisneach.
56. Lady Gregory, *Cuchulain of Muirthemne*, p. 112.
57. Ibid., p. 113.
58. *Works* IV, p. 209.
59. Ibid., p. 231.
60. Ibid., p. 235.
61. Ibid., p. 248.
62. Ibid., p. 265.
63. Lady Gregory, *Cuchulain of Muirthemne*, pp. 115f.
64. *Works* IV, p. 256.
65. Ibid., p. 269.
66. Ibid., p. 179: Yeats's Preface to *Deirdre*.
67. Ibid., p. xxvii.
68. Ibid., p. 224. Compare George Russell, *Deirdre* (Chicago, 1970).
69. George Russell, *Deirdre*, p. 12.
70. *Works* I, p. 38.
71. Compare George Russell, *Deirdre*, p. 11 and *Works* IV, pp. 185 and 187.
72. *Works* IV, p. 219.
73. George Russell, *Deirdre*, p. 17.
74. *Works* IV, pp. 207 and 231.
75. W.B. Yeats, *Collected Plays* (London, 1977), pp. 175, 189, 187 and 202.
76. Ibid., p. 179.
77. Ibid., p. 171.
78. Ibid., pp. 193 and 201.
79. See the dedication of Yeats's *Deirdre* and the memorandum which Synge wrote to Yeats in December 1906, *Works* IV, pp. xxxif.
80. T.S. Eliot, *Selected Essays* (London, 1951), p. 206.
81. *Works* IV, p. 179.
82. Ibid., p. 235.
83. See William Willeford, *The Fool and His Scepter* (Evanston, Illinois, 1969) pp. 11f.

Chapter V

1. George Steiner, *After Babel: Aspects of Language and Translation* (Oxford 1975), p. 235.
2. Letters to Louis Untermeyer and Leon Brodsky, quoted by Ann Saddlemyer, *Works* IV, p. xxvi.
3. Letter to Yeats, quoted by Robin Skelton, *Works* I, p. xv.

4. The rate of occurrence of Hiberno-English structures in Synge's language is treated by Alan Bliss in his essay on 'The Language of Synge' in *J.M. Synge: Centenary Papers*, ed. Maurice Harmon (Dublin, 1972), pp. 35–62; see especially pp. 41f. Declan Kiberd gives a list of Hiberno-English features of Synge's style on p. 81 of *Synge and the Irish Language*.

5. Works IV, pp. 191, 237, 249; and I, pp. 79 and 82. It is noteworthy that on occasion, in *Deirdre*, Synge used the unsyncopated form with quite different effect, e.g. 'It is I Deirdre will be crouching in a dark place' (IV, p. 261), and 'It is I am out of my wits' (IV, p. 267). In both cases, the effect is ironically dignified self-assertion.

6. Robin Skelton, *The Writings of J.M. Synge*, p. 135.

7. *Works* IV, pp. 211, 221, and 191.

8. *Works* III, p. 275.

9. *Works* I, pp. 80, 82, 93; and IV, pp. 191 and 247.

10. Bourgeois, *Synge and the Irish Theatre*, p. 226.

11. *Works* I, p. 79; and IV, pp. 189 and 261.

12. *Works* I, pp. 80, 84; and IV, pp. 221 and 223.

13. P.L. Henry, in *An Anglo-Irish Dialect of North Roscommon*, (Zurich, 1957), discusses the occurrence of such forms; and a concise introduction to the Irish language can be found in David Greene's booklet, *The Irish Language* (Cork, 1966). However, the infra-structure will be evident to the bilingual reader.

14. *Works* I, pp. 80, 82, 84, 91, and 99. It also occurs with (inadvertent?) comic effect at the opening of *The Shadow*, when Nora, making small talk with the tramp, who has indicated that he is walking from Brittas to Aughrim, says: 'Is it walking on your feet, stranger?', and he replies 'On my two feet, lady of the house . . .'.

15. *Works* I, pp. 79, 80, 100; and IV, pp. 185 and 189.

16. Kuno Meyer, *Ancient Irish Nature Poetry* (London, 1911), p. xi.

17. *Works* IV, pp. 193, 187, 195, 185, and 191.

18. *Works* IV, pp. 187, 183 and 193.

19. *Works* II, p. 60.

20. W.B. Yeats, *Essays and Introductions* (London, 1961), pp. 335f.

21. See Paul Zumthor, *Langue et techniques poétiques a l'époque romane* (Paris, 1963), p. 33; and 'Document et monument' in *Revue des sciences humaines* (Lille, Jan.–Mar. 1960), pp. 5–19. I am indebted to Margaret Bridges for bringing this author to my attention, and for enlightening exchanges on medieval literature.

22. See Zumthor, *Langue et techniques poétiques*, pp. 40 and 50.

23. A glossary for Synge's lexical peculiarities, compiled by Alan Bliss, can be found in S.B. Bushrui's *Sunshine and the Moon's Delight* (Gerrards Cross and Beirut, 1972), pp. 297–316.

24. Note, for example, the difficulties experienced by Yeats in overcoming his comic expectations of dialect: 'When I was a boy I was often troubled and sorrowful because Scottish dialect was capable of noble use, but the Irish of roystering humour only; and this error fixed on my imagination by so many novelists and rhymers made me listen badly.' (*Essays and Introductions*, p. 335.)

25. In the second volume of his *Histoire de la langue et de la littérature française* dealing with medieval literature, de Julleville himself wrote the chapter on poets, pp. 385–392.

189

26. See his *Notions générales sure les origines et sur l'histoire de la langue française*, p. 10.
27. Ibid., p. 5.
28. Preface to his poems, *Works* I, p. xxxvi.
29. Bourgeois, *Synge and the Irish Theatre*, p. 93.
30. Una Ellis-Fermor, *The Irish Dramatic Movement*, p. 164. Much of the Synge material now collected was not readily available to Miss Ellis-Fermor.
31. *Works* II, p. 353.
32. Padraic Colum, *The Road Round Ireland*, p. 25.
33. *Works* I, pp. 30, 33, 34, 39, 60 and 61.
34. Skelton, *The Writings of J.M. Synge*, p. 164.
35. See Ernest Hoepffner, *Les Troubadours* (Paris, 1955), p. 15.
36. Ibid., pp. 15, 16, and 199; see also E. Farsal, *Les Jongleurs en France au moyen-âge* (Paris, 1910), pp. 73–79.
37. See John Fox, *A Literary History of France: The Middle Ages* (London, 1974), p. 183.
38. See André Moret (ed.), *Anthologie du Minnesang* (Paris, 1955) p. 20.
39. See Olive Sayce, *Poets of the Minnesang* (Oxford, 1957), p. xi.
40. The Irish lyric tradition is described by Eleanor Knott in the booklet *Irish Classical Poetry* (Dublin, 1960), which is reprinted in *Early Irish Literature*, introduced by James Carney, (London, 1966).
41. Skelton, *The Writings of J.M. Synge*, p. 157.
42. See Whitley Stokes and John Strachan (eds.), *Thesaurus Palaeohibernicus* (Cambridge, 1905), pp. 354 and 296. Synge wrote about the hymn to Meyerfeld: see *Works* III, p. 90.
43. F.N. Robinson (ed.), *The Poetical Works of Chaucer* (Oxford, 1933), p. 635. On the Latin tradition see E.R. Curtius, *European Literature and the Latin Middle Ages*, transl. Willard Task (New York, 1953), pp. 470–473.
44. Richard Stanihurst, quoted by Eleanor Knott in *Irish Classical Poetry*, p. 73.
45. Cf. *Works* I, pp. 82f with Joseph Bédier (ed.), *Les Chansons de Colin Muset* (Paris, 1912), pp. 22–24.
46. For discussion of 'registers' in the medieval context, see Paul Zumthor, *Langue et techniques poétiques*, p. 141–145; motifs connected with the 'good life' register are dealt with on p. 156.
47. Details of editions with musical texts can be found in Joseph Bédier's Introduction to *Les Chansons de Colin Muset*, p. iv.
48. See de Julleville, *Les Comédiens*, p. 20.
49. A. Mary (ed.), *François Villon: Oeuvres* (Paris, 1970), pp.60f and *Works* I, p. 79.
50. Dante Gabriel Rossetti, *Poems*, ed. Oswald Doughty (London, 1957), p. 101, 'His Mother's Service to Our Lady'. Such reaction is the more likely since Synge's poem 'Queens' is a vigorous antidote to Rossetti's version of Villon's 'The Ballad of Dead Ladies', ibid., p. 100.
51. See A. Mary, *François Villon: Oeuvres*, ibid.
52. See Gerard Murphy (ed.), *Early Irish Lyrics* (Oxford, 1965), 'The Lament of the Old Woman of Beare', pp. 74–83; 'These Hands have been Withered', pp. 166f; and 'Once I was Yellow-haired', pp. 168f, for example.
53. Gerard Murphy, ibid., pp. 207f, writes that Kuno Meyer published a text based on a T.C.D. MS, together with a translation in *Otia Merseiana* I (1899), pp. 121–128.

54. Charles Algernon Swinburne, *The Poems* Vol. III (London, 1905), pp. 133–136.
55. Joerg Schaefer (ed.) *Walther von der Vogelweide: Werke* (Darstadt, 1972), p. 82. Thanks are due to Anne Oldcorn for help in translating from the German.
56. See Olive Sayce, *Poets of the Minnesang*, Introduction and pp. 92 and 98f.
57. Ibid., p. x; and André Moret, *Anthologie du Minnesang*, p. 35.
58. Synge MS 4412, f.9v.
59. Synge MS 4391, f.7.
60. Synge conveyed the depth of his feeling for his mother in a letter to Molly Allgood at the time: 'I cannot tell you how unspeakably sacred her memory seems to me There is nothing in the world better or nobler than a single-hearted wife and mother', Ann Saddlemyer, *Letters to Molly*, p. 299.
61. Jacques Crépet et Georges Blin (eds.), *Baudelaire: Les Fleurs du Mal* (Paris, 1968), 'Le Reniement de Saint Pierre', pp. 237–239. I am indebted to Professor Werner Stauffacher for suggesting this connection. Synge's reference to Baudelaire's morbidity appears in *Works* IV, p. 3.
62. Francesco de Sanctis, *Saggio critico sul Petrarca* (Bari, 1954), pp. 226–227.
63. Serafino Riva, *La Tradizione celtica e la moderna letteratura irlandese* (Rome, 1937), pp. 274 and 282.
64. See *Works* I, pp. 89, 90, 95, and 100 for examples of authorial self-consciousness; Ibid., pp. 101f for affected modesty; and for treatment of poetic conventions in the Latin Middle Ages, see Ernst Curtius, *European Literature in the Latin Middle Ages*, especially pp. 407–412. For discussion of Petrarchan conventions, see Leonard Forster, *The Icy Fire: Five Studies in European Petrarchism* (Cambridge, 1969), particularly pp. 1–60.
65. Giacomo Leopardi, *Opere* (Milan, 1956), pp. 93–95. Compare *Works* I, p. 81.
66. See Victor Hugo, *Théâtre Complet* I, pp. 438f and 442f.

Chapter VI

1. *I Corinthians*, iii: 19. See also *I Cor.*, i: 18; i: 25; iii: 18; and iv: 10; and *II Cor.*, xi: 19; and xvi: 17.
2. See Desiderius Erasmus, *Praise of Folly*, transl. Betty Radice (Harmondsworth, 1971), pp. 196–199.
3. *Works* II, p. 386.
4. See François Rabelais, *Gargantua and Pantagruel*, pp. 31–36; and for the influence of Erasmus on Rabelais see Walter Kaiser, *Praisers of Folly* (London, 1964), p. 104.
5. See Robin Skelton, *The Writings of J.M. Synge*, p. 117.
6. Bourgeois, *Synge and the Irish Theatre*, p. 51, fn.1.
7. For a history of the fool see Enid Welsford, *The Fool: His Social and Literary History* (New York, 1961); and for details of the Festival of Fools see Petit de Julleville, *Les Comédiens en France*, pp. 29–41, and *Le Théâtre en France*, p. 61; also A.P. Rossiter, *English Drama from Early Times to the Elizabethans* (London, 1950), p. 56.
8. *Works*, I, p. xxxvi.
9. See William Willeford, *The Fool and His Scepter,* pp. 79–81.

10. Enid Welsford, *The Fool*, pp. 266 and 323.
11. Barbara Swain, *Fools and Folly* (New York, 1972), p. 1.
12. Synge MS 4373, f.11.
13. *Works* III, p. 37.
14. *Works* II, p. 202.
15. Ibid., p. 209.
16. Ibid., pp. 209f.
17. Ann Saddlemyer, 'Synge to MacKenna', p. 66; and *Works* II, p. 223.
18. *Works* III, p. 47. The connection with Christ is further endorsed by the fact that it was 'the third day they found Darcy' after the tramp had last heard him, whereas Synge's original story had told of the madman being found the following morning: *Works* III, p. 39.
19. *Works* III, pp. 39 and 41, 51–55; 55, 57; 43 and 57.
20. Ibid., p. 149.
21. Ibid., pp. 103, 121, and 137.
22. Ibid., pp. 113, 119; 117, 119; 139; 141.
23. Ibid., p. 67.
24. See Enid Welsford, *The Fool*, p. 240. Martin's blindness, in addition to his imaginative vision suggests the traditional connection with the poet.
25. *Works* IV, pp. 29 and 35.
26. Ibid., pp. 7, 23, 31, 37, and 49.
27. See Walter Kaiser, *Praisers of Folly* (London, 1964), p. 130.
28. *Works* IV, pp. 37 and 49.
29. Ibid., p. 49. William Willeford points out that the fool is traditionally deprived of rights and responsibilities because of his deficiencies, while at the same time he remains dependent on the social group from which he is outlawed: *The Fool and His Scepter*, p. 14.
30. Alan Bliss glosses 'playboy' as apparently a translation of the Irish *buachaill báire*, meaning a trickster; he quotes a tentative definition as 'a tricky, independable sort of person', and indicates that in addition to such connotations there is also a note of admiration, which may be ironic in Synge's use of the term: 'A Synge Glossary', p. 311.
31. *Works* IV, pp. 294f.
32. Ibid., pp. 69 and 137.
33. Ibid., p. 79.
34. See William Willeford, *The Fool and His Scepter*, p. xx on the matter of the fool's uncertain identity; and p. 137 on his representing values which transcend those of non-fools.
35. Ibid., p. 38 on pairs of fools.
36. Compare *Works* IV, pp. 173 and 143 with Miguel de Cervantes Saavedra, *The Adventures of Don Quixote*, transl. J.M. Cohen (Harmondsworth, 1950), pp. 66f.
37. William Willeford, *The Fool and His Scepter*, p. 166.
38. Ann Saddlemyer, 'Deirdre of the Sorrows: Literature first . . . drama afterwards' in *J.M. Synge: Centenary Papers*, p. 104.
39. See William Willeford, *The Fool and His Scepter*, p. 208–225 on the fool in *King Lear*.
40. Ibid., pp. 174–199 and 222 on the fool and the woman.
41. Ibid. p. 188.
42. *Works* IV, p. 223.

43. Ibid., p. 382: Ann Saddlemyer, from the first indication of the later character of Owen in the drafts, records his reply to Ainnle's decision not to return with Fergus as 'There's wisdom. Now Ardan double that'. Ibid., p. 385 she notes the increasing distinction between the characters of Fergus and Owen, and with it the increasing emphasis on Owen's madness.
44. *Works* IV, p. 221.
45. Ibid., p. 235.
46. Ibid., p. 391.
47. Ibid., pp. 181, 221, 235, and 223.
48. Ibid., pp. 243 and 189.
49. Ibid., p. 197.
50. Ibid., pp. 219, 218, 221, and 219.
51. Ibid., pp. 193, 265, and 267.

Chapter VII

1. *Works* II, p. 70.
2. Ibid., p. 136.
3. Ibid., p. 159.
4. Mikhail Bakhtin, *Rabelais and his World*, pp. 26, 118, 320–322.
5. *Works* IV, p. 103.
6. Ibid., p. 89.
7. See Per Nykrog, *Les Fabliaux*, (Copenhagen, 1957), p. 97. Synge could readily have known this fabliau in R. de Montaiglon and G. Reynaud's *Recueil Général et Complet des Fabliaux des XIII et XIV Siècles* (Paris, 1872–1890). The genre enjoyed a considerable vogue around 1900, probably helped by Bédier's *Les Fabliaux* published in 1893, according to Nykrog, p. iv.
8. *Works* IV, pp. 223 and 221.
9. Ibid., p. 109.
10. Ibid., pp. 137, 139.
11. Ibid., p. 155; also on p. 153 Pegeen had found fault with Shawn for his lack of savagery; *Works* III, p. 113.
12. *Works* II, p. 275.
13. *Works* I, p. 56.
14. *Works* IV, pp. 97 and 171.
15. Ibid., p. 49.
16. Ibid., p. 73.
17. *Works* III, p. 133.
18. *Works* III, pp. 145 and 79.
19. *Works* IV, pp. 33 and 135.
20. *Works* II, p. 192.
21. Ibid., p. 214.
22. *Works* IV, p. 133.
23. Ibid., p. 135.
24. *Works* I, pp. 21, 36, 55, and 112.
25. *Works* IV, pp. 67 and 221.
26. Ibid., p. 153.

27. Ibid., p. 53.
28. *Works* IV, p. 83.
29. Synge's words, quoted by Ann Saddlemyer in ' "A Share in the Dignity of the World": J.M. Synge's Aesthetic Theory', p. 252.
30. *Works* I, p. 34; François Villon, *Oeuvres*, p. 000
31. *Works* IV, p. 23.
32. Ibid., pp. 205 and 223. On the Buridan reference see D.B. Wyndham Lewis, *François Villon* (New York, 1928), p. 350.
33. *Works* II, p. 336.
34. Ibid., p. 249.
35. On the emotional effects of incongruity see Arthur Clayborough, *The Grotesque in English Literature* (Oxford, 1965), pp. 70f.
36. T.R. Henn, *The Plays and Poems of J.M. Synge*, p. 62, quotation from fn.3.

Chapter VIII

1. W.B. Yeats, *Autobiographies* (London, 1955), p. 345.
2. *Works* I, pp. 56f.
3. Ann Saddlemyer, 'Synge to MacKenna', pp. 72f.
4. Quoted by Ann Saddlemyer in ' "A Share in the Dignity of the World": J.M. Synge's Aesthetic Theory', p. 243.
5. 'Vita Vecchia', *Works* II, p. 23.
6. *Works* III, p. 51.
7. Ibid., pp. 73 and 95.
8. Ibid., pp. 137 and 105.
9. Ibid., p. 145.
10. Quoted by Ann Saddlemyer in ' "A Share in the Dignity of the World": J.M. Synge's Aesthetic Theory', p. 243.
11. *Works* IV, p. 255.
12. Ibid., pp. 257f.
13. Alan Price, *Synge and Anglo-Irish Drama* (London, 1961), p. 207.
14. *Works* IV, pp. 267–9 and 223–5.
15. Ibid., pp. 223, 219, 223, 225, and 235.
16. *Works* IV, pp. 239, 211, 261, and 265.
17. *Christopher Marlowe: Works*, ed. Tucker Brooke (Oxford, 1910) p. 367.
18. *Works* III, p. 51.
19. Ibid., pp. 53 and 55.
20. Ibid., p. 97.
21. *Works* IV, pp. 247, 267, 243, 251, and 253.
22. *Works* III, pp. 141 and 149.
23. *Works* IV, p. 59.
24. See Synge's programme notes for the first production of *The Playboy, Works* IV, p. 363.
25. *Works* IV, p. 386.
26. W.B. Yeats, *Autobiographies*, p. 487.
27. *Works* IV, p. 179, fn 1.
   Herbert Fackler in 'J.M. Synge's *Deirdre of the Sorrows*: Beauty Only', *Modern*

Drama X (1969), pp. 404–409, mistakenly treats Yeats's statement that 'there is nothing grotesque but beauty only' as his ultimate assessment of *Deirdre*, in order to support his own view of the play as 'simple, almost stark'.

28. Ibid., p. 291.
29. Victor Hugo, *Théâtre Complet* I, p. 419.
30. Ibid., p. 450.

Chapter IX

1. Henri Bergson, *Le Rire* (Paris, 1972) p. 3. *Le Rire* first appeared in serial in the Revue de Paris in 1899, and the following year Bergson was appointed to a professorship at the Collège de France where Synge attended lectures.
2. Oscar Wilde, *The Importance of Being Earnest* in *Complete Works* (London, 1967), p. 333. King Lear, Act III, Scene 4.
3. *Works* IV, pp. 3 and 291.
4. Vivian Mercier, *The Irish Comic Tradition*, p. 1.
5. Luigi Pirandello, *L'Umorismo* (Florence, 1920), p. 223.
6. *Works* III, p. 291; and IV, p. 186.
7. François Rabelais, *Oeuvres Complètes*, ed. Pierre Joudra (Paris, 1962), p. 3; see also Thomas Urquart's translation of *Gargantua and Pantagruel* I, p. 2, and II, pp. 91f.
8. Petit de Julleville, *Comédie et Moeurs*, pp. 239 and 12; *Théâtre en France*, p. 423.
9. W.B. Yeats, *Autobiographies*, p. 473.
10. *Works* II, p. 163.
11. *Works* IV, p. 3.
12. Ibid. p. 4, fn.
13. *Comédie et Moeurs*, pp. 74 and 225f.
14. *Répertoire du Théâtre*, p. 232.
15. *The Plays and Poems of J.M. Synge*, p. 47.
16. See de Julleville, *Comédie et Moeurs*, p. 225 on this farce. Besides farces and *fabliaux*, one might also mention the parallels to these French genres in other European countries: see Derek Brewer, *Medieval Comic Tales* (Cambridge, 1972), p. 143; Chaucer's anti-clerical tales; Early Irish satires such as 'The Vision of MacConglinne'; and the related Middle English 'The Land of Cokaygne'.
17. *Works* IV, p. 19.
18. Ibid., p. 17.
19. See de Julleville, *Comédie et Moeurs*, p. 225 for an account of a 'priest' being beaten in a medieval French farce. It would be interesting to know whether Synge knew Jacques de Vitry's *exemplum* of an avaricious priest who refuses to bury the mother of a young woman without payment, and the dead mother was left in a sack with the priest as a pledge: Jacques de Vitry, *The Exampla or Illustrative Stories from the Sermones Vulgares*, ed. Thomas F. Crane (London, 1890).
20. *Works* V, p. 21.

21. Compare Ibid., p. 45 with Ben Jonson, *Bartholomew Fair*, Act V, Scene 3, ed. Brinsley Nicholson (London, 1894), pp. 151 and 153.
22. *Works* IV, p. 49.
23. *Works* III, p. 21.
24. *Works* IV, p. 173.
25. *Works* III, p. 145.
26. See Per Nykrog, *Les Fabliaux*, p. 133.
27. *Works* III, pp. 83 and 89.
28. *Works* IV, pp. 79 and 65.
29. Ibid., p. 173.
30. See Henri Bergson, *Le Rire*, pp. 32–36.
31. *Works* II, p. 95.
32. *Works* IV, pp. 67 and 73.
33. *Works* IV, pp. 109, 105, 75, 77, and 173.
34. *Works* II, p. 96.
35. See de Jubainville, *Cours de littérature celtique*, Vol. VII, entitled *Etudes sur le droit celtique*, pp. 84, 97–108, and 190–198; on pp. 14f the traditional oath by the forces of nature is treated, of which Synge makes use (without textual precedent) for the wedding of Deirdre and Naisi: see *Works* IV, p. 215. Old Irish law is also treated by de Jubainville in his *Senchus Mór* (Paris, 1881). Synge notes the treatises on Brehon law which are among surviving MSS in 'La Vieille Littérature Irlandaise': *Works* II, p. 353.
36. See Tom Peete Cross, *Motif-index of Early Irish Literature* (Bloomington, Indiana, 1952); D.P. Rotunda, *Motif-Index of the Italian Novella* (Bloomington, Indiana, 1942); and Per Nykrog, *Les Fabliaux*.
37. *Comédie et Moeurs*, pp. 287–329.
38. See *Works* II, p. 70.
39. Lady Gregory, *Our Irish Theatre* (London, 1914), p. 109.
40. Quoted by Greene and Stephens, *J.M. Synge,* p. 182.
41. David Greene, 'The Shadow of the Glen and the Widow of Ephesus', in *Publications of the Modern Languages Association*, Vol. LXII, March 1947, pp. 223–228.
42. See *Works* II, p. 65.
43. *Works* III, pp. 211f.
44. On the ambivalence of folk humour see Mikhail Bakhtin, *Rabelais*, pp. 10f.
45. *Works* II, p. 351.
46. Nicholas Grene, *Synge: A Critical Study of the Plays* (London, 1975), p. 146.
47. Quoted by Frances Barsach in her introduction to the reprint of Thomas Wright's *A History of Caricature and Grotesque in Literature and Art* (New York, 1968), p. viii. Source not identified.
48. Arthur Clayborough, *The Grotesque in English Literature*, p. 68.
49. Wolfgang Kayser, *The Grotesque in Art and Literature*, p. 54.

Chapter X

1. *Works* I, p. xxxvi.
2. *Works* II, p. 347.

3. Victor Hugo, *Théâtre Complet*, pp. 434f.
4. Quoted by Ann Saddlemyer, *Works* IV, p. xxiii.
5. See T.S.R. Boase, *English Art 1800–1870* (Oxford, 1959), p. 287. Raymond Johnson kindly provided bibliographical information on the Pre-Raphaelites.
6. See David Cecil, *Visionary and Dreamer* (London, 1969), p. 190.
7. Bourgeois, *Synge and the Irish Theatre*, p. 38.
8. *Works* IV, p. 269.
9. D.G. Rossetti, *Collected Works* (London, 1887), Vol. I, p. 232.
10. *Works* IV, pp. xxvii and xxvi.
11. Ruskin saw the danger that the Pre-Raphaelites might retreat into medievalism and hoped that they would not: See Nello Ponente, *The Structures of the Modern World*, transl. James Emmous (Geneva, 1965), p. 136.
12. T.S.R. Boase, *English Art 1800–1870*, p. 283.
13. Malcolm Kelsall, 'Synge in Aran', *Irish University Review*, Autumn 1975, p. 260.
14. See Ruby Cohn, *Samuel Beckett: The Comic Gamut* (New Brunswick, 1962), p. 270.
15. W.B. Yeats, *Autobiographies*, p. 345.
16. For Synge's view of Rembrandt as a great artist, see *Works* II, p. 349. Kenneth Clark, *The Nude* (London, 1956), p. 327.
17. Synge admired a bronze statuette by Rodin owned by his friend Stephen MacKenna, and took Molly Allgood to see his work: *Letters to Molly*, ed. Ann Saddlemyer, p. 272. Kenneth Clark, *The Nude*, p. 330.
18. See Mikhail Bakhtin, *Rabelais*, p. 398, n. 9.
19. *Works* II, p. 349.
20. Synge's reluctance to theorize is another instance of a parallel with Victor Hugo: compare *Works* II, p. 348 and *Théâtre Complet*, p. 434.
21. *Works* I, p. xxxvi.
22. *Works* IV, pp. 53f.
23. *Works* II, p. 349.
24. Victor Hugo, *Thèâtre Complet*, p. 416.
25. Ibid., and also pp. 418 and 421.

SELECT BIBLIOGRAPHY

J.M. SYNGE

Works by Synge:

J.M. Synge: Collected Works, General ed. Robin Skelton, London: Oxford University Press, 1962–68, reprinted Gerrards Cross: Colin Smythe, and Washington D.C.: The Catholic University of America Press, 1982

I. *Poems*, ed. Robin Skelton, 1962

II. *Prose*, ed. Alan Price, 1966

III. *Plays* I, ed. Ann Saddlemyer, 1968

IV. *Plays* II, ed. Ann Saddlemyer, 1968

Letters to Molly: John Millington Synge to Maire O'Neill, ed. Ann Saddlemyer, Cambridge, Massachusetts: Harvard University Press, 1971

Some Letters of John M. Synge to Lady Gregory and W.B. Yeats, selected by Ann Saddlemyer, Dublin: Cuala, 1971

'Synge to MacKenna: The Mature Years', ed. Ann Saddlemyer in *Irish Renaissance: A Gathering of Essays, Memoirs, Letters and Dramatic Poetry from the Massachusetts Review*, ed. Robin Skelton and David Clark, Dublin: Dolmen, 1968

Synge/Petrarch, ed. Robin Skelton, Dublin: Dolmen, 1971

Manuscripts

Synge Manuscript Collection, The Library, Trinity College, Dublin. Catalogue by Nicholas Grene, Dublin: Dolmen, 1971

MEDIEVAL TEXTS

Brewer, Derek (ed.), *Medieval Comic Tales*, Cambridge: D.S. Brewer, 1972

Chaucer, Geoffrey, *The Poetical Works*, ed. F.N. Robinson, London: Oxford University Press, 1933

Fournier, Edouard, *Le Théâtre français avant la renaissance*, Paris: Leplace, Sanchez et Cie., 1872

199

Henderson, George (ed. and transl.), *Fled Bricrend: The Feast of Bricriu*, Dublin: Irish Texts Society, 1899

Hull, Vernam (ed.), *Longes Mac N-Uislenn: The Exile of the Sons of Uisliu*, New York: Modern Language Association, 1949

Jacob, P.L. (ed.), *Recueil de Farces, sotties et moralités*, Paris: Garnier, 1882

Kinsella, Thomas (transl.), *The Tain*, London: Oxford University Press, 1970

Meyer, Kuno (transl.), *Ancient Irish Poetry*, London: Constable, 1911

Montaiglon, A. de and G. Reynaud, *Recueil Général et complet des fabliaux des XIII et XIV siècles*, Paris: Librairie des Bibliophiles, 1872–90

Moret, André (ed.), *Anthologie due Minnesang*, Paris: Aubier, 1955

Murphy, Gerard (ed. and transl.), *Early Irish Lyrics*, London: Oxford University Press, 1956

Muset, Colin, *Les Chansons de Colin Muset*, ed. Joseph Bédier, Paris: H. Champion, 1912

Roques, Mario (ed.), *Le Garçon et l'aveugle*, Paris: H. Champion, 1912

Sayce, Olive (ed.), *Poets of the Minnesang*, Oxford: Clarendon Press, 1957

Stokes, Whitley (ed.), *Irische Texte* II, Leipzig, 1887

Stokes, Whitley and John Strachan (eds.), *Thesaurus Palaeohibernicus*, Cambridge: Cambridge University Press, 1905

Strassburg, Gottfried von, *Tristan*, transl. A.T. Hatto, Harmondsworth: Penguin, 1960

Tolkein, J.R.R. and E.V. Gordon (eds.), *Sir Gawain and the Green Knight*, Oxford: Clarendon, 1968

Villon, François, *Oeuvres*, ed. André Mary, Paris: Garnier, 1970

Vitry, Jacques de, *The Exempla or Illustrative Stories from the Sermones Vulgares*, ed. Thomas F. Crane, London: The Folklore Society, 1890

Vogelweide, Walther von der, *Werke*, ed. Joerg Schaefer, Darmstadt: Wissenschaftliche Buchgeselleschaft, 1972

Windisch, Ernst, *Irische Texte* I, Leipzig, 1880

RELEVANT WORKS ON THE GROTESQUE

Bakhtin, Mikhail, *Rabelais and his World*, transl. Helen Iswolski, Boston: Massachusetts Institute of Technology, 1968

Bibliography

Clayborough, Arthur, *The Grotesque in English Literature*, Oxford: Clarendon, 1965

Erasmus, Desiderius, *Praise of Folly*, transl. Betty Radice, Harmondsworth: Penguin, 1971

Hugo, Victor, *Théâtre Complet* I, ed. J.-J. Thierry and J. Meleze, Paris: Gallimard, 1963–64 (Preface de 'Cromwell' pp. 409–454)

Kaiser, Walter, *Praisers of Folly*, London: Victor Gollanz, 1964

Kayser, Wolfgang, *The Grotesque in Art and Literature*, transl. Ulrich Weisstein, Indiana: Bloomington University Press, 1963

Swain, Barbara, *Fools and Folly*, New York: Columbia University Press, 1932

Willeford, William, *The Fool and his Scepter*, Evanston, Illinois: Northwestern University Press, 1969

Wright, Thomas, *A History of Caricature and Grotesque in Literature and Art*, Introduction by Frances K. Barsach, New York: Ungar, 1968

SECONDARY MATERIAL

Books:

Baudelaire, Charles, *Les Fleurs du Mal*, ed. Jacques Crépet and Beorges Blin, Paris: J. Corti, 1968

Beckett, Samuel, *Waiting for Godot*, London: Faber, 1979

Bergson, Henri, *Le Rire*, Paris: Presses univ. de France, 1972

Boase, T.S.R., *English Art 1800–1870*, London: Oxford University Press, 1959

Bourgeois, Maurice, *John Millington Synge and the Irish Theatre*, London: Constable, 1913

Bushrui, Suheil (ed.), *Sunshine and the Moon's Delight*, Gerrards Cross and Beirut: Colin Smythe and The American University of Beirut, 1972

Cecil, David, *Visionary and Dreamer*, London: Constable, 1959

Cervantes, Miguel de, *The Adventures of Don Quixote*, Transl. J.M. Cohen, Harmondsworth: Penguin, 1950

Clark, Kenneth, *The Nude*, London: John Murray, 1956

Cohn, Ruby, *Samuel Beckett: The Comic Gamut*, New Brunswick: Rutgers, 1962

Colum, Padraic, *The Road Round Ireland*, New York: Macmillan, 1926

Cross, Tom Peete, *Motif-Index of Early Irish Literature*, Indiana: Bloomington University Press, 1952

Curtius, Ernst R, *European Literature and the Latin Middle Ages*, transl. Willard Trask, New York and London: Routledge and Kegan Paul, 1953

Dillon, Miles (ed.), *Irish Sagas*, Cork: Mercier, 1968

Dodds, E.R., *Journal and Letters of Stephen MacKenna*, London: Constable, 1936

Eliot, T.S., *The Sacred Wood*, London: Methuen, 1976

—— *Selected Essays*, London: Faber, 1951

Ellis-Fermor, Una, *The Irish Dramatic Movement*, London: Methuen, 1939

Estill, Adelaide Duncan, *The Sources of Synge*, Philadelphia: University of Pennsylvania Press, 1939

Faral, E., *Les Jongleurs en France au moyen-âge*, Paris: H. Champion, 1910

Forster, Leonard, *The Icy Fire: Five Studies in European Petrarchism*, Cambridge University Press, 1969

Foucault, Michel, *Madness and Civilization: A History of Madness in the Age of Reason*, New York: Vintage Books, 1973

Fox, John, *A Literary History of France: The Middle Ages*, London: Benn, 1974

Greene, David and Edward Stephens, *J.M. Synge 1871–1909*, New York: Macmillan, 1959

Greene, David, *The Irish Language*, Cork: Mercier, 1972

Gregory, Lady Augusta, *Cuchulain of Muirthemne*, Gerrards Cross: Colin Smythe, 1973

—— *Our Irish Theatre*, London: Putnam, 1914

—— *Seventy Years: Being the Autobiography of Lady Gregory*, ed. Colin Smythe, Gerrards Cross: Colin Smythe, 1973

Grene, Nicholas, *Synge: A Critical Study of the Plays*, London: Macmillan, 1975

Harmon, Maurice (ed.), *J.M. Synge Centenary Papers 1971*, Dublin: Dolmen, 1972

Henn, T.R. (ed. and Introduction), *The Plays and Poems of J.M. Synge*, London: Methuen, 1963

Henry, P.L., *An Anglo-Irish Dialect of North Roscommon*, Zurich: Aschmann and Scheller, 1957

Hoepffner, Ernest, *Les Troubadours*, Paris: Colin, 1955

Hull, Eleanor, *The Cuchullin Saga in Irish Literature*, London: Grimm, 1898

Hyde, Douglas, *A Literary History of Ireland*, London: T. Fisher Unwin, 1899; Ernest Benn, 1967

—— *The Three Sorrows of Storytelling*, London: T. Fisher Unwin, 1895

—— *Love Songs of Connacht*, Shannon: Irish University Press, 1969

Jonson, Ben, *Works* II, ed. Brinsley Nicholson, London: T. Fisher Unwin, 1894

Jubainville, Henry d'Arbois de, *Introduction à l'étude de la littérature celtique*, Paris: Thorin, 1883

—— *Études sur le droit celtique: Le Senchus Mór*, Paris: L. Larose, 1881

—— *Le Cycle mythologique irlandais et la mythologie celtique*, Paris: Thorin, 1884

—— *Cours de littérature celtique*, Paris: Thorin, 1883–1902

—— *L'Epopée celtique en Irlande*, Paris: Thorin, 1892

—— *Elements de la grammaire celtique*, Paris: Fontemoing, 1903

Julleville, Louis Petit de, *Histoire de la Grèce sous la domination romaine*, Paris: Thorin, 1875

—— *Histore du théâtre en France: Les Mystères* I and II, Paris: Hachette, 1880

—— *Notions génerales sur les origines et sur l'histoire de la langue française*, Paris: Delelain Frères, 1883

—— *Les Comédiens en France au moyen-âge*, Paris: L. Cerf, 1885

—— *La Comédie et les moeurs en France au moyen-âge*, Paris: L. Cerf, 1886

—— *Répertoire du théâtre comique en France au moyen-âge*, Paris: L. Cerf, 1886

—— *Le Théâtre en France: L'Histoire de la littérature dramatique depuis ses origines jusqu'à nos jours*, Paris: A. Colin, 1886

—— *Histoire de la langue et de la littérature française* I–VIII, Paris: A. Colin, 1896–1902

Keating, Geoffrey, *Foras Feasa ar Éirinn: The History of Ireland*, ed. David Comyn, Dublin: Irish Texts Society, 1905

Kiberd, Declan, *Synge and the Irish Language*, London: Macmillan, 1979

Knott, Eleanor, *Irish Classical Poetry*, Dublin: Colm O'Lochlain, 1960

—— and Gerard Murphy, *Early Irish Literature*, Introduction James Carney, London: Routledge and Kegan Paul, 1966

Leopardi, Giacomo, *Opere*, ed. Francesco Flora, Milan: Mondadori, 1956

Lewis, D.B. Wyndham, *François Villon*, New York: The Literary Guild of America, 1928

MacCurtin, Andrew, *Oidhe Chloinne Uisnigh: The Fate of the Children of Uisneach*, Dublin: Society for the Preservation of the Irish Language, 1898

Marlowe, Christopher, *Works*, ed. Tucker Brooke, Oxford: Oxford University Press, 1910

Martin, W.G. Wood-, *Traces of the Elder Faiths in Ireland*, London: Longman, 1902

Meir, Colin, *The Ballads and Songs of W.B. Yeats: The Anglo-Irish Heritage in Subject and Style*, London: Macmillan, 1974

Mercier, Vivian, *The Irish Comic Tradition*, London: Oxford University Press, 1962

Murphy, Gerard, *Saga and Myth in Ancient Ireland*, Cork: Mercier, 1971

Nykrog, Per, *Les Fabliaux*, Copenhagen: Ejnar Munksgaard, 1957; Geneva: Droz, 1973

Pirandello, Luigi, *L'Umorismo*, Florence: Battistelli, 1920

Price, Alan, *Synge and Anglo-Irish Drama*, London: Methuen, 1961

Ponente, Nello, *The Structures of the Modern World*, transl. James Emmons, Geneva: Albert Skira, 1965

Rabelais, François, *Oeuvres Complètes*, ed. Pierre Joudra, Paris: Garnier Frères, 1962

—— *Gargantua and Pantagruel*, Transl. Thomas Urquart, London: Dent, 1929

Rafroidi, Patrick, ed., *Aspects of the Irish Theatre*, Paris, Lille: Editions Universitaires, 1972

Riva, Serafino, *La Tradizione celtica e la moderna letteratura irlandese*, Rome: Religio, 1937

Ronsard, Pierre de, *Poésies Choisies*, ed. Françoise Jonkovsky, Paris: Garnier, 1969

Rosetti, Dante Gabriel, *Poems*, ed. Oswald Doughty, London: Dent, 1957

Rossiter, A.P., *English Drama from Early Times to the Elizabethans*, London: Hutchinson's University Library, 1950

Rotunda, D.P., *Motif-Index of the Italian Novella*, Indiana: Bloomington University Press, 1942

Russell, George (Æ), *Deirdre*, Chicago: de Paul University, 1970

Sanctis, Francesco de, *Saggio Critica sul Petrarca*, ed. Nino Cortese, Naples: Morano, 1932

Skelton, Robin, *The Writings of J.M. Synge*, London: Thames and Hudson, 1971

——*J.M. Synge and his World*, London: Thames and Hudson, 1971

Steiner, George, *After Babel: Aspects of Language and Translation*, London: Oxford University Press, 1975

Stephens, Edward, *My Uncle John*, ed. Andrew Carpenter, London: Oxford University Press, 1974

—— and David Greene, *J.M. Synge 1871–1909*, New York: Macmillan, 1959

Swinburne, Charles Algernon, *The Poems* III, London: Chatto and Windus, 1905

Wade, Allan, *The Letters of W.B. Yeats*, London: R. Hart-Davis, 1954

Wilde, Oscar, *Complete Works*, ed. Vyvyan Holland, London: Collins, 1967

Yeats, W.B., *Autobiographies*, London: Macmillan, 1955

—— *Essays and Introductions*, London: Macmillan, 1961

—— *Collected Plays*, London: Macmillan, 1977

Zumthor, Paul, *Langue et techniques poétiques à l'époque romane*, Paris: Librarie C. Klincksieck, 1963

Articles

Bliss, Alan, 'The language of Synge' in *J.M. Synge Centenary Papers 1971*, ed. Maurice Harmon, Dublin: Dolmen, 1972

—— 'A Synge Glossary' in *Sunshine and the Moon's Delight*, ed. Suheil Bushrui, Gerrards Cross and Beirut: Colin Smythe and The American University of Beirut, 1972

Fackler, Herbert, 'J.M. Synge's *Deirdre of the Sorrows*: Beauty Only' in *Modern Drama XI*, February 1969

Gaskell, Ronald, 'The Realism of J.M. Synge' in *Critical Quarterly*, London, Autumn 1963

Green, David, '*The Shadow of the Glen* and the Widow of Ephesus' in *Publications of the Modern Language Association*, LXII, March 1967

Henn, T.R., 'John Millington Synge: A Reconsideration' in *Hermathena* CXII, Dublin, Autumn 1971

Kelsall, Malcolm, 'Synge in Aran' in *Irish University Review*, Dublin, Autumn 1975

Saddlemyer, Ann, 'A Share in the Dignity of the World: J.M. Synge's Aesthetic Theory' in *The World of W.B. Yeats: Essays in Perspective*, ed. Robin Skelton and Ann Saddlemyer, Dublin: Dolmen, 1965

—— 'Art, Nature, and the Prepared Personality' in *Sunshine and the Moon's Delight*, ed. Suheil Bushrui, Gerrards Cross and Beirut: Colin Smythe and The American University of Beirut, 1972

—— 'Deirdre of the Sorrows: Literature First . . . Drama Afterwards' in *J.M. Synge Centenary Papers 1971*, ed. Maurice Harmon, Dublin: Dolmen, 1972

Schoepperle, Gertrude, 'John Synge and his Old French Farce' in *North American Review* CCXIV, New York, October 1921

Sidnell, M.J., 'Synge's Playboy and the Champion of Ulster' in *Dalhousie Review* XXV, Spring 1965

Williams, Clive, 'Pestalozzi and John Synge' in *Hermathena*, Dublin, Spring 1968

Zumthor, Paul, 'Document et Monument' in *Revue des Sciences Humaines*, Lille, January-March 1960

Unpublished Theses:

Robinson, Paul N., 'Medieval Aspects in the Plays of J.M. Synge', University of Wisconsin, Madison, 1971

Smyth, Donna, 'The Figure of the Fool in the Works of W.B. Yeats, Samuel Beckett, and Patrick White', London University, 1972

INDEX